The Role of the United Kingdom Prime Minister

Prime Ministers are appointed based on their ability to command confidence in the House of Commons. If an election produces a clear majority for one party, then the leader of that party becomes Prime Minister. If it is the incumbent Prime Minister, then they just continue in office. If it is another party, then the incumbent formally resigns the morning after the election and they are replaced.

If no party wins a clear majority, then there may be a process of negotiation before it becomes clear who is likely to be Prime Minister. An incumbent Prime Minister is entitled to remain in office and test whether they can command confidence, or they may resign if it becomes obvious that they will not be able to do so.

However, it is vital that a Prime Minister is in place and there is an expectation they will not resign until it is clear who can take over.

In the mid-17th century, after the English Civil War (1642–1651), Parliament strengthened its position relative to the monarch, then gained more power through the Glorious Revolution of 1688 and the passage of the Bill of Rights in 1689. The monarch could no longer establish any law or impose any tax without its permission and thus the House of Commons became a part of the government. It is at this point that a modern style of Prime Minister begins to emerge.

The title 'Prime Minister' was originally a term of abuse rather than a description of an official role. It implied that an individual subject had risen improperly above others within the royal circle, and had echoes of a political institution imported from France, England's great enemy. When Robert Harley, a favourite of Queen Anne (1702-1714), was impeached in 1715, one of the charges against him was that he was a Prime Minister. The prevailing view at this time was that monarchs should be their own Prime Ministers.

Robert Walpole in 1721 is generally regarded as the first Prime Minister although the post was not yet firmly established in practice nor officially recognised. By 1805 The Times newspaper was beginning to use the phrase 'Prime Minister' in this sense and around this time it began to be employed in parliamentary debates.

The office of Prime Minister was widely accepted as a political reality by the mid-nineteenth century. But official acknowledgement of this development was slower to take place. In 1878 a significant development occurred when Benjamin Disraeli used the term 'Prime Minister' when signing the Treaty of Berlin.

In December 1905 the Prime Minister was granted a place in the official order of precedence. The first statutory reference to the Prime Minister came in the Chequers Estate Act 1917, which specified Chequers as a prime-ministerial residence.

The House of Commons - Debate proposals and make laws.

The House of Lords - Check proposed laws, make amendments.

The Crown, i.e. the Queen - Head of State, approves laws.

Contents

Contents

Sir Robert Walpole *(Earl of Orford)*
1st British Prime Minister

Born
26 August 1676, Houghton Hall, Norfolk
Died
18 March 1745, age 68, Arlington Street, London
Period in office as Prime Minister
20 years 315 days from 3 April 1721 – 11 February 1742
Political party
Whig
Constituencies Represented as MP
Castle Rising 1701-1702
King's Lynn 1702-1742
Ministerial offices held as Prime Minister
First Lord of the Treasury
Leader of the House of Commons
Chancellor of the Exchequer

Robert Walpole, 1st Earl of Orford, (26 August 1676 – 18 March 1745), known between 1721 and 1742 as **Sir Robert Walpole**, was a British politician and is generally regarded as the first 'de facto' (existing or holding a specified position in fact but not necessarily by legal right) Prime Minister of Great Britain and from a position in which he dominated politics in the reigns of George I and George II.

Walpole was born in Houghton, Norfolk into a wealthy landowning family. As a child, Walpole attended a private school at Massingham, Norfolk and entered Eton College in 1690.

Walpole was a member of the Whig party and his political career began not long after the death of his father in 1700, when in 1701 he won his father's previous seat as MP for Castle Rising. At the 1702 General Election he went on to represent King's Lynn and he rose rapidly in government, becoming a member of the Admiralty Board, Secretary of War and in 1709, Treasurer of the Navy. His rise was temporarily halted by the Tories, who came into power in 1710 under the leadership of Robert Harley. Walpole represented the constituency of King's Lynn from 1702 until February 1742 (with a short intermission in 1712). Walpole's father who had also been a Whig, had been a supporter of the 1688 to 1689 'Glorious Revolution' which gave Britain a constitutional monarchy.
.
The intermission in Walpole's political career came in 1712 when he was accused of *Venality* (being bribable, or willing to sell one's services of power) and Corruption with regards to a matter of two forage contracts for Scotland.
Although it was proven that Walpole had not retained any of the money, he was still pronounced 'guilty of high breach of trust and notorious corruption'. Walpole was impeached by the House of Commons and found guilty in the House of Lords. He was

subsequently imprisoned in the Tower of London for six months and expelled from Parliament.

Whilst in the Tower though, he was considered a political martyr and still retained support of the Whig leaders.

After his release Walpole again stood as candidate in Kings Lyn and was re-elected to Parliament in 1713.

HOUSE OF COMMONS CIRCA 1740

In 1715, Walpole became first Lord of the Treasury and Chancellor of the Exchequer. He resigned in 1717 after disagreements within his party but in 1720 was made Paymaster General.

Walpole avoided the scandal that surrounded the collapse of the South Sea Company (a British joint-stock company used for reducing the national debt) and was subsequently appointed First Lord of the Treasury and Chancellor of the Exchequer again. In this position he effectively became Prime Minister. Although the term was not officially used at the time, he remained in this position of dominance until 1742. In his first year serving as Prime Minister he uncovered the 'Atterbury Plot' which was named after the Tory Bishop, Francis Atterbury of Rochester, whose plan was to take control of the government. The Bishop was subsequently exiled for life and Walpole was able to consolidate power for the Whigs by branding the Tories as Jacobites (supporters of the deposed James II and his descendants). The failed plot cemented Walpole's position as leader, boosting his support and kept the Tories out of the political game for a long time. He also consolidated Whig power through a system of royal patronage. Walpole's government pursued a policy of peace abroad, offered low taxation while reducing the national debt.

After George I's death in 1727, Walpole was briefly superseded by George II's favourite, Spencer Compton, but succeeded in returning himself to favour, partly through the support of the new Queen, Caroline. After the General Election of 1734, Walpole's supporters still formed a majority in the House of Commons albeit in lesser numbers than before. Walpole lowered land taxes in the late 1720's and early 1730's but by then his popularity had begun to wane.

In 1735, King George II made Walpole a gift of 10 Downing Street, now the permanent London residence of the British Prime Minister.

In 1736 opposition eventually began to develop within Walpole's own party, a trade dispute with Spain was used by his critics to force him to declare war in 1739, known as the War of Jenkins' Ear. The war was between Great Britain and Spain that began in October 1739 and eventually merged into the War of the Austrian Succession (1740–48). It was precipitated by an incident that took place in 1738 when Captain Robert Jenkins appeared before a committee of the House of Commons exhibiting what he alleged to be his own amputated ear. Jenkins said the ear was cut off in April 1731 in the West Indies by Spanish coast guards, who had boarded his ship (Rebecca) pillaged it, and then set it adrift. Public opinion had already been aroused by other Spanish outrages on British ships.

SIR ROBERT WALPOLE

Also in this period Walpole attempted to raise the excise tax on wine and tobacco as well as shifting tax burdens to the merchants instead of landowners. This was met with great opposition which led to a poor General Election result in 1741, making his position weak and unstable. A number of Whig politicians opposed Walpole's conduct of the war and he resigned in February 1742.

He was created Earl of Orford in the same year and served in the House of Lords continuing to maintain influence over George II.

Walpole died aged 68 on 18 March 1745.

He was buried in the parish church of St Martin in Houghton, Norfolk. His earldom passed to his eldest son Robert who was in turn succeeded by his only son George.

Interesting Robert Walpole facts:

Walpole may be considered the first 'Prime Minister', but in those days the title implied an unwarranted usurpation of royal authority, so Walpole disclaimed it.

In the United States, the towns of Walpole, Massachusetts (founded in 1724), and Orford, New Hampshire (incorporated in 1761), take their respective names from Sir Robert Walpole, Earl of Orford.

Walpole Street in Wolverhampton is named after Sir Robert Walpole.

Walpole Island, named for Sir Robert Walpole, comprises an island and an Indian reserve in South Western Ontario, Canada, on the border between Ontario and Michigan. It lies at the mouth of the St. Clair River on Lake St. Clair, approximately thirty miles (50 km) northeast of Detroit, Michigan, and of Windsor, Ontario.

Walpole is immortalised in St Stephen's Hall, where he and other notable Parliamentarians look on at visitors to Parliament.

Spencer Compton *(1ˢᵗ Earl of Wilmington)* 2nd British Prime Minister

Born
1673 Or 1674 (date unknown), Comton Wynyates, Warwickshire

Died
2 July 1743, age 70, St. James' Square, London

Period in office as Prime Minister
1 year 137 days from 3 April 1742 – 2 July 1743

Political party
Whig

Constituencies Represented as MP
Eye 1698-1710
East Grinstead 1713-1715
Sussex 1715-1728

Ministerial offices held as Prime Minister
First Lord of the Treasury

Spencer Compton, 1st Earl of Wilmington, (c. 1674 – 2 July 1743) was a British Whig statesman who served continuously in government from 1715 until his death in 1743.

Spencer Compton, Earl of Wilmington, was a compromise First Lord of the Treasury during a period of political instability. Born around 1674 to aristocratic parents (his father was third Earl of Northampton), he was educated at St Paul's School and the Middle Temple and Trinity College, Oxford. Compton's family background suggested allegiance to the Tories – his uncle was Bishop of London – but, following a quarrel with his elder brother, Compton shifted his affections to the Whigs.

Compton first stood for Parliament at East Grinstead on the interest of his kinsman the Earl of Dorset at the 1695 English General Election but was unsuccessful. He was later returned unopposed as Member of Parliament for Eye in Suffolk at a by-election on 3 June 1698. In Parliament he soon stood out as prominent figure amongst the Whigs and began a partnership with Robert Walpole that would last for over forty years.

Compton was appointed Chairman of the Commons election and privileges committee in 1705. This reflected his interest in parliamentary process and it was here, rather than in the oratory, that Compton's skills lay. He was involved in the impeachment of the incendiary Tory preacher Henry Sacheverell (an Anglican clergyman who achieved nationwide fame in 1709 after preaching an incendiary 5 November sermon) in 1710, but consequently found it difficult to acquire a new seat when a dispute with Lord Cornwallis, patron of the Eye seat, prevented him from standing there again. Following the Hanoverian succession that brought George I to the British throne in 1714, Compton had hoped for rapid political advancement and was eventually rewarded with roles as Treasurer of the Prince of Wales's household and Speaker of the House of Commons in 1715 and a member of the Privy Council (a formal body of advisers to the Sovereign of the United Kingdom) in 1716.

Compton's knowledge of parliamentary practice and precedent proved invaluable as Speaker of the House. His connections with both the Prince of Wales and Walpole however placed him in a difficult position when relations broke down between the Prince and his father, George I, in 1717.

SPENCER COMPTON

Compton became Paymaster of the Forces in 1722 but the Prince made no secret of his desire to replace Walpole with Compton when he succeeded to the throne. Thus, on receiving news of his father's death from Walpole in June 1727, the new King made clear his preference for Compton to head the government, but a combination of Walpole's hard work and Compton's timidity meant, however, that Walpole was able to continue as First Lord of the Treasury.

Compton was ennobled (as Baron, and later Earl of Wilmington) in 1728, perhaps because Walpole was keen to remove him as a potential rival in the Commons. He retained a strong dislike of Walpole and maintained contacts with a number of opposition figures, but he joined the administration as Lord Privy Seal and then Lord President of the Council in 1730. He remained a loyal minister for much of the 1730s. Yet his loyalty came at a price – following hints he might join the opposition during the Excise Crisis of 1733, he was made a Knight of the Garter.

As Walpole's power ebbed away following the declaration of war with Spain in 1739, Compton urged George II to reconstruct the ministry on a broader base. He became an aging compromise candidate for the prime ministry in 1742, when the real power lay with the Duke of Newcastle and John Carteret (later Earl Granville). He attempted to bring in oppositional Whigs and Tories to reconstruct the ministry but failed in the face of resistance both from George II and Walpole's followers. Compton is credited with having been Britain's second Prime Minister, a preferment almost entirely due to the inflated view in which King George II held of his abilities.

He remained the titular head of the administration until his death age 70 in July 1743. Unmarried, his estates were left to his nephew, James Compton, fifth Earl of Northampton and his titles became extinct.

Interesting Spencer Compton fact:

The cities of Wilmington, Delaware, Wilmington, North Carolina and Wilmington, Vermont are named in Compton's his honour.

Henry Pelham
3rd British Prime Minister

Born
Early 1696 (though some sources say 1694), Laughton, Sussex
Died
6 March 1754 age 59, Arlington St, London
Period in office as Prime Minister
10 years and 191 days from 27 August 1743 until 6 March 1754
Political party
Whig
Constituencies Represented as MP
Seaford 1717-1722
Sussex 1722-1754
Ministerial offices held as Prime Minister
First Lord of the Treasury
Leader of the House of Commons
Chancellor of the Exchequer

Henry Pelham (c. September 1694 – 6 March 1754) was a British Whig statesman, who served as Prime Minister of Great Britain from 27 August 1743 until his death in March 1754. He was the younger brother of Thomas Pelham-Holles, 1st Duke of Newcastle, who served in Pelham's government and succeeded him as Prime Minister.

Pelham was the second surviving son of Thomas Pelham, first Baron Pelham of Laughton, and his second wife Lady Grace Holles. Born in London, Pelham was educated at Westminster School and Hart Hall (now Hertford College), Oxford matriculating on 6 September 1710.

His father's death in 1712 brought him cash and land in the family's home county of Sussex. The Pelham family had traditionally been Whigs and both Henry and his elder brother, Thomas Pelham-Holles, the Duke of Newcastle, maintained this allegiance.

Pelham volunteered for the army during the pro-Stuart Jacobite rising of 1715, commanding dragoons at the Battle of Preston. He spent time travelling in Europe before becoming MP for Seaford in Sussex in a by-election on 28 February 1717.
In 1721 on the recommendation of Robert Walpole, he was chosen as Lord of the Treasury and at the 1722 General Election he was returned as MP for Sussex County. In 1724 he entered the ministry as Secretary at War, where he remained until 1730 when he moved to the more lucrative position of Paymaster of the Forces.

In 1742 a union of parties resulted in the formation of an administration in which Pelham became First Lord of the Treasury on 27th August 1743, succeeding the Earl of Wilmington after his death in July 1743.
Pelham served as First Lord of the Treasury, Chancellor of the Exchequer and Leader of the House of Commons.

Though he became First Lord of the Treasury in 1743, he really only emerged as Prime Minister in 1746 after a prolonged and desperate struggle with his rival Lord Carteret. Carteret possessed more brilliant talents, and above all had the strong support of the King himself, George II. But Pelham was firmly in control of the Commons, and with his experience and his connections in the City he also had a firm hold of the national purse strings. 'No Pelham, no money', was the cry when George II actually attempted to replace him with a Carteret ministry in 1746. Pelham emerged victorious with a government so powerful that there was no opposition to speak of in either House of Parliament

The Augustan era was essential to the development of prime ministerial power as being entirely dependent on a Commons majority, rather than royal prerogative interventions.
The Prime Minister called an early poll by asking the King to dissolve parliament in 1747.
The General Election was held during late June and July 1747. There were contests in only 62 out of the 314 English, Welsh and Scottish constituencies. After consideration of disputed elections, the new parliament consisted of 443 Whigs and 115 Tories. Of the Whigs, 351 were accounted government supporters (including a small handful of Tory defectors), while 92 were deemed opponents. The result gave the government a healthy overall majority of 144.

Pelham was a skilled administrator and financial manager and he helped to introduce a period of peace and prosperity by bringing to an end the expensive War of the Austrian Succession (1740–1748). Pelham was determined to retain the upper hand in the Commons and lost no time in initiating drastic cuts in the army and the navy. Over the next few sessions he obtained parliamentary approval for other areas of financial reconstruction and retrenchment. He reduced annual expenditure, eased the burden of direct taxation on the gentry, and cut the annual cost of financing the national debt which had soared from £46 million in 1739 to £77 million in 1748.

The Calendar (New Style) Act 1750 was to change England's traditional calendar to that of parity with Europe's but was controversial and caused a fracas between the Whigs and the Tories. The bill eventually passed through Parliament On September 2nd 1752 which was immediately followed by Thursday 14th technically removing eleven days out of the month. Subsequently, New Year's Day, previously beginning on March 25th would now fall on January 1st under the phrase 'The New Style the True Style'.

Two of Pelham's final acts were the Jew Bill of 1753, which allowed Jews to become naturalised by application to Parliament, and the Marriage Act of 1753, which enumerated the minimum age of consent for marriage.
'No marriage of a person under the age of 21 was valid without the consent of parents or guardians. Clergymen who disobeyed the law were liable for 14 years transportation'.
Pelham died on 6 March 1754 and was buried in All Saints' Church, Laughton, East Sussex.
On Pelham's death King George II himself was driven to observe, prophetically, 'Now I shall have no more peace'.

Interesting Henry Pelham facts:

Pelham was played by Roger Allam in the film Pirates of the Caribbean: On Stranger Tides.

Pelham was the first British Prime Minister who never acceded to the peerage in his lifetime.

Thomas Pelham-Holles *(1ˢᵗ Duke of Newcastle)*
4th British Prime Minister

Born
21 July 1693, Lincoln Inn Fields, London
Died
17 November 1768, age 75, Lincoln Inn Fields, London
Periods in office as Prime Minister
7 years and 205 days (2 terms) from 16 March 1754 – 11 (2 years 241 days) November 1756 and 29 June 1757 until 26 May 1762 (4 years 332 days)
Political party
Whig
Constituencies Represented as MP
East Grinstead 1678-1679
Lewes 1679- 1702
Sussex 1702-1705
Ministerial offices held as Prime Minister
First Lord of the Treasury
Leader of the House of Lords

Thomas Pelham-Holles, 1st Duke of Newcastle upon Tyne and 1st Duke of Newcastle-under-Lyme, (21 July 1693 – 17 November 1768) was a British Whig statesman, who lived throughout the Whig supremacy of the 18th century. He is commonly known as the **Duke of Newcastle**. A protégé of Sir Robert Walpole, he served under him for more than 20 years until 1742. He held power with his brother, Prime Minister Henry Pelham, until 1754 and served as a Secretary of State for 30 years dominating British foreign policy. Thomas Pelham-Holles, Duke of Newcastle, was one of the eighteenth century's great political survivors and served as First Lord of the Treasury through peace and war.

Born in Sussex in July 1693, he was the eldest son of Thomas Pelham, first baron Pelham of Laughton, and his second wife, Lady Grace Holles. He was educated at Westminster School and matriculated in 1709 at Clare College, Cambridge.

In 1711 Thomas Pelham received a large estate from his uncle John Holles 1st Duke of Newcastle who died from injuries he received in a fall from his horse while hunting. One stipulation of his uncle's will was that his nephew add Holles to his name, which he faithfully did, thereafter styling himself as Thomas Pelham-Holles. After his father's death in February 1712 he received another large inheritance, making him a considerable landowner and granting him substantial influence over the election of at least a dozen MPs in his native Sussex and also in Nottinghamshire and Yorkshire. His strong support for the Whig cause and the Hanoverian succession was rewarded by George I with a series of noble titles, including the Dukedom of Newcastle, previously held by his uncle.

In 1714 he became Lord-Lieutenant of the Counties of Middlesex and Nottingham and a Knight of the Garter. In his new position, he was in charge of suppressing Jacobitism in the counties under his control. In Middlesex, he arrested and questioned 800 people and drew up a Voluntary Defence Association to defend the County. In 1715, he became involved in a riot that ended with two men being killed, and Pelham-Holles having to flee along rooftops.

THOMAS PELHAM-HOLLES

The succession of George I was secured in late 1715 by the defeat of a Jacobite army at the Battle of Preston and the subsequent flight of James Francis Edward Stuart (the Old Pretender).

During the Whig split of 1717, Pelham-Holles remained loyal to the Sunderland-Stanhope grouping (the British government under Lord Stanhope and Lord Sunderland) and he was appointed Lord Chamberlain shortly afterwards. Earlier in that year he had secured the election of his brother, Henry Pelham, as an MP. Pelham-Holles initially used his skills as a courtier and to build up good relations with George I. However, following Walpole's ascent to power, he moved into a more directly political role. He became Secretary of State for the Southern Department in 1724, becoming (along with his Northern Departmental colleague Viscount Townshend) one of the ministers charged with the direction of British foreign policy. Pelham-Holles served as Townshend's junior colleague until the latter's resignation in 1730 made him the senior secretary and second only to Walpole within the administration. Pelham-Holles's brother Henry Pelham had now attained the lucrative position of Paymaster General and had effectively replaced Townshend as the third man of the government. The three men continued what had become dubbed as the Norfolk Congress by meeting regularly at Houghton Hall, Sir Robert Walpole's country house in Norfolk. The three men would hold private meetings, draw up wide-ranging policies on foreign and domestic issues and then present them to Parliament for their seal of approval, which their vast majority allowed them to do. Slowly, however, Pelham-Holles and his brother were moving out of the shadow of Walpole and being more assertive. Pelham-Holles was particularly annoyed both by what he saw as the abandonment of Austria and by the suggestion that Walpole no longer trusted him.

By 1735, Pelham-Holles had largely assumed control of colonial affairs, further increasing the amount of patronage he controlled. A devout Anglican, he was also given control over ecclesiastical matters, especially the appointment of bishops and lucrative positions in the Church of England.

Pelham-Holles became more powerful when his younger brother Henry Pelham became Prime Minister in 1743. Together, the two brothers and their supporters (known as the 'Old Whigs') made a coalition with the 'New Whigs', who were previous opponents of the Walpole government. However, there still remained a strident opposition, led vocally by men like William Pitt and Lord Sandwich.

After the death of his brother Henry, Pelham-Holles was persuaded to head the government by the King and became First Lord himself in March 1754. In April and May 1754 Pelham-Holles oversaw a General Election, largely adopting the electoral strategy drawn up by his brother and winning a large majority. He remained in power until 1756, when his government collapsed following the fall of Minorca. The ignominious loss of Minorca to France led Pelham-Holles to resign in November 1756 after fierce criticism he received for his handling of the war that was engulfing Europe.

His retirement from public life was however only temporary. He returned as First Lord in June 1757. His management of finances and marshalling of MPs underpinned William Pitt the Elder's strategic vision as Secretary of State, ultimately leading to British success in the Seven Years War (1756-63).

1759 became known as the "Annus Mirabilis" after Britain enjoyed victories on several continents as well as at sea. In November a French fleet planning to invade England was defeated at Quiberon, much of the credit went to Pitt, rather than Pelham-Holles. War-weariness and a change of monarch created tensions within the ministry and George III's promotion of John Stuart, Earl of Bute, led first to Pitt's resignation and then in November 1756 Pelham-Holles resignation.

In 1762, Pelham-Holles was created Baron Pelham of Stanmer.

He remained in active opposition but accepted he would not hold office again. He continued to wield enormous patronage and influence, but his health swiftly gave way after a stroke in

December 1767, which left him lame and impaired in speech and memory.

Pelham-Holles did return briefly to office as Lord Privy Seal in the Marquess of Rockingham's first administration. He died in November 1768 aged 75 at his London home in Lincoln's Inn Fields.

Interesting Thomas Pelham-Holles facts:

Thomas Pelham-Holles was played in the 1948 film *Bonnie Prince Charlie* by G. H. Mulcaster. He also features in the British television series *City of Vice*, which covers the early years of the Bow Street Runners.

He was also portrayed in the novel *Humphry Clinker* by Tobias Smollett as a bungling fool, ignorant of all geography, who is convinced that Cape Breton is not an island.

Newcastle House is a mansion in Lincoln's Inn Fields in central London which Pelham-Holles inherited from his uncle in 1711, it was used as his primary London residence (preferring it to 10 Downing Street when he was Prime Minister) often throwing lavish parties which were attended by much of London society.

Pelham-Holles was among the historical figures depicted in the painting 'The Two Georges' by Thomas Gainsborough.

In 1717 Pelham-Holles was given responsibility of overseeing theatres and suppressing any plays or playwrights who were belived to be too critical of the Hanoverian succession or the Whig government.

He married Lady Henrietta Godolphin in April 1717.

William Cavendish *(4th Duke of Devonshire)* 5th British Prime Minister

Born
Baptised 1 June 1720, Baptised St Martin's in the Fields, Westminster

Died
2 October 1764, age 44, Spa, the Austrian Netherlands (now Belgium)

Period in office as Prime Minister
225 days from 16 November 1756 until 29 June 1757

Political party
Whig

Constituency Represented as MP
Derbyshire 1741-1751

Ministerial offices held as Prime Minister
First Lord of the Treasury
Leader of the House of Lords
Lord Treasurer of Ireland

William Cavendish, 4th Duke of Devonshire, (8 May 1720 – 2 October 1764), styled **Lord Cavendish** before 1729 and **Marquess of Hartington** between 1729 and 1755, he was a British Whig statesman and nobleman who was briefly nominal Prime Minister of Great Britain.

William Cavendish, Duke of Devonshire, was a compromise choice as First Lord of the Treasury. His tenure coincided with a period of political infighting and external threat. Cavendish's status as a major landowner and his membership of a major political family allowed him to look after the affairs of state while Thomas Pelham-Holles (the Duke of Newcastle) and William Pitt the elder resolved their differences.

Cavendish was elected as MP for Derbyshire in 1741 through familial interest. Inheriting his father's staunch support for the Whigs, Cavendish worked hard to support Walpole in the dying days of his administration. Following Walpole's resignation in early 1742, Devonshire shifted his support to the Old Corps Whig grouping, led by the Duke of Newcastle, his brother Henry Pelham and the Earl of Hardwicke. He remained loyal to them throughout their struggle to displace John, Lord Carteret in George II's affections.

Cavendish was appointed Lord Lieutenant of Ireland in March 1755. Irish politics in this period was divided between supporters of the administration and a patriot faction, keen to demonstrate independence from London. Cavendish was an Irish landowner himself and spent a lot of time in Ireland.

In December 1755 Cavendish's father died and his Dukedom passed on to him. He remained in Ireland until October 1756 when the political crisis triggered by the outbreak of war with France and the loss of Minorca was reaching its height. Following Pelham-Holles resignation in November 1756, Cavendish was asked to form an administration with William Pitt the Elder. As in Ireland, Cavendish hoped to reconcile factions and bring people together. It was widely felt that his tenure as First Lord was temporary, ideally, some sort of new arrangement needed to be reached between Pelham-Holles, Pitt and George II. By April 1757, George had grown tired of waiting for Pelham-Holles to come back into the fold. He sacked Pitt, provoking a protracted period of negotiations which Robert Walpole's son Horace called the 'interministerium'.

WILLIAM CAVENDISH

Cavendish was given the Garter and appointed First Lord of the Treasury (most historians consider him Prime Minister during this service) in November 1756, and he served as First Lord until May 1757 in an administration effectively run by William Pitt. Cavendish's administration secured increased money for the war, troops were sent to America and a Militia Act was passed.

By late June 1757 an accommodation had been reached and Pitt returned as Secretary of State, while Pelham-Holles resumed office as First Lord of the Treasury.

Cavendish became Lord Chamberlain but continued to attend ministerial meetings. Following Pelham-Holles second resignation in May 1762, over the conduct of the war and the growing problem of Lord Bute's influence on the King, Cavendish did not resign himself but refused to attend meetings. This led to him losing office in November 1762.

Cavendish resigned his Lord Lieutenancy of Derbyshire in solidarity with Newcastle and Rockingham when they were dismissed from their Lord Lieutenancies.

For a long time he had a weak constitution and he gradually grew more ill in his last couple of years. He ultimately died in the Austrian Netherlands where he had gone to take the waters at Spa.

His death was a large political loss to his allies, the Whig magnates such as the Duke of Newcastle. Dying at the age of 44 years and 147 days, he remains the shortest lived British Prime Minister. Cavendish was buried at Derby Cathedral.

Interesting William Cavendish fact:

Through his marriage to Lady Charlotte Boyle the Cavendish's inherited estates which included: Burlington House Piccadilly London, (now the Royal Academy of Arts); Chiswick House London, Londesborough Hall Yorkshire, Bolton Abbey Yorkshire, Lismore Castle County Waterford Ireland. The Cavendish's main residence was Chatsworth House a stately home in Derbyshire, it has been home to the Cavendish family since 1549.

John Stuart *(3rd Earl of Bute)*
6th British Prime Minister

Born
25 May 1713, Parliament Square, Edinburgh
Died
10 March 1792, age 78, South Audley Street, London
Period in office as Prime Minister
318 days from 26 May 1762 until 8 April 1763
Political party
Tory
Ministerial offices held as Prime Minister
First Lord of the Treasury
Leader of the House of Lords

John Stuart, 3rd Earl of Bute, 25 May 1713 – 10 March 1792) was a British nobleman who served as Prime Minister of Great Britain from 1762 to 1763 under George III. He was the first Prime Minister from Scotland following the Acts of Union in 1707 and the first Tory to have held the post. He was also elected as the first President of the Society of Antiquaries of Scotland when it was founded in 1780.

John Stuart, third Earl of Bute, was a Scottish aristocrat who rose, through his royal connections to a position of political pre-eminence. Bute's grandfather had been an MP for Buteshire in the Scottish parliament and was created Earl of Bute in April 1703. Bute's father died in 1723 and the family estates were placed under the guardianship of Bute's uncles, the Duke of Argyll and the Earl of Ilay, the major political power brokers of early Hanoverian Scotland.

His first real political experience came with election as one of the sixteen Scottish representative peers in the House of Lords in 1737. Bute was only an occasional attendee, however, and aligned against his support for Argyll **against Walpole** he failed to secure re-election in 1741. Having spent time improving his Scottish estates, Stuart moved to London after the outbreak of the 1745 pro-Stuart Jacobite rebellion. He came into the circle of Frederick, Prince of Wales, and quickly achieved his confidence. He retained the trust of Frederick's wife, Augusta, after the Prince's death in 1751 and he became tutor to their eldest son, the future George III. Stuart's relationship with Prince George was a close one – he was a father-like figure for the young Prince. Following George II's death in October 1760, the new King promoted Stuart quickly. He became a Privy Counsellor, Secretary of State for the Northern department and was created a British peer. Stuart's new colleagues, particularly William Pitt the Elder and the Pelham-Holles, resented Stuart's rapid rise. With the country in the throes of the Seven Years War (1756-63), they feared that Stuart would persuade the new King to bring the war to a swift close, despite Britain having achieved substantial victories across the globe, such as the conquest of Canada. Pitt eventually resigned in October 1761. Stuart undoubtedly wanted to bring the war to a close. He was less attached to the Prussian alliance than either Pitt or Pelham-Holles and his abandonment of Prussia caused Pelham-Holles to resign in May 1762.

JOHN STUART

This left the way clear for Stuart to become First Lord of the Treasury. With the backing of George III he pressed ahead with negotiations with France and he was able to steer a peace agreement through both Houses of Parliament. Pitt remained vehemently opposed to the terms of the peace and Stuart was the subject of sustained personal attacks in the public sphere.

Stuart's premiership was notable for the negotiation of the Treaty of Paris (1763) which concluded the Seven Years' War. In so doing, Stuart had to soften his previous stance in relation to concessions given to France in that he agreed that the important fisheries in Newfoundland be returned to France without Britain's possession of Guadeloupe in return.

After peace was concluded, Stuart and the King decided that Britain's military expenditure should not exceed its pre-war levels, but they thought a large presence was necessary in America to deal with the French and Spanish threat. They therefore charged the colonists for the increased military levels, thus catalysing the resistance to taxes which led to the 'American Revolution'. Stuart also introduced a cider tax of four shillings per hogshead in 1763 to help finance the Seven Years' War.

His popularity was damaged by the imposition of the new Cider Tax and there were fears that the new tax would lead to an unacceptable degree of government intrusion into the lives of the population at large.
Shortly after the bill passed in April 1763, Stuart tendered his resignation which George III reluctantly accepted and Stuart's relationship with the King cooled after Pitt returned to office in 1766. In his political retirement he devoted himself to scholarship and used his considerable wealth as a patron of literary and scientific endeavour.
For the remainder of his life, Stuart remained at his estate in Hampshire, where he built himself a mansion called High Cliff near Christchurch and continued in his pursuit of botany.

He died aged 78 at his home in South Audley Street, Grosvenor Square Westminster, from complications suffered in a fall, he was buried at Rothesay on the Isle of Bute.

Interesting fact:

The flowering plant genus *Stewartia* is named after John Stuart.

George Grenville
7th British Prime Minister

Born
14 October 1712, Wotton, Buckinghamshire
Died
13 November 1770, age 58, Bolton Street, Piccadilly, London
Period in office as Prime Minister
2 years 85 days from 16 May 1763 until 10 July 1765
Political party
Whig
Constituency Represented as MP
Buckingham 1741-1770
Ministerial offices held as Prime Minister
First Lord of the Treasury
Chancellor of the Exchequer
Leader of the House of Commons

George Grenville (14 October 1712 – 13 November 1770) was a British Whig statesman who rose to the position of Prime Minister of Great Britain. Grenville was born into an influential political family and first entered Parliament in 1741 as an MP for Buckingham. He emerged as one of Cobham's Cubs, a group of young members of Parliament associated with Lord Cobham.

Grenville was educated at Eton and Christ Church, Oxford. He did not graduate but entered the Inner Temple and qualified as a barrister in 1735. His elder brother, Richard (later the 2nd Earl Temple), had entered Parliament through Cobham's influence in 1734, joining the group of Walpole's opponents known as 'Cobham's Cubs'. William Pitt the Elder was another prominent member of this group which Grenville also joined when he became MP for Buckingham in 1741.

When Grenville entered Parliament in 1741 it was as one of the two members for Buckingham, and he continued to represent that borough for the next twenty-nine years (until his death in 1770). Although at first he was disappointed to be giving up what appeared to be a promising legal career for the uncertainties of opposition politics, he soon rose in the world of politics.

In December 1744 he became a Lord of the Admiralty in the administration of Henry Pelham. He spoke on naval matters in the Commons but hoped for further promotion. He joined the Treasury Board in 1747, further developing his financial and administrative skills. He allied himself with his brother Richard and with William Pitt (who became their brother-in-law in 1754) and forced Pelham into giving them promotion by rebelling against his authority and obstructing business. In June 1747, Grenville became a Lord of the Treasury.

Grenville married Elizabeth Wyndham in May 1749. Elizabeth's father was Sir William Wyndham, a leading Tory politician of the

Walpole era. Her grandfather, the Duke of Somerset, disapproved of the marriage and settled very little property on her. The couple had four sons and five daughters. Their youngest son, William Wyndham Grenville, eventually became Prime Minister himself in 1806.

After Pelham's death in 1754, Grenville was promoted to Treasurer of the Navy and joined the Privy Council. Grenville was aligned to the political faction led by William Pitt the elder in the Commons and Richard Grenville (now Earl Temple) in the Lords. Pitt was Paymaster of the Forces but had a difficult relationship with Pelham's successor, Pelham-Holles. Grenville followed his lead, acting as Pitt's deputy in the Commons. The bonds between them were strengthened when Pitt married Grenville and Temple's sister, Hester, in November 1754.

Grenville who had been made Treasurer of the Navy and Privy Councillor, was dismissed in 1755, along with Pitt and several other colleagues after speaking out and voting against the government on a debate about a subsidy treaty with Russia which they believed was unnecessarily costly, and would drag Britain into Continental European disputes. Opposition to European entanglements was a cornerstone of Patriot Whig thinking.

He and Pitt joined the opposition, haranguing the Newcastle government. Grenville and Pitt both championed the formation of a British militia to provide additional security rather than the deployment of Hessian mercenaries favoured by the government. As the military situation deteriorated following the loss of Minorca, the government grew increasingly weak until it was forced to resign in autumn 1756.

In 1758, as Treasurer of the Navy, Grenville introduced and carried a bill which established a fairer system of paying the wages of seamen and supporting their families while they were at sea, which was praised for its humanity if not for its effectiveness. He remained in office during the years of British victories, notably the 'Annus Mirabilis' of 1759 for which the credit went to the government of which he was a member. However his seven-year-old son died after a long illness and Grenville remained by his side at their country house in Wotton and rarely went to London.

In 1761, when Pitt resigned upon the question of the war with Spain, in the administration of Lord Bute, Grenville's role was seen as an attempt to keep someone closely associated with Pitt involved in the government, in order to prevent Pitt and his supporters actively opposing the government. However, it soon led to conflict between Grenville and Pitt. Grenville was also seen as a suitable candidate because his reputation for honesty meant he commanded loyalty and respect amongst independent MPs.

In May 1762, Grenville was appointed Northern Secretary, where he took an increasingly hard line in the negotiations with France and Spain designed to bring the Seven Years' War to a close and in October 1762 he was made in First Lord of the Admiralty.

In April 1763, Grenville became First Lord of the Treasury and Chancellor of the Exchequer succeeding John Stuart as first Minister after Henry Fox had rejected the job. King George III eventually lost patience with Grenville. Irritated by Grenville's assertive attitude towards him and his desire to control all official appointments. When Marquess of Rockingham agreed to accept office, the King dismissed Grenville in July 1765. Grenville died on 13 November 1770, aged 58 and is buried at Wotton Underwood in Buckinghamshire.

Interesting George Grenville facts:

The town of Grenville, Quebec, was named after George Grenville.

Grenville was one of the relatively few prime ministers who never acceded to the peerage.

Charles Watson-Wentworth *(2nd Marquess of Rockingham)* 8th British Prime Minister

Born
13 May 1730, Wentworth Woodhouse, near Rotherham Buckinghamshire

Died
1 July 1782, age 52, Wimbledon, London

Periods in office as Prime Minister
Total 1 year 115 days over 2 Terms: from 13 July 1765 – 30 July 1766 (1 year 18 days) and 27 March 1782 – 1 July 1782 (97 days)

Political party
Whig

Ministerial offices held as Prime Minister
First Lord of the Treasury
Leader of the House of Lords

Charles Watson-Wentworth, 2nd Marquess of Rockingham, (13 May 1730 – 1 July 1782), styled The Hon. Charles Watson-Wentworth before 1733, Viscount Higham 1733 - 1746, Earl of Malton 1746 - 1750 and The Marquess of Rockingham in 1750.

Watson-Wentworth was a British Whig statesman, most notable for his two terms as Prime Minister of Great Britain. He became the patron of many Whigs, known as the Rockingham Whigs, and served as a leading Whig grandee and was one of the leading opposition figures during George III's reign . He served in only two high offices during his lifetime (Prime Minister and Leader of the House of Lords).

Watson-Wentworth was born in May 1730 at the family seat of Wentworth Woodhouse near Rotherham. His father, Thomas, had served as an MP, siding with the court Whigs, and had been raised to the peerage. After his father's death in December 1750 he became a Marquess, and on 13 May 1751 (his 21st birthday), and inherited his father's estates.
In addition to the estates in Yorkshire, Watson-Wentworth was also a major landowner in both Northamptonshire and Wicklow. He added further to this fortune with his marriage to Mary Bright in 1752.
Watson-Wentworth's maiden speech was on 17 March 1752 in support of the Bill which disposed of Scottish lands confiscated in the aftermath of the Jacobite rising of 1745. His speech was not well received, with Horace Walpole criticising him for venturing into "a debate so much above his force".
During the 1750s, his direct involvement in national politics was limited. His interests, instead, were in improving his estates and horse racing.
Watson-Wentworth became a Knight of the Garter in 1760.
When George III tired of George Grenville, Watson-Wentworth was one of the opposition leaders who wanted to accept office in the summer of 1765. He was suggested as a possible candidate

for various offices but ultimately became First Lord, his first national political office of any sort. Rockingham's rapid rise was partly due to the absence of other plausible candidates, the Duke of Devonshire had died in 1764 and Thomas Pelham-Holles was considered too old to take major office again.

The administration, like most eighteenth-century governments, was a coalition. Its major political task was to deal with the emerging crisis in the North American colonies following the imposition of stamp duties, bitterly resisted by the colonists. Rockingham, mindful of the disruption to Atlantic trade, was keen to repeal the Stamp Act that Grenville had imposed. Nevertheless, he also wanted to reassert the principle that Parliament had the right to tax the colonists, which he duly did with a Declaratory Act.

CHARLES WATSON-WENTWORTH

In the mid 1760's George III's support for Rockingham began to waver. The King was unhappy with Rockingham's refusal to admit some of John Stuart's friends to office and was determined to change his ministry again. This he did by replacing Rockingham with William Pitt the Elder in July 1766.

From 1766 to 1782 Rockingham spent the next sixteen years in opposition.

In March 1782 he was appointed Prime Minister for a second time and, upon taking office, pushed for an acknowledgement of the independence of the United States, initiating an end to British involvement in the American War of Independence.

Due to rising unemployment, in this second premiership, Rockingham's administration saw the passage of the Relief of the Poor Act 1782 (also known as Gilbert's Act), a poor relief law proposed by Thomas Gilbert which aimed to organise poor relief on a county basis, this saw the creation of unions of civil parishes, later officially called *unions under Gilbert's Act*, to provide outdoor relief and set up workhouses.

Rockingham's second term was unfortunately short-lived, for Lord Rockingham died at the beginning of July during an Influenza epidemic, fourteen weeks after taking office. He was replaced as Prime Minister by Lord Shelburne, who was more reluctant to accept the total independence of America and proposed a form of Dominion status, however by April 1783 he succeeded in securing peace with America and this feat remains his legacy.

Interesting Charles Watson-Wentworth facts:

Passionate about horse racing and breeding, Watson-Wentworth owned Allabaculia the first horse to win "the oldest classic turf race" the St Leger at Doncaster in 1776.

Places named after Lord Rockingham:

Canada

Rockingham, Nova Scotia

United States

Rockingham, North Hampshire

William Pitt the Elder (1st Earl of Chatham) 9th British Prime Minister

Born
15 November 1708, Westminster, London
Died
11 May 1778, age 69, Hayes, Middlesex
Period in office as Prime Minister
2 years 76 days from 30 July 1766 – 14 October 1768
Political party
Whig
Constituencies Represented as MP
Old Sarum 1735-1747
Seaford 1747-1754
Aldborough 1754-1756
Okehampton 1756-1757
Bath 1756-1766
Ministerial offices held as Prime Minister
First Lord of the Treasury
Lord Privy Seal

William Pitt, 1st Earl of Chatham, (15 November 1708 – 11 May 1778) was a British statesman of the Whig group who served as Prime Minister of Great Britain in the middle of the 18th century. Historians call him Pitt of Chatham, or William Pitt the Elder, to distinguish him from his son, William Pitt the Younger, who also became Prime Minister. Pitt was also known as the Great Commoner, because of his long-standing refusal to accept a title until 1766.

Pitt was the grandson of Thomas Pitt (1653–1726), the Governor of Madras, known as "Diamond" Pitt for having discovered a diamond of extraordinary size and sold it to the Duke of Orléans for around £135,000. This transaction, as well as other trading deals in India, established the Pitt family fortune. After returning home the Governor was able to raise his family to a position of wealth and political influence, in 1691 he purchased the property of Boconnoc in Cornwall, which gave him control of a seat in Parliament. He made further land purchases and became one of the dominant political figures in the West Country, controlling seats such as the rotten borough of Old Sarum.

Pitt was Born in November 1708, his grandfather and father had both been MPs and his grandfather, Thomas, had been Governor of Madras. Pitt was a pupil at Eton from 1719 until 1726. He entered Trinity College, Oxford in 1727 but rapidly moved on to study in Utrecht. His elder brother Thomas, inherited the family estates and William had to seek other employment. His Etonian friend, George Lyttelton, introduced him to Richard Temple, Viscount Cobham in 1731 and Pitt gained a commission in Temple's regiment.

Pitt's elder brother Thomas was returned at the General Election of 1734 for two separate seats, Okehampton and Old Sarum, and chose to sit for Okehampton, passing the vacant seat to William. Accordingly, in February 1735, William Pitt entered Parliament as member for Old Sarum. He quickly sided with the opposition to Walpole, joining Cobham's nephews Richard Grenville and Lyttelton as a member of the group known as 'Cobham's Cubs'. Opposition to the ministry in the eighteenth century was frequently associated with the heir to the throne and Pitt and the cubs moved closer to Frederick, Prince of Wales. Pitt was very critical of Walpole's handling of relations with Spain in the late 1730s and spoke strongly in the debates in early 1742 that ultimately led to Walpole's resignation.

William Pitt the Elder 1st Earl of Chatham

Pitt's maiden speech in the Commons was delivered in April 1736, in the debate on the congratulatory address to George II on the marriage of his son Frederick, Prince of Wales.

Owing to public pressure, the British government was pushed towards declaring war with Spain in 1739. Britain began with a success at Porto Bello. However the war effort soon stalled, and Pitt alleged that the government was not prosecuting the war effectively.

Pitt considered the war a missed opportunity to take advantage of a power in decline, although later he became an advocate of warmer relations with the Spanish in an effort to prevent them forming an alliance with France. Many of Pitt's attacks on the government were directed personally at Sir Robert Walpole who had now been Prime Minister for twenty years. He spoke in favour of the motion in 1742 for an inquiry into the last ten years of Walpole's administration. In February 1742, following poor election results and the disaster at Cartagena, Walpole was at last forced to succumb to the long-continued attacks of opposition, he resigned and took a peerage. In 1744 Pitt was hoping for a position in government with the administration formed by the Pelhams, but was disliked by the King and leading Whigs over his views on the subsidies offered to Hanover (where the King had spent the first thirty years of his life) and was therefore thwarted. Also In 1744 Pitt received a large boost to his personal fortune when the Dowager Duchess of Marlborough died leaving him a legacy of £10,000 as an "acknowledgment of the noble defence he had made for the support of the laws of England and to prevent the ruin of his country".

It was with deep reluctance that in February 1746 the King finally agreed to give Pitt a place in the government, with Pitt being appointed as Vice Treasurer of Ireland and subsequently in May of 1746, Paymaster of the Forces, neither of which office required personal contact with the King. Pitt was elected as MP for Seaford in 1747 and then Aldborough in 1754. Pitt married Lady Hester Grenville, sister of Richard Grenville, Earl Temple, and George Grenville, in November 1754. Their marriage yielded five children, including William Pitt the Younger.

In 1766, following the collapse of the first Rockingham ministry, Pitt finally agreed to lead an administration but as Lord Privy Seal, rather than First Lord. Poor health, which had been a recurrent feature of his political career, led him to accept a peerage and he became Earl of Chatham. He had hoped to revive Britain's alliances in northern Europe which he felt had been fatally damaged at the end of the Seven Years War. In this, and in attempts to resolve the American crisis, he was unsuccessful. By October 1768, having failed to achieve his aims, a weary Pitt begged the King to allow him to resign. George III accepted, determined to keep him out of office henceforth. Pitt has a distinctive place among English statesmen as he was the first minister whose main strength lay in the support of the nation at large as distinct from its representatives in the Commons.

His final appearance in the House of Lords was on April 7, 1778, on the occasion of the Charles Lennox, the Duke of Richmond's motion for an address praying the King to conclude peace with America on any terms.

He died in May 1778 aged 69, and received a funeral in Westminster Abbey at public expense.

Interesting Pitt the Elder facts:

Pitt the Elder married Lady Hester Grenvilleon October 16, 1754 and had five children (three boys and two girls) including future Prime Minister Pitt the Younger.

The American metropolis of Pittsburgh in Pennsylvania was named after the British Prime Minister William Pitt the Elder.

Pitt's parliamentary skills led him to be known as the 'Great Commoner'. The Commons voted for a state funeral for him although the Lords didn't attend.

Pitt's London house, in St. James's Square, is now the home of the international affairs think tank called Chatham House. Whose aim is to help governments and societies build a sustainably secure, prosperous and just world.

Augustus Fitzroy, (3rd Duke of Grafton)
10th British Prime Minister

Born
28 September 1735
Died
14 March 1811, age 75, Euston Hall, Suffolk
Period in office as Prime Minister
2 years 76 days from 14 October 1768 – 28 January 1770
Political party
Whig
Constituencies Represented as MP
Boroughbridge 1756
Bury St Edmunds 1756-1757
Ministerial offices held as Prime Minister
First Lord of the Treasury
Leader of the House of Lords

Augustus Henry FitzRoy, 3rd Duke of Grafton (28 September 1735 – 14 March 1811), styled Earl of Euston between 1747 and 1757, was a British Whig statesman of the Georgian era. He is one of a handful of Dukes who have served as Prime Minister.

Born in 1735 he was a son of Lord Augustus FitzRoy, a Captain in the Royal Navy, and Elizabeth Cosby, daughter of Colonel William Cosby, who served as a colonial Governor of New York. His father was the third son of the 2nd Duke of Grafton and Lady Henrietta Somerset, which made FitzRoy a great-grandson of both the 1st Duke of Grafton and the Marquess of Worcester. He was notably a fourth-generation descendant of King Charles II and the 1st Duchess of Cleveland, the surname FitzRoy stems from this illegitimacy. His younger brother was the 1st Baron Southampton. After the death of his uncle in 1747, he was styled Earl of Euston as his grandfather's heir apparent.

FitzRoy was educated at Newcome's School in Hackney and at Westminster School, made the Grand Tour - a 17th- and 18th-century custom of a traditional trip through Europe undertaken by upper-class young European men of sufficient means and rank (typically accompanied by a chaperone, such as a family member when they had come of age), and he obtained a degree at Peterhouse, University of Cambridge.

1756 was an eventful year personally and politically for Fitzroy. He married a wealthy heiress, Anne Liddell, in January and in November he was appointed Lord of the Bedchamber to the Prince of Wales and elected MP for both Boroughbridge and Bury St Edmunds. Given the familial connection with Suffolk he chose to sit for the latter. Although the marriage produced three children, it was not a happy one, the couple separated in 1764, and by Act of Parliament were granted a divorce in 1769. Fitzroy's tenure as an MP was short too. His grandfather's death in May 1757 led to his elevation to the Lords with his promotion to Lord Lieutenant of Suffolk.

In 1765, Fitzroy was appointed a Privy Counsellor, then, following discussions with William Pitt the Elder he was eventually offered the role of Secretary of State for the Northern Department (a precursor to the modern Foreign Secretary) in the Rockingham administration.

FitzRoy joined the government believing that Watson-Wentworth would make serious efforts to find an accommodation with Pitt the Elder. When it became clear that this was not the case, he resigned in May 1766. Watson-Wentworth's administration collapsed a few months later and Pitt was finally persuaded to come into office. Pitt had accepted a peerage and chose to be Lord Privy Seal. He therefore, needed someone else to become First Lord of the Treasury. FitzRoy accepted, initially relying heavily on Pitt for direction and advice.

AUGUSTUS HENRY FITZROY

However, Pitt's ill-health and inability to provide a lead on a day-to-day basis increasingly hampered the effectiveness of the administration. FitzRoy emerged from Pitt's shadow during 1767 and royal support persuaded him to take on greater responsibility himself. He was already effectively leader of the administration when Pitt stepped down in October 1768.

Fitzroy had to deal with many problems during his two-year ministry. On 10 May 1768 government soldiers opened fire on demonstrators that had gathered at St George's Field's, Southwark, in South London. The protest was against the imprisonment of the radical Member of Parliament John Wilkes for writing an article that severely criticised King George III. FitzRoy's decision to debar Wilkes from Parliament during the Middlesex elections resulted in the emergence of the Petitioning Movement, so-called because it produced petitions for the dissolution of Parliament that were signed by a quarter of the electorate. FitzRoy disregarded the petitions as irrelevant. The Wilkes affair also saw the emergence of the Society for the Supporters of the Bill of Rights, which campaigned for the extension of the franchise and shorter Parliaments. The year 1768 also saw poor harvests with consequent food shortages and soaring prices. High unemployment and a severe winter provoked riots among the Spitalfields silk-weaver and East End coal-heavers. Merchant seamen in Hull, Tyneside and London went on strike for higher wages. These problems merely added to FitzRoy's burdens.

Ministerial resignations in early 1770 sapped FitzRoy's willingness to continue in office and on 28 January 1770 he resigned. Although he maintained an interest in politics for the rest of his life he devoted increasing attention to his second wife, his Suffolk estates and theological matters.

He died in March 1811 aged 75.

Interesting Augustus FitzRoy facts:

FitzRoy would be the only Prime Minister to divorce and remarry whilst in office until Boris Johnson in 2020.

FitzRoy also had horse racing interests with his racing silks being sky blue, with a black cap.

Frederick North (Lord North, Earl of Guilford)
11th British Prime Minister

Born
13 April 1732, Piccadilly, London
Died
5 August 1792, age 60, London
Period in office as Prime Minister
12 years 59 days from 27 March 1770 – 28 January 1782
Political party
Tory
Constituency Represented as MP
Banbury 1754-1790
Ministerial offices held as Prime Minister
First Lord of the Treasury
Chancellor of the Exchequer
Leader of the House of Commons

Frederick North, 2nd Earl of Guilford, (13 April 1732 – 5 August 1792), better known by his courtesy title **Lord North**, which he used from 1752 to 1790, was Prime Minister of Great Britain from 1770 to 1782. He led Great Britain through most of the American War of Independence. He also held a number of other cabinet posts, including Home Secretary and Chancellor of the Exchequer.

Lord North was born in London on 13 April 1732 at the family house at Albemarle Street, just off Piccadilly, though he spent much of his youth at Wroxton Abbey in Oxfordshire. North's father, the First Earl, was at the time Lord of the Bedchamber to Prince Frederick, who stood as godfather to North.
North was educated at Eton College between 1742 and 1748 and at Trinity College, Oxford, wherein 1750 he was awarded an MA. After leaving Oxford, he travelled in Europe on a Grand Tour with Lord Dartmouth. They stayed in Leipzig for nearly nine months, studying under the constitutional scholar Johann Jacob Mascov. They continued through Austria and Italy, staying in Rome from December 1752 to Easter 1753, then through Switzerland to Paris, returning to England in early 1754.

Lord North was the son of a Tory nobleman, the 1st Earl of Guilford, was elected Member of Parliament for Banbury at the age of 22. He went on to represent the town (of which his father was high steward) for nearly 40 years. Thomas Pelham Holles, when Prime Minister, made him a Lord of the Treasury in 1759, and North held this office under the succeeding Prime Ministers, John Stuart and George Grenville until 1765.
In November 1763, he was chosen to speak for the government concerning radical MP John Wilkes. Wilkes had made a savage attack on both the Prime Minister and the King in his newspaper The North Briton, which many thought libellous. North's motion that Wilkes be expelled from the House of Commons passed by 273 votes to 111. Wilkes' expulsion took

place in his absence, as he had already fled to France following a duel.

On the fall of Watson-Wentworth's first ministry in 1766, North was sworn as a member of the Privy Council and made Paymaster General by the next Prime Minister, Augustus FitzRoy. On the death of Charles Townshend in September 1767 North became Chancellor of the Exchequer and in early 1768, he became Leader of the House of Commons.

LORD NORTH

When FitzRoy resigned as Prime Minister in January of 1770 it was to North that the King turned to as his new premier. North's successful handling of the Falkland Islands crisis in February 1771 marked the establishment of his authority as Prime Minister. His first year in office had been a triumph of coolness, courage, and determination, and he had revealed qualities of leadership few had suspected. North had become an exceptionally conscientious First Minister, continuing simultaneously as Chancellor of the Exchequer, he helped establish budget day as a major date in the political calendar. He maintained his supremacy in the House of Commons against a divided opposition, and such was George III's confidence in his minister that in 1772 North became the first commoner since Robert Walpole to receive the Order of the Garter. North himself reduced the National Debt by some £10 million by 1775, but the impact of the American War of Independence meant that it soon rose by £75 million.

Most of North's government was focused first on the growing problems with the American colonies. Later on, it was preoccupied with conducting the American War of Independence that broke out in 1775 with the Battle of Lexington. Following the Boston Tea Party in 1773, Lord North proposed a number of legislative measures that were supposed to punish the Bostonians. These measures were known as the Coercive Acts in Great Britain, while dubbed the Intolerable Acts in the colonies. Underestimating the colonists' powers of resistance, he faced war half-heartedly, and with the British defeat at Saratoga in 1777 his ministry was on the defensive. After another British capitulation at Yorktown in 1781 he clung on to power, but on 20 March 1782 he resigned shortly after a motion demanding an end to the war in America which saw the ministry defeated in the Commons, before peace was concluded.

For a short period North was an effective critic of William Pitt the Younger's administration from the opposition benches, but with ill health and sight loss he made a gradual withdrawal from public life.

North died in Grosvenor Square, London, on 5 August 1792 aged 60.

Interesting Frederick North facts:

Lord North Street and Guilford Street in London are named after Frederick North.

Lord North never used the term 'Prime Minister' of himself.

William Petty (2nd Earl of Shelburne)
12th British Prime Minister

Born
2 May 1737, Dublin, Ireland
Died
7 May 1805, age 68, London
Period in office as Prime Minister
266 days from 4 July 1782 – 26 March 1783
Political party
Whig
Constituency Represented as MP
Wycombe 1760-1761
Kerry 1761-1762 (Parliament of Ireland)
Ministerial offices held as Prime Minister
First Lord of the Treasury
Leader of the House of Lords

William Petty, (1st Marquess of Lansdowne), (2 May 1737 – 7 May 1805; known as **The Earl of Shelburne** between 1761 and 1784, (by which title he is generally known to history) was an Irish-born British Whig statesman who was the first Home Secretary in 1782 and then Prime Minister in 1782–83 during the final months of the American War of Independence. He succeeded in securing peace with America and this feat remains his most notable legacy. He was also well known as a collector of antiquities and works of art.

Petty was born in Dublin on 2 May 1737 to a Kerry landed family, the Fitzmaurices (his father changed the family name to Petty in 1751 on inheriting estates in High Wycombe, shortly before being created Earl of Shelburne in 1753). Petty had an unhappy Irish childhood, he wrote 'Arrived at the age of sixteen I had nobody to teach me, and everything to learn, of which I was fully aware, but I had, what I was not at all aware of, everything to unlearn; no such easy matter'. He studied at Christ Church, Oxford (he left Oxford at 20) and then went into military service.

Fitzmaurice (as he then was) distinguished himself in the battles of Minden and Kloster Kampen in the Seven Years' War. While still abroad, he was returned on 2 June 1760 for the seat at Chipping Wycombe which his father had held and after his father's death in 1761 he inherited his title and was elevated to the House of Lords. In 1761 the King prevented the Prime Minister, Thomas Pelham-Holles (the Duke of Newcastle), from using public money to fund the election of Whig candidates, Pelham-Holles simply used his private fortune to ensure that his ministry gained a comfortable majority.

Petty became First Lord of Trade in the Grenville ministry (1763) but resigned, a few months later and he attached himself to William Pitt, under whom, in 1766, he served as Secretary of State for the Southern Department. However differences with his colleagues on colonial questions caused him to resign in 1768.

Petty followed Pitt into opposition in 1768, where he emerged as a prominent but independent figure alongside Rockingham and Grenville during Lord North's ministry.
He continued to prefer conciliation to coercion in America, though his own oratory was often extremely combative (in 1780 he was wounded in a resulting duel with the MP William Fullarton).

WILLIAM PETTY

In domestic politics he found himself at odds with Rockingham's Whig faction over his support for parliamentary reform and sympathy for the anti-Catholic Gordon riots of 1780.
Following the fall of the North government in March 1782, Petty joined its replacement under Watson-Wentworth. Petty was made Prime Minister in July 1782 following Watson-Wentworth's death (he died in office after 97 days of his second term), with the American War still being fought.

Petty's government lasted only 266 days and was brought down largely due to the terms of the Peace of Paris which brought the conflict to an end.

Although only Prime Minister for just eight months (only three of which Parliament was in session) it was notable for introduction of William Pitt the Younger to high office as Chancellor of the Exchequer.

Petty resigned as Prime Minister on 26 March 1783.

The 45-year-old ex-premier remained active in Parliament for more than two decades, but not even Pitt, formerly his protégé, wished (or could afford to) offer him major office, especially after Lord Lansdowne (as Petty became in November 1784) proved conciliatory to the French revolutionaries and to domestic extra-parliamentary opposition.

After his resignation he still gave general support to the policy of Pitt, but ceased to take an active part in public affairs. He was elected a Foreign Honorary Member of the American Academy of Arts and Sciences in 1803.

William Petty had married twice and was a father to three children (a son from his first marriage and a son and daughter from his second marriage).

Petty died in London aged 68, on 7 May 1805.

Interesting William Petty facts:

Petty's brother, The Hon. Thomas Fitzmaurice (1742–1793) of Cliveden, was also a Member of Parliament.

Benjamin Disraeli said of Petty 'he is one of the suppressed characters of English history'.

Petty was Britain's first Irish born Prime Minister

William Cavendish-Bentinck
(3rd Duke of Portland)
13th British Prime Minister

Born
14 April 1738
Died
30 October 1809, age 79, Bulstrode, Buckinghamshire
Periods in office as Prime Minister
Total 3 years 84 days over 2 Terms: from 2 April 1783 – 18 December 1783 (261 days) and 2 years 188 days from 31 March 1807 – 4 October 1809 (2 years 188 days)
Political party
Whig
Constituency Represented as MP
Weobley 1761-1762
Ministerial offices held as Prime Minister
First Lord of the Treasury
Leader of the House of Lords

William Cavendish-Bentinck, 3rd Duke of Portland, (14 April 1738 – 30 October 1809) was a British Whig politician during the late Georgian era. He served twice as the Prime Minister of Great Britain (1783 and 1807–09) on both occasions he was merely the nominal head of a government controlled by stronger political leaders. The twenty-four years between his two terms as Prime Minister is the longest gap between terms of office of any British Prime Minister.

William Bentinck was the youngest son of the second Duke of Portland, and was born on 14 April 1738. He attended Westminster School and Christ Church, Oxford (where he added 'Cavendish' to his surname) and where he graduated with an MA in 1757. He then undertook a tour of Europe, towards the end of which, in 1761, through his family's interest, he was elected MP for Weobley, Herefordshire. The following year he entered the Lords when he succeeded his late father as Duke of Portland.

Following his elevation to the House of Lords, the 3rd Duke's political influence developed quickly. He aligned himself with the Whigs and in 1765 became Lord Chamberlain in Rockingham's (Watson-Wentworth's) ministry. After Watson-Wentworth's ministry fell, Cavendish-Bentinck played an influential role in organising the party and used his extensive electoral influence to secure the return of a number of MP's. It was to be sixteen years, however, before he returned to government with Rockingham. In 1782 when Watson-Wentworth died, Cavendish-Bentinck was surprised to be chosen as party leader and found himself at the head of a coalition government as First Lord of the Treasury. By the end of 1783, however, the coalition government had been dismissed, and Cavendish-Bentinck found himself in opposition once again. In 1793, after a bitter struggle within the Whig party, and after protracted manoeuvrings, Cavendish-Bentinck and his followers managed to secure five cabinet places in the Pitt administration. This gave them a share of power which had previously seemed unobtainable.

In the later years of his political career Cavendish-Bentinck began to move towards the emerging 'Toryism'. He was hostile to both parliamentary reform and to Catholic Emancipation and remained a loyal supporter of the royal prerogative.

William Cavendish-Bentinck

The lack of leadership from the Prime Minister and military setbacks in the war with Napoleon in Spain and Portugal encouraged serious ministerial rivalries to develop. Cavendish-Bentinck himself became Secretary of State for the Home Department in 1794, a post which he was to hold until 1801. His tenure at the Home Office coincided with the suppression of the Irish Rebellion of 1798, and it seems that Cavendish-Bentinck was a central figure in secret negotiations to secure the passing of the legislation. From 1801 to 1805 he served as Lord President of the Council and then as a Minister without Portfolio. He continued to serve in the cabinet until Pitt's death in 1806.

In 1807, despite suffering badly from gout and kidney stones Cavendish-Bentinck once again held the post of First Lord of the Treasury, though his age and illnesses really meant he was unfit for the task. Due to his ailments much work was left to Spencer Perceval, who even took up residence in No. 10 Downing Street. His second ministry though was dominated by the Foreign Secretary, George Canning, and the Secretary for War, Viscount Castlereagh (later 2nd Marquess of Londonderry). When Castlereagh discovered in September 1809 that Canning had made a deal with Cavendish-Bentinck to have him removed from office, he was furious. Castlereagh challenged Canning to a duel, which was fought on 21 September 1809. Canning had never fired a pistol and completely missed, whilst Castlereagh wounded his opponent in the thigh. Both men resigned as a result of the incident. Their disagreements and Cavendish-Bentinck's ill health caused him to resign, by the end of the following month. In October 1809, shortly after having an operation to remove a kidney stone, Cavendish-Bentinck died.

Interesting William Cavendish-Bentinck fact:

Portland Canal and Portland Channel on the British Columbia Coast are named after William Cavendish-Bentinck 3rd Duke of Portland.

William Pitt the Younger
14th British Prime Minister

Born
28 May 1759, Hayes Place, near Hayes Kent
Died
23 January 1806, age 46, Putney Heath, London
Periods in office as Prime Minister
Total 18 years 345 days (2 Terms) from 19 December 1783 – 14 March 1801 (17 years 86 days) and 10 May 1804 – 23 January 1806 (1 year 259 days)
Political party
Tory and Whig
Constituencies Represented as MP
Appleby 1781-1784
Cambridge University 1784-1806
Ministerial offices held as Prime Minister
First Lord of the Treasury
Chancellor of the Exchequer
Leader of the House of Commons

William Pitt the Younger (28 May 1759 – 23 January 1806) was a prominent British Tory statesman (although he referred to himself as an 'Independent Whig') of the late eighteenth and early nineteenth centuries. He became the youngest Prime Minister of Great Britain in 1783 at the age of 24 and the first Prime Minister of Great Britain and Ireland as of January 1801. He left office in March 1801, but served as Prime Minister again from 1804 until his death aged 46 in 1806. He was also Chancellor of the Exchequer for all of his time as Prime Minister.

William Pitt, was the second son of William Pitt, 1st Earl of Chatham, and was born at Hayes Place in the village of Hayes, Kent. Pitt was from a political family on both sides. His mother, Hester Grenville, was sister to former Prime Minister George Grenville. Pitt suffered from occasional poor health as a boy, he was educated at home by the Reverend Edward Wilson, and was an intelligent child who quickly became proficient in Latin and Greek. He was admitted to Pembroke College, Cambridge, on 26 April 1773, a month before his fourteenth birthday where he studied political philosophy, classics, mathematics, trigonometry, chemistry and history.

While at Cambridge, he befriended the young William Wilberforce, (later the leader of the movement to abolish the slave trade) who became a lifelong friend and political ally in Parliament. Pitt who was still plagued by poor health, took advantage of a little-used privilege available only to the sons of noblemen, and chose to graduate without having to pass examinations. He then went on to acquire a legal education at Lincoln's Inn and was called to the bar in the summer of 1780. During the General Elections of September 1780, at the age of 21, Pitt contested the University of Cambridge seat, but lost. Still intent on entering Parliament, Pitt (with the help of his university friends) stood in a by-election in Appleby (a former county of Westmorland) winning the seat which sent Pitt to the House of Commons in January 1781.

In Parliament, the youthful Pitt cast aside his tendency to be withdrawn in public and in 1782 he was appointed Chancellor of the Exchequer. The following years were marked by the battle between George III and the radical Charles Fox, whom the King detested. Matters deteriorated when Fox forged an alliance with the previously loyal Lord North. The two men defeated the government and King George was forced to ask them to take control. Fox became Pitt's lifelong political rival.

WILLIAM PITT THE YOUNGER

In December 1783, George III dismissed the Lord North/Fox ministry that had succeeded Petty's government, and it was to the 24-year-old Pitt that the King turned to serve as both Prime Minister and Chancellor.

At 24 Pitt was the youngest man to become Prime Minister, and although he was immediately defeated in parliament he refused to resign, and George III was prepared to abdicate rather than let Fox in again.

Therefore in 1784, Parliament was dissolved for a General Election which Pitt won (he contested and won the University of Cambridge's seat). His government worked to restore public finances which were severely strained by the cost of the American War of Independence and later by the war with France. Pitt imposed new taxes - including Britain's first income tax - and reduced both smuggling and frauds. He also simplified customs and excise duties. In 1785 he introduced a bill to remove the representation of thirty-six rotten boroughs (a borough that was able to elect an MP despite having very few voters, the choice of MP typically being in the hands of one person or family). He also tried to extend, the electoral franchise to more individuals, but this was abandoned after a parliamentary defeat. Among Pitt's initiatives were financial and administrative reforms with an eye to efficiency and the elimination of corrupt practices. A serious attempt was made to reduce the national debt through the creation of a sinking fund in 1786. In 1788 Pitt faced a major crisis when King George fell victim to a mysterious illness at the time classed as "madness" which was down to the physical and genetic blood disorder called 'porphyria' (the 1994 film The Madness of King George was based on this period). With the King incapacitated, Parliament had to look to appoint a regent to rule in his place. All factions agreed that the only viable candidate was the King's eldest son, Prince George, Prince of Wales. The Prince, however, was a supporter of Charles Fox and had the Prince come to power, he would almost surely have dismissed Pitt. Parliament spent months debating legal technicalities relating to the regency and fortunately for Pitt, the King recovered in February 1789, just after a Regency Bill had been introduced and passed in the House of Commons. Pitt continued in government after the 1790 General Election which ran from 16 June until 28 July. Ninety-two of the 314 constituencies (29 per cent) were contested, an increase of five on the figure for 1784. Roughly the figures were 558 Members of which 340 might be classed as government, 183 opposition, and 35 independent or doubtful. The French

Revolution remained a great concern in the early 1790's and in 1793, the French declared war on Britain. The wartime situation made it difficult for Pitt to pursue his administrative reforms, and financial restraints forced Pitt into a series of recourses to raise the vast sums necessary to sustain the war effort, including in 1799 Britain's first income tax. Pitt oversaw a major triumph with the Act of Union of 1800, which saw the United Kingdom of Britain and Ireland come into being on 1 January 1801 with the Irish Parliament being closed down. But with opposition from the King to his supplementary proposals for Catholic emancipation and state provision for Catholic and Dissenting clergy, it resulted in Pitt resigning on February 3, 1801. Although now physically failing, in May 1804 Pitt returned to head a second ministry, albeit weaker in its basis than his first. He saw Nelson's victory at Trafalgar in 1805 which provided a welcome and rare moment of success in Pitt's continental war strategy. Unfortunately the exhausted premier had to witness Napoleon's decisive victory at Austerlitz before he died aged 46 (suspected liver failure), in office on 23 January 1806 at his house on Putney Heath, he was unmarried and left no children.

Interesting Pitt the Younger facts:

Pitt Street in Glasgow is named after William Pitt the Younger.

At 24 Pitt is still the youngest person ever to become Prime Minister.

Robert Donat portrays Pitt in the 1942 biopic *The Young Mr. Pitt*, which chronicles the historical events of Pitt's life.

Pitt Street is the main financial precinct street in the Central business district of Sydney.

Henry Addington (1st Viscount Sidmouth) 15th British Prime Minister

Born
30 May 1757, Holborn, London

Died
15 February 1844, age 86, London, buried Mortlake, Surrey

Period in office as Prime Minister
3 years 55 days from 17 March 1801 – 10 May 1804

Political party
Tory

Constituency Represented as MP
Devizes 1784- 1805

Ministerial offices held as Prime Minister
First Lord of the Treasury
Chancellor of the Exchequer
Leader of the House of Commons

Henry Addington, 1st Viscount Sidmouth, (30 May 1757 – 15 February 1844).

Henry Addington was British Prime Minister from March 1801 to May 1804. He replaced William Pitt the Younger, who left office on March 14, 1801, to which the King chose Addington, who was an uncompromising Anglican, as opposed to Pitt who whose position was favouring Roman Catholic emancipation. He is best known for obtaining the Treaty of Amiens in 1802, but the peace only lasted a year and he struggled to cope with the problems of the Napoleonic Wars.

Henry Addington was the first British Prime Minister to emerge from the middle classes. He was the son of Anthony Addington a leading physician who had treated William Pitt the Elder, which resulted with him becoming friends with William Pitt the Younger. Addington studied at Reading School, Winchester and Brasenose College, Oxford, and then studied law at Lincoln's Inn becoming a barrister in 1784.

Later in 1784 when Pitt the Younger called his first election, he suggested to Addington that he should enter politics, and with Pitt's help, Addington secured a seat in the House of Commons as a member for Devizes in Wiltshire. By 1789 Pitt made Addington Speaker of the House which was commended by the King.

The King and Addington opposed Pitt's plans in 1801 for Catholic emancipation and although they tried, they couldn't get him to change his mind so the King asked Addington to form his own ministry. Pitt however remained in support and in March 1801 Addington became Prime Minister and Chancellor of the Exchequer. His first cabinet included three future Prime Ministers: Spencer Perceval, Robert Jenkinson and William Cavendish-Bentinck.

Once in office he declared the pursuit of peace as his government's priority, not least on the grounds that further military conflict was financially unaffordable. Addington's domestic reforms doubled the efficiency of the Income tax.

By early 1803 Britain's financial and diplomatic positions had recovered sufficiently to allow Addington to declare war on France (Addington making the declaration in the Commons wearing military uniform), but the administration was attacked in Parliament by Pitt, who eventually declared open opposition to Addington's ministry.

Henry Addington

Although the king stood by him, it was not enough because Addington did not have a strong enough hold on the two houses of Parliament. By May 1804, partisan criticism of Addington's war policies provided the pretext for a parliamentary coup by the three major factions – Grenvillites, Foxites, and Pittites – who had decided that they should replace Addington's ministry.

And so on 10 May 1804 Addington resigned.

Addington, was invited back into cabinet in 1805 in Pitt's second administration as Lord President of the Council and was given a peerage as Viscount Sidmouth (county of Devon).

After Pitt's death in 1806 Addington served in William Grenville's ministry as Lord Privy Seal. In 1812, Robert Jenkinson (Lord Liverpool) asked him to become Home Secretary which he accepted. He continued in this office throughout the years of economic distress and radical political activity that marked the period after the battle of Waterloo in 1815. Addington held the post of Home Secretary for almost ten years until Robert Peel took over in 1822. Addington remained in the Cabinet as Minister without Portfolio for the next two years before moving on to the House of Lords. Addington's achievement as premier during a difficult period of international conflict has been underestimated. He rose to the premiership from a family background in the lesser gentry and professions, and he can claim to have delivered the first budget speech.

Addington died in London on 15 February 1844 at the age of 86, and was buried in the churchyard at St Mary the Virgin Mortlake, now in Greater London.

Interesting Henry Addington facts:

Addington donated to the town of Reading, the four acres of land that is today the site of the Royal Berkshire Hospital.

Addington/Viscount Sidmouth's name is commemorated in the town's Sidmouth Street and Addington Road as well as in Sidmouth Street in Devizes (Wiltshire).

William Wyndham Grenville (1st Baron Grenville) **16th British Prime Minister**

Born
25 October 1759, Buckinghamshire
Died
12 January 1834, age 74, Buckinghamshire
Period in office as Prime Minister
1 year 43 days from 11 February 1806 – 25 March 1807
Political party
Whig
Constituencies Represented as MP
Buckingham 1782-1784
Buckinghamshire 1784-1790
Ministerial offices held as Prime Minister
First Lord of the Treasury
Leader of the House of Lords

William Wyndham Grenville, 1st Baron Grenville (25 October 1759 – 12 January 1834) Born in Buckinghamshire he was British Prime Minister from 11 February 1806 – 25 March 1807.

Grenville was one of seven children and the youngest son of George Grenville (Prime Minister 1763-65). William Grenville was initially educated at East Hill School in Wandsworth and went on to study Eton College. Both his parents died within a year of each other just as he started at Eton. He also studied at Christ Church, Oxford University (1776-80) and then went on to Lincoln's Inn (1780-1782) but was never called to the bar and abandoned plans for a legal career, instead choosing politics. Through the influence of his elder brother George he was elected MP for Buckingham in 1782 and then Buckinghamshire in 1784.

Grenville was related to the Pitt family by marriage. William Pitt, 1st Earl of Chatham had married his father's sister Hester, and thus the younger Grenville was the first cousin of William Pitt the Younger. Grenville supported the Whigs but in 1784 he was appointed Postmaster-General by Pitt, (who was now Prime Minister) becoming Pitt's principal advisor for the following years. In August 1786 Grenville also became vice-president of the Board of Trade as he was as fully committed as Pitt was to the task of financial and commercial reconstruction, following the loss of the American colonies and the removal of statutory control over Irish legislation.

In 1790 he was granted the title Lord Grenville and entered in the House of Lords. Grenville received further promotion under William Pitt and served in his government as Home Secretary (1790-91) and Foreign Secretary (1791-1801). Grenville was a strong supporter of Catholic Emancipation and in 1801 he resigned along with Pitt when George III blocked proposed legislation on the subject.

Grenville's opposition to the 1802 Peace of Amiens negotiated by the Addington ministry saw him become a focus for opposition and he worked with the Whig leader Charles James Fox, whom he came to regard as necessary to any government in which he could serve. Following Pitt's death in 1806, it was to Grenville that the King turned to form a coalition ministry embracing several political factions – known as the 'Ministry of All the Talents' and included Grenville's cousin William Windham who served as Secretary of State for War and the Colonies, and also his younger brother, Thomas Grenville, who served briefly as First Lord of the Admiralty.

William Wyndham Grenville

The coalition was not successful apart from the one notable and lasting achievement was the abolition of the slave trade in 1807, of which Grenville had been an abolitionist of long-standing.

William Wilberforce had introduced the 1807 Abolition of the Slave Trade Act (a bill he had been attempting to pass since 1791).

With the support of Grenville and the Foreign Secretary (Charles Fox) he led a campaign in the House of Commons to ban the slave trade in captured colonies. There was little opposition in the House of Commons and the bill was passed by an overwhelming 114 to 15 vote. In the House of Lords Lord Greenville made a passionate speech that lasted three hours where he argued that the trade was "contrary to the principles of justice, humanity and sound policy" and criticised fellow members for "not having abolished the trade long ago". When the vote was finally taken the bill was passed in the House of Lords by 41 votes to 20. The bill was passed and the 'Abolition of the Slave Trade' received Royal Assent on 30th March 1807.

Grenville's government fell in March 1807, when it clashed with George III over its proposal to allow Roman Catholics to serve in the army up to the rank of general. The monarch demanded a pledge from his ministers not to raise the Catholic question in future. Out of office, Grenville became leader of a Whig opposition (although it was said he had moved closer to the Tories) and in 1817 he retired from the role. A stroke in 1823 did not prevent his occasional and effective intervention in political debates. He had married the Honourable Anne, daughter of Thomas Pitt, 1st Baron Camelford, in 1792, with the marriage being childless. He died on 12 January 1834 aged 74 at his estate in Dropmore, Buckinghamshire.

Interesting **William Grenville fact**:

William Grenville had from the 1780's until it's passing in 1807, long argued for the abolition of slavery, with the Act coming under his premiership in 1807.

Spencer Perceval
17th British Prime Minister

Born
1 November 1762, Audley Square, London
Died
11 May 1812, age 49, Lobby of the House of Commons
Period in office as Prime Minister
2 years 221 days from 4 October 1809 – 11 May 1812
Political party
Tory
Constituency Represented as MP
Northampton 1796-1812
Ministerial offices held as Prime Minister
First Lord of the Treasury
Leader of the House of Commons
Chancellor of the Duchy of Lancaster
Chancellor of the Exchequer
Commissioner of the Treasury of Ireland (1810-1812)

Spencer Perceval (1 November 1762 – 11 May 1812) was a British Tory statesman who served as Prime Minister of the United Kingdom from October 1809 until his assassination in May 1812. Perceval is the only British Prime Minister to have been murdered. He was also the only Solicitor General or Attorney General to become Prime Minister.

Spencer Perceval was born in Audley Square, Mayfair London on 1 November 1762, he was the second son of the second marriage of the second Earl of Egmont (which made him a man of comparatively slender means). *Perceval was educated at Harrow School and Trinity College, Cambridge, where he associated with others who shared Anglican evangelicalism which later marked him out among his political peers. He studied Law at Lincoln's Inn, and practised as a barrister on the Midland circuit. In 1796 he became a King's Counsel.* In the same year of 1796, at the age of 33, Perceval was elected MP for Northampton. In the House of Commons Perceval became a strong supporter of William Pitt and the Tory group in Parliament. In August 1798 he was appointed Solicitor to the Ordinance, and then in 1799 Solicitor-General to the Queen. From 1801 he served Prime Minister Henry Addington as Solicitor General and then Attorney General, he was then Pitt's chief law officer in the Commons during a series of important political trials (he prosecuted the revolutionary Colonel Edward Despard who was executed for high treason in 1803 after being accused of plotting both the seizure of the Tower of London and the assassination of George III known as the 'Despard Plot'). When King George III dismissed William Grenville's ministry in March 1807, Perceval, who was an ardent opponent of Catholic emancipation, became Chancellor of the Exchequer. He also became the Chancellor of the Duchy of Lancaster.

On 30 September 1809 Perceval's was recommended by the Cabinet to the King for the role of Prime Minister (he continued as the unpaid Chancellor of the Exchequer).

Against expectations, he skilfully kept his government afloat for three years despite a severe economic downturn and the continuing war with Napoleon. His government introducing repressive methods against the Luddites. This included the Frame-Breaking Act (Criminal Damage) which made the destruction of machines a capital offence.

Perceval was shot dead in the lobby of the House of Commons on 11 May 1812.

Assassination of Spencer Perceval

At around 5pm on the 11 May 1812 Spencer Perceval entered the House of Commons to an inquiry into the Orders in Council that had placed embargoes upon French trade. The Commons wasn't very busy with around 60 of the 658 members present, as Perceval entered the lobby a number of people were gathered around. No one had noticed a quiet man named John Bellingham walk calmly towards the Prime Minister and from a short distance draw his pistol from a specially designed pocket in his overcoat and shot Perceval in the chest. The sound of the gunshot inside the chamber was intense and a thick smell of gunpowder filled the air.

Perceval was carried to an adjoining room but was pronounced dead within a short time.

Bellingham was restrained and claimed he had shot the Prime Minister for what he saw as the unjust refusal of the government to assist him when he was wrongly imprisoned in Russia, and subsequently not pay him any compensation. Bellingham was hanged for murder on 18 May 1812.

Spencer Perceval is the only Prime Minister in history to be assassinated. He received the accolade of a monument in Westminster Abbey.

Interesting Spencer Perceval facts:

Perceval was assassinated 6 months before his 50th birthday and left a wife and 12 children.

In July 2014, a memorial plaque was unveiled in St Stephen's Hall of the Houses of Parliament, close to where he was killed.

Author Denis Gray wrote a biography on Spencer Perceval entitled: Spencer Perceval: The Evangelical Prime Minister 1762-182 in 1963.

Robert Banks Jenkinson (2nd Earl of Liverpool) 18th British Prime Minister

Born
7 June 1770, London
Died
4 December 1828, age 58, Kingston-upon-Thames, Surrey
Period in office as Prime Minister
14 years 306 days from 8 June 1812 – 9 April 1827
Political party
Tory
Constituencies Represented as MP
Appleby 1790
Rye 1790-1803
Ministerial offices held as Prime Minister
First Lord of the Treasury
Leader of the House of Lords

Robert Banks Jenkinson, 2nd Earl of Liverpool (7 June 1770 – 4 December 1828), was a British statesman and Prime Minister (1812–1827).

Jenkinson was the son of George III's close adviser Charles Jenkinson, later the first Earl of Liverpool, and his first wife, Amelia Watts. He was educated at Charterhouse School and Christ Church, Oxford. In the summer of 1789, Jenkinson spent four months in Paris to perfect his French and enlarge his social experience. He returned to Oxford for three months to complete his terms of residence, and in May 1790 was created Master of Arts.

At the age of twenty Jenkinson was granted the seat of Appleby, a pocket borough owned by Sir James Lowther and later that year won election to the House of Commons for Rye (East Sussex), a seat he would hold until 1803. At the time, however, anyone under the age of 21 (in 1800, nobody under 21 could vote or sit in Parliament, and fewer than 5% in a population of approx 10.5 million had a political vote), so he refrained from taking his seat and spent the following winter and early spring in an extended tour of the continent. Once in Parliament with the help of his father's influence and his own political talent, he rose relatively fast in the Tory government.

In 1792 he delivered several speeches during the parliamentary session and he served as a member of the Board of Control for India from 1793 to 1796. With the outbreak of hostilities with France, Jenkinson, was one of the first of the ministers in government to enlist in the militia. He became a Colonel in the Cinque Ports Fencibles in 1794, and his military duties led to frequent absences from the Commons.
Jenkinson was a member of the Board of Control for India (1793–96), master of the Royal Mint (1799–1801) and entered the cabinet in 1801 as Secretary of State for Foreign Affairs, in which capacity he negotiated the short lived Treaty of Amiens with France.

He was home secretary twice (1804–06, 1807–09) and when William Pitt died in 1806, it was said that the King asked Jenkinson to accept the post of Prime Minister, but he refused, as he believed he lacked a governing majority.

After the death of his father in December 1808 Jenkinson took the title as 2nd Earl of Liverpool.

From 1809-12 Jenkinson was the Secretary for War and the Colonies.

After the assassination of Spencer Perceval in 1812, Jenkinson was asked to form a government, which he reluctantly did. Few expected him to survive in office very long, as at first his government seemed very insecure. But the opposition provided by the Whig party was weak and disunited and Jenkinson stayed in office for 14 years and 306 days.

As Prime Minister Jenkinson, steered the country through the period of radicalism and unrest that followed the Napoleonic Wars. After the war, unrest broke out at home, partly caused by an economic recession that started in 1817. Unemployment, a bad harvest and high prices produced riots and protests. The repeal of income tax and the creation of the Corn Laws tended to make the situation worse. Jenkinson's government reacted by suspending habeas corpus (the legal procedure that keeps the government from holding you indefinitely without showing cause) for 2 years. Things became even worse in summer 1819, when large gatherings in favour of parliamentary reform culminated in a massive public meeting in Manchester on 16 August. Soldiers attacked the crowds, killing 11 and wounding many more. The shocking event became known as the 'Peterloo Massacre'.

The end of the Napoleonic Wars with France in 1815, aided by the Duke of Wellington's victories in the field, boosted support for Jenkinson who after the 'Peterloo Massacre' introduced the 'Six Acts' limiting the right to hold radical meetings. This crackdown on liberty prompted an attempt by radicals in 1820 to murder Jenkinson and his Cabinet, and start a radical revolution. But the 'Cato Street Conspiracy' (Cato Street was where the gang last met) proved unsuccessful. Five of the conspirators were hung for high treason and five were transported (one policeman was killed in the arrests).

During the 1820s Jenkinson became more liberal, and a period of economic prosperity began. He also returned Britain to the Gold Standard in 1819. The anti-trade union laws were repealed, and many trading restrictions were removed. Jenkinson found the heavy burden of running a divided country increasingly stressful and he began to suffer health problems. On 17th February, 1827, he had a stroke and was forced to resign. Although he lived for nearly two more years, he was rarely conscious and he died on 4th December 1828, age 58.

Interesting Robert Jenkinson facts:

Jenkinson was the first British Prime Minister to regularly wear long trousers instead of knee breeches and adopt a short haircut.

Liverpool Street and Liverpool Road in London are named after Jenkinson (Lord Liverpool).

Jenkinson's first wife, Louisa, died at 54. He soon married again, on 24 September 1822, to Lady Mary Chester, a long-time friend of Louisa.

Having died childless, he was succeeded as Earl of Liverpool by his younger half-brother Charles.

Jenkinson was the longest-serving Prime Minister of the 19th century.

George Canning
19th British Prime Minister

Born
11 April 1770, Marylebone, London
Died
8 August 1827, age 57, Chiswick House, Middlesex
Period in office as Prime Minister
119 days from 12 April 1827 – 9 August 1827
Political party
Tory
Constituencies Represented as MP
Newtown (Isle of Wight) 1793-1796, 1806-1807, 1826-1827
Wendover 1801-1802
Tralee 1802-1806
Hastings 1807-1812
Petersfield 1812
Liverpool 1812-1823
Harwich 1823-1826
Seaford 1827
Ministerial offices held as Prime Minister
First Lord of the Treasury
Leader of the House of Commons
Chancellor of the Exchequer

George Canning (11 April 1770 – 8 August 1827) was a British Tory statesman who served as British Prime Minister from April to August 1827. He occupied various senior cabinet positions under numerous Prime Ministers, finally becoming Prime Minister for the last 118 days of his life which is the record for the shortest period of time held by a Prime Minister.

Canning's father, the eldest son of an Irish landowner, was disinherited for his marriage to a beautiful but penniless girl and died in 1771 leaving his wife and year-old son entirely destitute. The widow became an actress and in 1783 she married another actor. As this was seen as an unsatisfactory environment (acting was not considered a respectable profession), George Canning was taken away by his wealthy uncle, Stratford Canning, who raised him along with his own children.

Canning was educated at Eton College and at Christ Church, Oxford. After graduating in 1791 he decided on a political career. In July 1792, he came under the influence of the Prime Minister, William Pitt the Younger, who undertook to find him a seat in Parliament. In July 1793 Canning was elected for the privately controlled borough of Newtown on the Isle of Wight. Canning was highly regarded and became Paymaster of the forces in 1800, but with Pitt's resignation in 1801 Canning also left office. When Pitt formed his last ministry in 1804 Canning became the Treasurer of the Navy, and after Pitt's death in 1806 Canning again left office. He returned to cabinet as Foreign Secretary in 1807 under William Cavendish Bentinck. Canning's greatest success was outmanoeuvring Napoleon at Copenhagen by seizing the Danish navy, but a vicious argument ensued with the War Minister, (Robert Stewart Viscount Castlereagh), over the deployment of troops. When Castlereagh discovered in September 1809 that Canning had made a deal with Cavendish-Bentinck to have him removed from office, he was furious.

Demanding redress, Castlereagh challenged Canning to a duel, which was fought on 21 September 1809 on Putney Heath. Canning having never fired a pistol completely missed, whilst Castlereagh wounded Canning in the thigh. There was much outrage that two cabinet ministers had resorted to such a method, that they both felt compelled to resign from the government. After Perceval's assassination in 1812, the new Prime Minister, Robert Jenkinson offered Canning the position of Foreign Secretary once more. Canning refused, as he was reluctant to serve in any government with Castlereagh.

However, after a spell as ambassador to Portugal, Canning returned to join the government in 1816 as President of the Board of Control.

GEORGE CANNING

Canning resigned from office once more in 1820 in opposition to the treatment of Queen Caroline, the estranged wife of the new King George IV, as Canning and Caroline were personal friends. In 1822, when Castlereagh committed suicide, Canning succeeded him as both Foreign Secretary and Leader of the House of Commons and despite his personal issues with Castlereagh, he continued many of his foreign policies.

During this period he was incremental in preventing South America from falling into the influence of France.
In 1827 Robert Jenkinson was forced to stand down as Prime Minister after suffering a severe stroke and on April 10 1827, Canning being Jenkinson's right hand man was chosen by George IV to succeed him. The Duke of Wellington (Arthur Wellesley) resigned from the cabinet and the command of the army, followed by Sir Robert Peel and three other 'Protestant' peers. Consequently the Tory party was now heavily split between the 'High Tories' (supporters of a very traditionalist form of conservatism) and the moderates supporting Canning, often called 'Canningites'. As a result, Canning found it difficult to form a government and chose to invite a number of Whigs to join his Cabinet creating a coalition with his 'Canningites'.
From the early part of 1827 Canning's health went into steep decline and he finally succumbed to pneumonia on August 8 1827 at the age of 57.

His total period in office remains the shortest of any Prime Minister, at 119 days. Canning was buried in Westminster Abbey in London.

Interesting George Canning facts:

'Canning Street' in Hinckley named after him and a Blue Plaque place on the side of his home in Burbage.

A square in downtown Athens, Greece, is named after Canning (Πλατεία Κάνιγγος, *Plateía Kánningos*, Canning Square), in appreciation of his supportive stance toward the Greek War of Independence (1821–1830).

Canning Street in Belfast is named after George Canning.

Frederick John Robinson (Viscount Goderich) 20th British Prime Minister

Born
1 November 1782, London
Died
28 January 1859, age 76, Putney Heath, London
Period in office as Prime Minister
131 days from 31 August 1827 – 8 January 1828
Political party
Tory
Constituencies Represented as MP
Carlow 1806-1807
Ripon 1807-1827
Ministerial offices held as Prime Minister
First Lord of the Treasury
Leader of the House of Lords

Frederick John Robinson, 1st Earl of Ripon, 1 November 1782 – 28 January 1859), styled **The Honourable F. J. Robinson** until 1827 and known between 1827 and 1833 as **Viscount Goderich** was Prime Minister of the United Kingdom between August 1827 and January 1828.

Frederick John Robinson was the younger son of the 2nd Baron Grantham and Lady Mary Yorke the daughter of the 2nd Earl of Hardwicke. He was raised mainly by his mother after his father died when he was only three years old. He was educated at a preparatory school at Thames, then attended Harrow School from 1796 to 1799, followed by St John's College, Cambridge from 1799 to 1802. After graduating in 1802 he was admitted to Lincoln's Inn. He remained a member there until 1809, but did not pursue a legal career and was not called to the bar.

Robinson's political career was initially sponsored by his uncle, the 3rd Earl of Hardwicke, who as Lord Lieutenant of Ireland made him his private secretary in Dublin in 1804 and then secured him a parliamentary seat at Carlow in 1806 (in the 1807 General Election he was elected MP for Ripon thanks to another relative). By then Robinson had developed an association with Lord Castlereagh whom he served as under-secretary in the War Office from May 1809. In October 1809, Robinson resigned along with Castlereagh as they were unwilling to serve under the new Prime Minister (Spencer Perceval). Although in June 1810, Robinson was subsequently persuaded to serve as a member of the Admiralty board in Perceval's government. After Perceval's assassination in 1812 Castlereagh was appointed in Jenkinson's cabinet and appointed Robinson the vice-presidency of the Board of Trade with a privy councillorship and a seat at the Treasury (which he exchanged for one of the joint paymaster-generalships in 1813). Robinson served under Jenkinson as Vice-President of the Board of Trade between 1812 and 1818 and as and as joint-Paymaster of the Forces between 1813 and 1817. From this position he sponsored the Corn Laws of 1815. The Corn Laws made the price of wheat artificially high, to the benefit of the landed classes but to the detriment of the working classes. The controversial Corn Laws provoked attacks on Robinson's home by protestors, in which a nineteen year old midshipman named Edward Vyse was shot and killed.

FREDERICK JOHN ROBINSON

As time went on Robinson emerged as a leading architect of 'Liberal Tory' economic policy, first as President of the Board of Trade from January 1818 and then Chancellor of the Exchequer from January 1823. The first three years as Chancellor were regarded as a success but this was overshadowed in the fourth year when a run on the banks led to a financial crisis. In January 1827 Prime Minister Jenkinson gave Robinson the change he asked for with a peerage as Viscount Goderich, although Robinson found the upper house no less stressful than the Commons.

In February 1827 Jenkinson resigned due to ill health and George Canning took over the leadership, but when Canning died in August 1827, King George IV, who was said to favour the Tories over the Whigs announced his intention of appointing Robinson to the Premiership. Robinson led a coalition of moderate Tories and Whigs from 31 August 1827 which constituted his government. His fragmented ministry was at odds over the demands of the King and those of his Whig allies. The pressure of government and personal problems (his wife suffered from hypochondria and depression) became too much and on 11 December he wrote to the King stating that his own health and, more importantly, that of his wife, were so poor that he felt unfit for the duties of his post. The King chose to construe this as a resignation and immediately set about finding an alternative Prime Minister. On 8 January 1828 Robinson's ministry came to an end. Despite the distress of his prime ministership, Robinson remained a front-bench politician for a further twenty years.

In April 1833, as the newly created Earl of Ripon, he joined Lord Grey's ministry as Lord Privy Seal, having already served the Whig premier as Colonial Secretary from 1830. In 1834 he resigned over the government's policies on the Irish Church and in 1836 joined the Conservative Party. In 1841 he was back as Sir Robert Peel's president of the Board of Trade, and in May 1846 he took his final government post as president of the India Board. In a fitting finale to his political career he moved the abolition of the Corn Laws, a month before his resignation. Robinson died at Putney Heath, London, in January 1859, aged 76. He was succeeded by his only son, George who became a noted Liberal statesman and cabinet minister.

Interesting Frederick John Robinson fact:

Robinson has the unique distinction of being the only Prime Minister in history to never face a session of Parliament.

Arthur Wellesley (1st Duke of Wellington) 21st British Prime Minister

Born
1 May 1769, Dublin, Ireland
Died
14 September 1852, age 83, Walmer Castle, Kent
Periods in office as Prime Minister
2 years 322 days (2 terms) from 22 January 1828 - 16 November 1830 (2 years 299 days) 17 November 1834 – 9 December 1834 (23 days)
Political party
Tory
Constituencies Represented as MP
Trim (Ireland) 1790-1795
Rye 1806
Newport (Isle of Wight) 1807
Ministerial offices held as Prime Minister
First Lord of the Treasury
Leader of the House of Lords

Arthur Wellesley, 1st Duke of Wellington, (1 May 1769 – 14 September 1852) was an Anglo-Irish soldier and Tory statesman who was one of the leading military and political figures of 19th-century Britain, serving twice as Prime Minister. He ended the Napoleonic Wars when he defeated Napoleon at the Battle of Waterloo in 1815.

Wellesley was born in Dublin, the fourth son of the 1st Earl of Mornington. He always denied being Irish, however, saying that 'being born in a barn does not make one a horse'. Wellesley's father died when he was 12 and his domineering mother thought him inferior to his elder brothers. He played the violin and was good at arithmetic but made little academic progress during his time at Eton College (1781-4). In 1785, due to financial issues he went to Brussels with his mother where he learnt French.

Wellesley, the Duke of Wellington is more famous today as a soldier than as a politician. Fearless at an early age, he entered the French military academy at Angers, in Anjou in 1786. Through his eldest brother's influence, Wellington gained his first commission in the army as an ensign in March 1787 and on Christmas Day, 1787, he was promoted to lieutenant.

Shortly before the General Election of 1789, he went to the rotten borough of Trim to speak against the granting of the title "Freeman" of Dublin to the parliamentary leader of the Irish Patriot Party, Henry Grattan. Succeeding, he was later nominated and duly elected as a Member of Parliament for Trim in the Irish House of Commons, voting with the government in the Irish parliament over the next two years.

He became a captain on 30 January 1791, in the 58th Regiment of Foot unit in the British Army.

Wellesley then became a 'major by purchase' (a commission as an officer could be secured by paying money, avoiding the need to wait to be promoted for merit or seniority), in the 33rd Regiment in 1793, and a few months later, in September, he purchased a lieutenant-colonelcy in the 33rd where he fought with the Duke of York at Flanders in 1794. Returning to England in March 1795, he was returned as a member of parliament for Trim for a second time.

Wellesley was promoted to full colonel by seniority on 3 May 1796 and a few weeks later set sail for Calcutta in India with his regiment. In 1797 he was joined by his eldest brother Richard (now known as Lord Mornington) who had been appointed Governor General and his younger brother Henry who was his secretary. Wellesley was promoted to major-general in 1802 during the 2nd Maratha War (1803-05). He returned to England in 1805. In 1806 he was elected Member of Parliament for Rye in East Sussex and continued his political career before serving at Copenhagen in 1807.

In 1808, Wellesley was made lieutenant-general and sent to Portugal, where he defeated the French at Roliça and Vimeiro.

During the latter engagement, he checked the French columns with the reverse slope defence, a tactic that became his trademark.

In 1809 Wellesley was in command of the British expeditionary force destined for Portugal for the Iberian Peninsula campaign, and spent the next five years trying to expel the French from the Peninsula. Napoleon abdicated and was sent into exile on the island of Elba. Hailed by the public as the nation's conquering hero, Arthur Wellesley was rewarded with the title, Duke of Wellington. The following year Napoleon escaped from Elba and returned to France where he resumed control of the government and army. In June 1815 he marched his troops into Belgium where the British and Prussian armies were encamped. On 18th June at a place called Waterloo, the French and British armies met for what was to be the final battle. Wellington inflicted an overwhelming defeat on Napoleon, but the victory cost a staggering number of lives. Wellington is said to have wept when he learned of the numbers of men slaughtered that day. The British had suffered 22,000 casualties and the French nearly 40,000. Napoleon was defeated. He was forced to abdicate when the Allies entered Paris on 7 July. He spent the rest of his life in exile on the island of St Helena in the South Atlantic. Waterloo was Wellesley's last battle. When he returned to Britain he was treated as a hero, formally honoured, and presented with both an estate in Hampshire and a fortune of £400,000.

After the Battle of Waterloo, Wellesley became Commander in Chief of the army in occupied France until November 1818. He then returned to England and Parliament, and joined Robert Jenkinson's government in 1819 as Master General of the Ordnance, a position he held until 1827. In 1828, after twice being overlooked in favour of Canning and Robinson, Wellesley was finally invited by King George IV to form his own government.

As Prime Minister, although he was known for his measures to repress reform, one of his first achievements was overseeing Catholic emancipation in 1829, which was the granting of almost full civil rights to Catholics in the United Kingdom. This led to a dual between Wellesley and Lord Winchilsea who was an opponent of the bill, in Battersea Park on 21 March 1829. In the duel however, honour was satisfied when Wellington deliberately shot wide and Winchilsea shot in the air before writing Wellington an apology. The nickname "Iron Duke" originates from this period. Wellesley's government fell in 1830, after a wave of riots swept the country in the summer and autumn of that year. The Whigs who had been out of power for most of the years since the 1770s, saw the chance for political reform in response to the unrest, and as the key to their return. Wellington stuck to the Tory policy of no reform and no expansion of suffrage, and as a result, lost a vote of no confidence on 15 November 1830. Despite Wellington's opposition, Lord Grey's government still passed the Reform Act in 1832. Wellesley was again to be Prime Minister though for three weeks in November and December 1834, acting as interim leader, before stepping aside for Sir Robert Peel with the party evolving into the Conservatives. Wellesley took on the role of Foreign Secretary in Peel's first cabinet (1834–1835) and he was a Minister without Portfolio and Leader of the House of Lords in the second (1841–1846). He retired from political life in 1846. Wellesley died at Walmer Castle in Deal on 14 September 1852 aged 83.

Interesting Arthur Wellesley facts:

Officers under his command called Wellesley *"The Beau"* as he was a fine dresser.

His name was given to Wellington boots, after the custom-made boots he wore instead of traditional Hessian boots.

Charles Grey (2nd Earl Grey)
22nd British Prime Minister

Born
13 March 1764, Falloden, Northumberland
Died
17 July 1845, age 81, Howick Hall, Howick, Northumberland
Period in office as Prime Minister
3 years 230 days from 2 November 1830 – 9 July 1834
Political party
Whig
Constituencies Represented as MP
Northumberland 1786-1807
Appleby May-July 1807
Tavistock July-November 1807
Ministerial offices held as Prime Minister
First Lord of the Treasury
Leader of the House of Lords

Charles Grey, 2nd Earl Grey, (13 March 1764 – 17 July 1845), known as **Viscount Howick** between 1806 and 1807, was Prime Minister of the United Kingdom from November 1830 to July 1834 and oversaw four years of political reform that had enormous impact on the development of democracy in Britain.

Charles Grey was the son of General Charles Grey (1729–1807) and his wife, Elizabeth (1743/4–1822), daughter of George Grey of Southwick, County Durham. He had four brothers and two sisters. Little is known of Grey's childhood other than that he was sent to a private school in Marylebone, where he was unhappy, and then to Eton College. Grey proceeded to Trinity College, Cambridge, where he spent three years and acquired a facility in Latin and in English composition but did not take a degree.

On 18 November 1794 Grey married Mary Elizabeth Ponsonby (1776–1861) and between 1797 and 1819 the couple had eleven sons, (the eldest of whom, Henry George Grey, became a politician like his father), and four daughters.

In September 1786 whilst Grey was abroad on his travels he was first elected to the Commons aged just 22, he was nominated for a vacancy for the county of Northumberland by his uncle Sir Henry Grey, and although he professed no political allegiance he was expected to follow the family tradition of back-bench toryism. But Grey took opposition to William Pitt the younger and came under the influence of the Whig leader Charles James Fox, throwing himself characteristically wholeheartedly into Whig politics.

The outbreak of the French Revolution in 1789 aroused radical societies and publications such as Thomas Paine's *The Rights of Man*, which declared that all citizens possessed equal political rights and that democracy was the only foundation of legitimate government. This led to Grey playing a major role in the foundation of the 'Society of the Friends of the People' in 1792. In the late 18th century, The House of Commons was dominated largely by those from aristocratic and powerful backgrounds, and although Grey did not approve the ideas of Thomas Paine, he argued that Britain should set its own house in order to forestall any extremism, and that the leadership of respectable and moderate men would keep the reformers on a constitutional path.

Charles Grey

In 1792 Grey gave notice in the House of Commons, stating that he would present a motion for parliamentary reform in the next session, and on 6 May 1793 he did so. He based his proposals for reform on a petition drawn up by the Friends of the People. The petition highlighted the level of influence in elections, the small amount of voters in some constituencies, and the lack of representation for industrial towns. The motion was lost by 282 votes to 41. For the following years, Grey and a few remaining friends were left in opposition, regularly opposing measures introduced by Pitt to defend the monarchy and constitution from radical groups. In January 1806 Pitt died and Grey joined the Grenville Administration, serving as First Lord of the Admiralty. On 14th November 1807, Charles Grey's father died and Grey inherited the title of Earl Grey, he continued in opposition for the next 23 years. In 1810 Grey took up the cause of Catholic emancipation and there were times during this period when Grey came close to joining the Government, but he declined because the Prince Regent refused to make concessions on the Catholic issue.

After years of struggling and failing to achieve political change, in 1830, enthusiasm for reform was building again in Britain with younger members of the Whig party eager to take up the issue. In his first speech in the new Parliament of 1830, Grey spoke passionately for reform. The speech provoked Prime Minister Wellesley to his famous assertion that not only was reform not necessary, but that a better system than the present could hardly be conceived. Wellesley was seen as out of touch and his popularity plummeted to such an extent that he had little option but to resign on 15 November 1830, mainly on the question of Parliamentary reform. On 16 November William IV appointed Grey as Prime Minister at the age of sixty-six.

In June 1832, the Reform Act finally passed into law after 15 torrid months of debate. It extended the vote to just 7% of the adult male population, based on a series of lowered property qualifications. Introduced in March 1831, the bill scraped through the Commons by a single vote, but was thrown out at the committee stage (when the bill is debated in detail - sometimes called the 'second reading'). Parliament was dissolved and the General Election was fought on the single issue of the Reform Act - an unprecedented event in British political history. The Whigs won the election and passed the bill, but the House of Lords (with a majority of Tories) threw it out, sparking riots and civil disobedience across the country. With the spectre of France's bloody revolution clearly in mind, William IV eventually agreed to create 50 Whig peers to redress the balance in the Lords if the bill was rejected again. The Lords conceded and the Act was finally passed on 7th June 1832, and became known as the Great Reform Act. The effect of this Act was to enable the middle classes of the big industrial towns to share in political power. Fifty-six towns with less than 2,000 inhabitants ('rotten boroughs') lost separate representation and 31 further towns were reduced to one MP. Sixty-seven new constituencies were created.

Other reforming measures in Greys ministry included restrictions on the employment of children, and the abolition of slavery in the British Empire in 1833.

Grey resigned in July 1834 mainly over Irish policy and in his resignation speech to the House of Lords on 9 July he stated:

'With the satisfaction, at least, that in having used my best endeavours to carry into effect those measures of reform that the country required, I have not shrunk from any obstacles, nor from meeting and grappling with the many difficulties that I have encountered in the performance of my duty'.

The speech was received with loud cheers and applause. Grey enjoyed a peaceful retirement and died on 17 July 1845 aged 81.

Interesting Charles Grey facts:

Earl Grey tea, a blend which uses bergamot oil to flavour the brew, is named after Grey.

Earl Grey's statue stands on the column at the top of Grey Street in Newcastle

William Lamb (2nd Viscount Melbourne)
23rd British Prime Minister

Born
15 March 1779, London
Died
24 November 1848, age 69, Brocket, Herts
Periods in office as Prime Minister
6 years 257 days (2 terms) from 16 July 1834 - 14 November 1834
(122 days) 18 April 1835 – 30 August 1841 (6 years 135 days)
Political party
Whig
Constituencies Represented as MP
Leominster 1806
Haddington Burghs 1806-1807
Portarlington 1807-1812
Peterborough 1816-1819
Hertfordshire 1819-1826
Newport (Isle of Wight) 1827
Bletchingley 1827-1828
Ministerial offices held as Prime Minister
First Lord of the Treasury
Leader of the House of Lords

William Lamb, 2nd Viscount Melbourne, (15 March 1779 – 24 November 1848), in some sources called **Henry William Lamb,** a British Whig statesman who served as Home Secretary (1830–1834) and Prime Minister twice (1834 and 1835–1841).

William Lamb was born in London in 1779 to an aristocratic Whig family, and was the son of the 1st Viscount Melbourne and Elizabeth, Viscountess Melbourne (although Lady Melbourne had many affairs and it is believed that George Wyndham, 3rd Earl of Egremont was the father of William Lamb). Lamb was educated at Eton College and at Trinity College, Cambridge. At Cambridge, Lamb became acquainted with a group of romantic radicals including the poets Percy Bysshe Shelley and George Gordon Byron. Lamb was admitted to Lincoln's Inn in 1797, and he was called to the bar in 1804. After taking his degree in July 1799 Lamb spent a period of time in Glasgow being mentored by Scottish philosopher John Millar.

On his return from Scotland Lamb quickly became a darling of Whig society. With the death of his older brother, Peniston, on January 24 1805, Lamb became heir to his father's title. He married Lady Caroline Ponsonby, an Anglo-Irish aristocrat on 3rd June 1805, a marriage which was to bring scandal. Within a few years of marriage Caroline had launched into a series of public liaisons, most disastrously with the poet Lord Byron, from 1812 into 1813 with the resulting scandal being the talk of Britain. In 1816 Lady Caroline published a novel, Glenarvon, containing obvious lurid portraits of herself, her husband, Byron and many others. Embarrassed and disgraced, Melbourne decided to part from his wife, though the formal separation did not occur until 1825.

Lady Caroline died in 1828, aged 42, her death hastened by drink and drugs. Lamb, not yet Prime Minister, was by her bedside.

Lamb joined Brooks's Club in April with Charles Fox as his sponsor, and in January 1806 was brought into parliament as a Whig MP for Leominster (Herefordshire) before he moved to the seat of Haddington Burghs. For the 1807 election he successfully stood for Portarlington, a seat he held until 1812. In 1816, Lamb was returned for Peterborough by Whig grandee Lord Fitzwilliam, and stated that he was committed to the Whig principles of the Glorious Revolution.

WILLIAM LAMB

Although a Whig, Melbourne was made secretary for Ireland from 1827-1828 in a Tory government. In 1829, his father's death meant he inherited his title and moved to the House of Lords. He had spent twenty-two years in the House of Commons but was not well known politically. In November 1830, the Whigs came to power under Lord Grey and Lamb was made Home Secretary, where he reluctantly supported the parliamentary Reform Act of 1832, but forcibly repressed agrarian and industrial radicals notably the Tolpuddle Martyrs in 1834. In a bid to repress trade unions, Lambs introduced legislation against 'illegal oaths'. As a result, the Grand National Consolidated Trades' Union failed. In March of the same year, six labourers were transported to Australia for seven years for attempting to provide a fund for workers in need. They became known as the 'Tolpuddle Martyrs' and the foundation of modern day trade unionism.

In July 1834, Lord Grey resigned as Prime Minister and King William IV was forced to appoint another Whig to replace him because the Tories were not strong enough to support a government. Lamb was deemed the one most likely to be acceptable to King William IV and to hold the Whig party together. Lamb reluctantly took on the role of Prime Minister but with King William IV's opposition to the Whigs' reforming ways, after only 122 days, he dismissed Lamb and the government in November 1834. With Sir Robert Peel's Conservatives still failing to win a parliamentary majority, in 1835, Lamb took office as Prime Minister once more, although without any strong political convictions, he held together a difficult and divided cabinet. He managed to sustain support in the House of Commons through an alliance of Whigs, Radicals and Irish MPs.

When the young Victoria ascended to the throne in 1837, she and Lamb developed a close relationship, with the Prime Minister tutoring the new Queen in government and politics. The Queen's reliance on Melbourne resulted in a political crisis in 1839, when Melbourne resigned after a defeat in parliament. The Queen invited the Conservative leader Sir Robert Peel to form a government, but he insisted that the Queen's Whig ladies of the bedchamber be replaced with Tory ones, which was the usual practice. The Queen refused, so Peel declined to form a government and Lamb returned to office.

Queen Victoria came to regard Lamb as a mentor and personal friend, and he was given a private apartment at Windsor Castle.

During Lamb's ministry Chartism became popular, taking its name from the People's Charter of 1838, it was a working-class movement for parliamentary reform. The Chartists also fought against the New Poor Law of 1834. In June 1839, a petition, signed by 1.3 million working people, was presented to the House of Commons, but MPs voted not to hear the petitioners.

In the later stages of his premiership, Lamb's support in Parliament declined and in 1840 it grew difficult for him to hold the Cabinet together. His unpopular and scandal-hit term along with a series of parliamentary defeats, ended following a vote of no confidence initiated by Conservative MP John Stuart-Wortley, and Lamb's government fell. He resigned as Prime Minister on 30 August 1841.

Lamb survived a stroke on October 23, 1842, fourteen months after his departure from politics. In retirement, he lived at Brocket Hall, Hertfordshire, where he died on 24 November 1848 aged 69. He was buried nearby at St Etheldreda's Church, Hatfield, Hertfordshire.

Interesting William Lamb facts:

William Lamb is portrayed by Jon Finch in the film Lady Caroline Lamb (1972).

Melbourne, the capital city of Victoria, Australia, was named in his honour in March 1837. He was the Prime Minister of the United Kingdom at the time.

Lamb was the last Prime Minister to be dismissed by a monarch in his first term in November 1834.

Sir Robert Peel (2nd Baronet)
24th British Prime Minister

Born
15 February 1788, Bury, Lancashire
Died
2 July 1850, age 62, Westminster, London
Periods in office as Prime Minister
5 years 59 days (2 terms) from 10 December 1834 - 8 April 1835
(120 days) 30 August 1835 – 29 June 1846 (4 years 304 days)
Political party
Conservative
Constituencies Represented as MP
Cashel 1809-1812
Chippenham 1812-1817
Oxford University 1817-1829
Westbury 1829-1830
Tamworth 1830-1850
Ministerial offices held as Prime Minister
First Lord of the Treasury
Leader of the House of Lords
Chancellor of the Exchequer

Sir Robert Peel, 2nd Baronet, (5 February 1788 – 2 July 1850) was a British Conservative statesman who was twice British Prime Minister (1834–35 and 1841–46). His period in government saw landmark social reforms and the repeal of the Corn Laws. He is regarded as the father of modern British policing, owing to his founding of the Metropolitan Police Service. Peel was one of the founders of the modern Conservative Party.

Peel was born on February 5, 1788, in Bury, Lancashire. He was the eldest son and the third of the eleven children of Sir Robert Peel, 1st Baronet and his first wife Ellen Yates. Peel senior was one of the early textile manufacturers of the Industrial Revolution and a Member of Parliament for Tamworth. Peel was educated at Bury Grammar School, then Hipperholme Grammar School, and in February 1800 Harrow School. At Harrow he was a contemporary of Lord Byron. In 1805 he attended Christ Church, Oxford where he excelled, gaining a double first in 1808, studying classics and mathematics. After Oxford, Peel studied law at Lincoln's Inn.

In 1809 at the age of 21, using his father's influence, Peel secured the vacant seat at Cashel (County Tipperary in Ireland), and entered the Commons immediately. His mentor in Parliament was Arthur Wellesley, the future 1st Duke of Wellington (Peel named one of his sons after the Duke of Wellington). Peel quickly rose in power and in 1817 he gained the coveted honour of election as Member of Parliament for the University of Oxford. He served as Chief Secretary for Ireland (1812–1818), twice as Home Secretary (1822-1827 and 1828-1830), Chancellor of the Exchequer (1834–1835) and Leader of the Opposition when William Lamb was Prime Minister (1835–1841).

When George Canning succeeded as Prime Minister in 1827, Peel, who opposed Catholic emancipation, resigned on the issue, although he returned to office in 1828 under Arthur Wellesley. It was as Home Secretary In 1829, when Peel introduced the Metropolitan Police Act, which set up the first disciplined police force for the Greater London area. It was far-ranging criminal law and prison reform, and established the Metropolitan Police Force based at Scotland Yard in London. The constables were nicknamed "Bobbies" or "Peelers" after Robert Peel, and Peel became known as the father of modern policing, devising the Peelian Principles which defined the ethical requirements police officers must follow. The Peelian Principles have been used not only in the United Kingdom but in Canada, Australia, New Zealand and the United States.

Sir Robert Peel

The Wellesley government in which Peel had been Home Secretary fell in 1830, and Peel was now in opposition to a new administration, headed by Earl Grey. Though not opposed to moderate parliamentary reform, Peel argued against Grey's sweeping measures. Nonetheless, in 1832 the Reform Act was passed. The Whig Government of William Lamb was dismissed in November 1834 by William IV, who appointed Peel as the new Prime Minister. Also in 1834, under the direction of Peel (who is also considered the founder of today's Conservative Party), the name Conservative Party was officially adopted. In his Tamworth Manifesto, Peel outlined his support for the Reform Act, a shift which highlighted his adoption of a more enlightened Conservatism. Although in power, Peel's Tories remained a minority in the House of Commons, a situation which Peel found increasingly intolerable, and in April 1835, defeated by a combination of Whigs, radicals, and Irish nationalists, he resigned his office. During the next six years, aided by his astute and cautious tactics, he signalled a significant shift from staunch, reactionary 'Tory' to progressive 'Conservative' politics. The Conservative Party steadily increased in numbers and confidence. Following the General Election of June 1841, in which he gained a majority of more than 70 in the House of Commons, Peel formed his second administration which was one of the most memorable of the century. Although Peel was faced with war in China and Afghanistan, as well as strained relations with France and the United States, severe commercial distress at home, agitation by the workingmen's reform movement of the Chartists and the Anti-Corn Law League, O'Connell's campaign for the repeal of the union of Ireland and Great Britain, and a five-year accumulation of budgetary deficits, Peel still managed to pass some ground-breaking legislation. Such as the Mines Act of 1842 that banned the employment of women and children underground, and The Factory Act 1844 that limited working hours for children and women in factories. In 1845, he faced the defining challenge of his career - failed harvests led much of the population to call for the repeal of the 30-year-old Corn Laws, which banned the import of cheap foreign grain, a crisis triggered by the Irish potato famine. Unable to send sufficient food to Ireland to stem the famine, he eventually decided the Corn Laws must be repealed. Landowners saw the attempt as an attack on them, and fiercely protested in the House of Commons. Peel's Conservative Party which was very sensitive to the issue of Corn Laws, would not support him and the debate lasted for 5 months. Also in 1845, the bold reintroduction of the income tax (originally instituted during the Napoleonic Wars) established internal revenue on a sound footing and enabled him to make sweeping reductions of duties on food and raw materials entering the country. Eventually, in June 1846, the Corn Laws were repealed, an undertaking which was to split the Conservative Party in two. In the unsavoury atmosphere that followed, the protectionists amongst the Conservatives combined with the Whigs to defeat the government's Irish Coercion Bill. Peel promptly resigned and was cheered by crowds as he left the Commons.

On June 29, 1850, Peel went out for his usual evening ride on a new horse, the horse acted up throwing Peel off and landing on the prostrate Peel. Doctors found that Peel had broken his left collar-bone and probably several ribs. They also suspected severe internal bleeding. Peel's condition worsened and he died at his London home Whitehall Gardens on July 2, 1850 aged 62.

Interesting Robert Peel facts:

Peel was the first serving British Prime Minister to have his photograph taken.

Peel is featured on the cover of The Beatles' Sgt. Pepper's Lonely Hearts Club Band album.

There are 14 statues in British towns of Robert Peel.

There is a Sir Robert Peel Community Hospital in Tamworth.

'Peelites' was a breakaway faction of the Conservative Party which eventually joined with the Whigs and Radicals to form the Liberal Party.

Lord John Russell (1st Earl Russell)
25th British Prime Minister

Born
18 August 1792, Mayfair, London
Died
28 May 1878, age 85, Richmond Park, London
Periods in office as Prime Minister
6 years 113 days (2 terms) from 30 June 1846 – 21 February 1852 (5 years 237 days) 29 October 1865 – 26 June 1866 (241 days)
Political party
Whig/Liberal
Constituencies Represented as MP
Tavistock 1813-1820
Huntingdonshire 1820-1826
Bandon 1826-1830
Bedford 1830-1831
Devonshire 1831-1832
South Devon 1832-1835
Stroud 1837-1841
City of London 1841-1861
Ministerial offices held as Prime Minister
First Lord of the Treasury
Leader of the House of Commons (first term)
Leader of the House of Lords (second term)

John Russell, 1st Earl Russell (18 August 1792 – 28 May 1878), known by his courtesy title **Lord John Russell** before 1861, was an aristocratic Whig and Liberal politician who served as Prime Minister of Great Britain in 1846–1852, and 1865–1866 during the early Victorian era.

Russell was born on 18 August 1792 he was the youngest of three sons to John Russell, 6th Duke of Bedford and MP for Tavistock. He was born prematurely and consequently was often ill during childhood. He started to attend Westminster School but his ill health caused him to withdraw. Due to his health it was decided that he would be educated at home by tutors. From 1809-1812, Russell attended the University of Edinburgh, but left without taking a degree and travelled around Europe.

In 1813, while Russell was still abroad, he was elected as Whig MP for the borough of Tavistock at the age of 21, the borough being controlled by his family and he made his maiden speech in May 1814. He resigned on health grounds in 1817 but was returned again the following year. From 1819 onwards he was a passionate supporter of parliamentary reform and at the General Election of 1820 he abandoned his secure seat in the family borough of Tavistock to stand for Huntingdonshire, having been recommended by his friend Lord Milton.

In the years which followed, when the Whigs were in opposition he turned to writing. He started with *The Life of William Lord Russell* (1819), one of the Whig martyrs who had been executed in 1683. The next year he published *Essays and Sketches of Life and Character by a Gentleman who has Left his Lodgings* (1820); a novel, *The Nun of Arrouca* (1820), and a five-act play, *Don Carlos, or, Persecution* (1820), which was written in blank verse and dedicated to Lord Holland. These were followed by *An Essay on the History of the English Government and Constitution, from the Reign of Henry VIII to the Present Time* (1821), *Memoirs of*

the Affairs of Europe from the Peace of
Utrecht (1824), *Establishment of the Turks in Europe* (1828), a
second volume of *Memoirs of the Affairs of Europe* (1829),
and *The Causes of the French Revolution* (1832).

When the Whigs came to power in 1830 in Earl Grey's
government, Russell entered the parliament as Paymaster of the
Forces, and was soon elevated to the Cabinet. He was one of the
principal leaders of the fight for the Reform Act 1832. In 1834,
when the leader of the Commons, Lord Althorp, succeeded to the
peerage as Earl Spencer, Russell became the leader of the Whigs
in the Commons. This appointment prompted King William IV to
terminate William Lamb's government, which was the last time in
British history that a monarch dismissed a Prime Minister.

JOHN RUSSELL

In 1835 Russell was appointed by William Lamb as Home
Secretary and Leader of the House of Commons. In 1839 he
became Colonial Secretary. When Lamb's government fell in 1841
he became leader of the Opposition.

In 1845, as leader of the Opposition, Russell came out in favour of free trade and the repeal of the Corn Laws. This forced Conservative Prime Minister Sir Robert Peel to follow him. In December 1845, with the Conservatives split over the issue, Queen Victoria asked Russell to form a government, but he was unable to do so as Lord Grey refused to serve with Lord Palmerston as Foreign Secretary.

The Great Irish Potato Famine (1845-1852 a result of *P. infestans* infection) had caused a disastrous fall in food supplies after which Conservative Prime Minister Sir Robert Peel decided to join with Whigs and Radicals to repeal the Corn Laws, which imposed tariffs and other trade restrictions on imported food and grain. Peel's Conservative Party failed to support the bill but it passed with Whig and Radical support and Arthur Wellesley persuaded the House of Lords to pass it. Following the repeal of the Corn Law, Peel resigned as Prime Minister on June 29, 1846, and Russell became Prime Minister. Russell's solutions to the Potato Famine proved inadequate and during his first term as Prime Minister around one million Irish starved to death or died of diseases caused by malnutrition, and one million more were forced to leave their homeland as refugees, reducing the population of Ireland by 25%.

Russell was seen as shy and having no interest in cultivating the rapidly expanding media. His impression of aloofness added to the criticisms of his premiership. He was unable to compete with the popularity that his Foreign Secretary, Lord Palmerston had with his vigorous, assertive and fashionably liberal foreign policy.

During this administration (1846–52) Russell was able to establish the Factories Act 1847 which restricted the working hours of women and young persons (aged 13–18) in textile mills to 10 hours per day, and founded a national board of public health (1848). On 2 December 1851 Russell with the backing of

Queen Victoria and Prince Albert, forced Lord Palmerston to resign. This ultimately led to the downfall of Russell's ministry as on 21 February 1852 when Palmerston turned a vote on a militia bill into a vote of confidence on the Government. Russell resigned as Prime Minister but remained in the Cabinet, briefly as Foreign Secretary, and from 1853-1855 as a Minister without Portfolio. From 1855 to 1859, Russell retired from public life and devoted more and more of his time to literature.

In 1859 following another short-lived Conservative government, Palmerston and Russell made up their differences, and Russell consented to serve as Foreign Secretary in a new Palmerston cabinet, supporting the unification of Italy, he was elevated to the peerage as Earl Russell in 1861 and he became Prime Minister for a second time on Palmerston's death in 1865. In June 1866 again due to party disunity he resigned, and took no further active government posts. However, he continued to attend the House of Lords.

John Russell died May 28, 1878 aged 85.

Interesting John Russell facts:

A Tale of Two Cities by Charles Dickens was dedicated to Lord John Russell *"In remembrance of many public services and private kindness"*

John Russell was the last Whig Prime Minister.

His Public Health Act 1848 improved the sanitary conditions of towns and populous places.

In all, John Russell participated in twenty-two parliamentary elections.

Edward Smith Stanley (14th Earl of Derby)
26th British Prime Minister

Born
29 March 1799, Knowsley Hall, Prescot, Lancashire
Died
23 October 1869, age 70, Knowsley Hall, Prescot, Lancashire
Periods in office as Prime Minister
3 years 289 days (3 terms) from 23 February 1852 to 17
December 1852
(299 days), 20 February 1858 – 11 June 1859 (1 year 112 days)
28 June 1866 – 25 February 1868 (1 year 243 days)
Political party
Conservative
Constituencies Represented as MP
Stockbridge 1822-1826
Preston 1826-1830
Windsor 1831-1832
North Lancashire 1832-1844
Ministerial offices held as Prime Minister
First Lord of the Treasury
Leader of the House of Lords

Edward George Geoffrey Smith-Stanley, 14th Earl of Derby (29 March 1799 – 23 October 1869) was a British statesman, three-time Prime Minister of the United Kingdom and to date, the longest-serving leader of the Conservative Party. He was known before 1834 as **Edward Stanley**, and from 1834 to 1851 as **Lord Stanley**.

Smith-Stanley was born at Knowsley Hall, Prescot, Lancashire on 29 March 1799. He was the eldest son and first of seven children born to Edward Smith Stanley, 13th Earl of Derby and his wife Charlotte Margaret Hornby. He was educated at Eton between 1811 and 1817, before being admitted to Christ Church College, Oxford. In 1819 he was awarded the Chancellor's Latin verse prize for his poem Syracuse. Stanley did not take his Degree, but from an early age seemed destined for a political career.

In July 1822, Stanley, who at that point in his political career regarded himself as a 'constitutional Whig', took his seat in Parliament as the MP for Stockbridge (a rotten borough of Knowsley in Merseyside), a seat bought for him by his grandfather, the 12th Earl of Derby. He later went on to represent Preston, Windsor and then North Lancashire.

On 31 May 1825 he married Emma Caroline Bootle-Wilbraham and they had two sons and one daughter.

Smith-Stanley voted for Catholic Emancipation in 1829, and spoke briefly in favour of parliamentary reform in 1830. On the death of George IV in June 1830, a General Election was called and took place in July/August 1830, Smith-Stanley was re-elected for Preston. Having accepted office as Grey's Chief Secretary for Ireland, he was defeated at the December by-election by Henry 'Orator' Hunt (3,730 votes to 3,392, majority 338). However a vacancy was made for him at Windsor in February 1831. One of his measures as Chief Secretary of Ireland was to introduce the Irish Education Act, which created the Irish Board of National Education. Under the auspices of this Board, children of all denominations were admitted to schools receiving government grants and religious education was to be of an 'uncontroversial' nature. In April 1833, Stanley was moved from his post to that of Under-Secretary of State for War and the Colonies where he was responsible for drawing up the Abolition of Slavery Bill, presenting the final Bill to parliament which gave slaves their freedom on 1 August 1834. Smith-Stanley who was a religiously devout Anglican, opposed the alienation of Church property but Lord John Russell was determined to reduce the amount of land owned by the Anglican Church in Ireland. Smith-Stanley resigned his post as Colonial Secretary in 1834 before the seriousness of government splits became too obvious. In 1841, Smith-Stanley became a member of the Conservative Party and in 1844 he was elevated to the House of Lords with the title 'Lord Stanley of Bickerstaffe', (on his father's death on June 30, 1851, he inherited his title as the 14th Earl of Derby). He resigned from government in 1845 in protest at the proposed repeal of the Corn Laws, and in 1846 became leader of the Protectionist Conservatives (he served as Leader of the Conservative Party from 1846 – 1868). In February 1852 he formed a minority government and became Prime Minister following the collapse of Lord John Russell's Whig Government. But Smith-Stanley's first term as Prime Minister was a short-lived affair, he resigned in December of the same year, following the defeat of the first budget by his Chancellor of the Exchequer, Benjamin Disraeli, which got voted down in a "no confidence" vote. After resigning Smith-Stanley stayed on as the Leader of the Opposition until 1858. After Lord Palmerston resigned in 1858 Smith-Stanley formed another minority government, a ministry which passed the Jews Relief Act that ended the exclusion of Jews from taking their seats in Parliament. Once again his government was short-lived, in 1859, after just over one year, Stanley resigned having narrowly lost a vote of no-confidence brought by Lord

Hartington on behalf of various Whig and Radical factions which had come together at the Willis's Rooms meetings on 6 June 1859 in St James's Street which marked the birth of the Liberal Party. A further seven years in opposition followed, after which Stanley formed his third and final ministry in 1866. Once again it was a minority government. His final term was most noted for the Reform Act 1867, an electoral reform by which the new industrial cities, had for the first time, received a significant representation in the House of Commons. The Act extended the vote to all adult male householders (and lodgers paying £10 rental or more, resident for a year or more) living in a borough constituency. It created more than 1.5 million new voters. Versions of the Reform Act had been under serious discussion since 1860, but had always foundered on Conservative fears. Many considered it a 'revolutionary' move that would create a majority of 'working class' voters for the first time. In proposing the Reform Act, Benjamin Disraeli, Conservative Leader of the House of Commons, had warned his colleagues that they would be labelled the 'anti-reform' party if they continued to resist. The legislation was passed, and also received the backing of the Liberals under their new leader, William Gladstone. On 25 February 1868, Stanley resigned as Prime Minister on advice from his doctor and in 1869 he was appointed Knight Grand Cross of the Order of St Michael and St George in recognition of his former role as Secretary of State for War and the Colonies. He continued to serve in the House of Lords until his death aged 70 in October 1869.

Interesting Edward Smith Stanley fact:

In October 1831, Edward Stanley as Chief Secretary for Ireland addressed a letter to the Duke of Leinster setting out the details of a plan for education in Ireland. It famously became known as the 'Stanley Letter'.

George Hamilton Gordon (4th Earl of Aberdeen) 27th British Prime Minister

Born
28 January 1784, Edinburgh
Died
14 December 1860, age 76, St James', London
Period in office as Prime Minister
2 years 43 days from 19 December1852 until 30 January 1855
Political party
Conservative
Ministerial offices held as Prime Minister
First Lord of the Treasury
Leader of the House of Lords

George Hamilton-Gordon, 4th Earl of Aberdeen, (28 January 1784 – 14 December 1860), styled **Lord Haddo** from 1791 to 1801, was a British statesman, diplomat and Scottish landowner. A Conservative and Peelite politician who specialised in foreign affairs.

George Hamilton-Gordon was born in Edinburgh, the eldest son and first of seven children born to George Gordon (Lord Haddo), and the grandson of George Gordon, 3rd Earl of Aberdeen. His early years were divided between the family home at Haddo House in Aberdeenshire and Edinburgh. He was orphaned at the age of 11 after his father died falling from a horse in 1791 and his mother died in 1795. At the age of fourteen Hamilton-Gordon exercised his right under Scottish law to choose his guardians and he chose Pitt the younger and Henry Dundas. He was brought up by Dundas, 1st Viscount Melville (Dundas was War Secretary in the 1790s and was impeached in 1806, on the charge of misappropriation of public *money, he was the last British politician to face impeachment...he was acquitted).*

Hamilton-Gordon was educated at preparatory schools in Barnet and Parsons Green, London. In 1795 he went to Harrow, and in 1800 was admitted to St. John's College, Cambridge where he studied for only two sessions. At this time noblemen were able to obtain a Degree without sitting an examination and so he was awarded his MA in 1804. In 1802 Gordon took advantage of the peace of Amiens to set out on the grand tour where he kept a careful journal of his travels. His observations on the political and economic state of France are particularly mature for a man of barely nineteen. He was pleasantly surprised by the freedom of speech but distressed by evidence of the ravages of the revolution and his connection with William Pitt ensured him a meeting with Napoleon Bonaparte in Paris. He returned to England in 1804. Pitt had promised to give Gordon an English peerage which would have given him an automatic seat in the

House of Lords. Scottish peers did not have the right to a seat in the Lords but could elect sixteen of their number to represent them. Gordon, aged only twenty-two, did remarkably well to be returned as one of the representative peers in the General Election of 1806, and he was the only successful candidate not on the king's list. He was re-elected in 1807 and 1812. He made his maiden speech in April 1807, and in 1813 he was appointed Special Ambassador to Austria. He was a central figure in European diplomacy at that time, helping to form the coalition that defeated Napoleon I. He was an observer at the decisive Coalition victory of the Battle of Leipzig in October 1813, and he was one of the British representatives at the Congress of Châtillon in February 1814. He was at the negotiations which led to the Treaty of Paris in May of the same year. Later in 1814 he was created Viscount Gordon of Aberdeen in the peerage of the United Kingdom, and made a member of the Privy Council. For the period 1815 to 1828, Hamilton-Gordon was distracted by family problems and the care of his Scottish estates, therefore took a less prominent part in public affairs. In January 1828 Gordon accepted the post of Chancellor of the Duchy of Lancaster in Wellesley's first ministry, and he became Foreign Secretary later that year. By the end of 1830 though he had left office with the collapse of Wellesley's ministry.

In 1834 he took up the post of Secretary of State for War and the Colonies in Peel's short-lived first ministry, having to deal with problems in Canada, South Africa and the West Indies due to compensation arising from the abolition of slavery in 1833 (the bill was grandly titled '*An Act for the Abolition of Slavery throughout the British Colonies; for promoting the industry of manumitted Slaves; and for compensating the Persons hitherto entitled to the Services of such Slaves*').

In Peel's second government, Hamilton-Gordon again became Foreign Secretary and settled long-standing disputes over the eastern and western boundaries between Canada and the United

States, by the Webster-Ashburton Treaty (1842) and the Oregon Treaty (1846).

After Peel's death in 1850 Hamilton-Gordon formed a coalition Cabinet of Peelites (of whom he had been acknowledged leader) Whigs, and a Radical (which eventually, in 1859, become the Liberal Party). In December 1852 Disraeli submitted his budget to Parliament on behalf of Stanley's minority government, the Peelites, the Free Traders, and the Irish Brigade were all alienated by the proposed budget, but they side-lined their differences and voted with the Whigs against the proposed budget. The vote was 286 in favour of the budget and 305 votes against the budget. Because the leadership of the minority government had made the vote on the budget a "vote of confidence", the defeat of the Disraeli budget became a "vote of no confidence" in the minority government and meant its downfall. Accordingly, Gordon was asked to form a new government. In 1853, as his ministry reluctantly neared war with Russia over conflicts of interest in the Middle East, it became inevitable after Hamilton-Gordon sent the British fleet to Constantinople on September 23 1853, and then, three months later, into the Black Sea. Both Great Britain and France declared war (the war would eventually be called the Crimean War, but was initially referred to as the "Eastern Question") against Russia on March 28, 1854. Although he was ill-informed by the British generals in the Crimean War, Hamilton-Gordon was constitutionally responsible for their mistakes, and rather than face a Committee of Inquiry to investigate the conduct of the war, he resigned on January 29, 1855. It was something of a cruel irony that Hamilton-Gordon came to be blamed for the uncoordinated and frightful Crimean War. Hamilton-Gordon had made a successful career as a diplomat and had done much to normalise Britain's relationships with its powerful neighbours. But graphic reports from the front through a combination of the telegraph, and the new profession of war correspondent led to the Crimean being styled the first 'media war'. The reports publicised the squalor and disease that appeared to be claiming more soldiers' lives than the fighting. The reports inspired Florence Nightingale to volunteer and take the first 38 nurses out to treat the wounded. Hamilton-Gordon never held office after February 1855, although he assisted Palmerston in forming the next administration by asking his fellow Peelites to stay on. After the war he continued to advise the Foreign Secretary Lord Clarendon on the conduct of foreign affairs, and co-operated with Sidney Herbert in persuading Gladstone (whom he was convinced must one day lead the Liberal Party) not to re-join the Conservatives.

Hamilton-Gordon, who had been an historian before he became a politician, was convinced that posterity would redress any balance. He meticulously preserved all his papers and left his youngest son, Arthur Charles Hamilton-Gordon, (later Baron Stanmore), the task of publishing them. Unfortunately, Hamilton-Gordon also gave Sir James Graham and William Gladstone final powers of veto to avoid indiscretions. Gladstone who was still an active politician sabotaged the entire publication to suppress the revelation that he had opposed parliamentary reform in 1853.

Gordon died at Argyll House, Argyll Street, London, on 14 December 1860 aged 76, and was buried in the old church at Stanmore on 21 December.

Interesting George Hamilton Gordon facts:

The English poet, peer and politician George Gordon Byron, 6th Baron Byron, (known simply as Lord Byron), was Gordon's cousin, and was referred to by Byron in his *English Bards and Scotch Reviewers* (1809) as "the travell'd thane, Athenian Aberdeen."

In 1994 the novelist, columnist, and politician Ferdinand Mount used George Gordon's life as the basis for a historical novel, *Umbrella*.

Henry John Temple (3rd Viscount Palmerston) 28th British Prime Minister

Born
20 October 1784, Westminster, London
Died
18 October 1865, age 80, Brocket Hall, Hertfordshire
Periods in office as Prime Minister
9 years 143 days (2 terms) from 6 February 1855 until 19 February 1858 (3 years 14 days) and 12 June 1859 until 18 October 1865 (6 years 129 days)
Political party
Whig/Liberal
Constituencies Represented as MP
Newport (Isle of Wight) 1807-1811
Cambridge University 1811-1831
Bletchingley 1831-1832
Hampshire South 1832-1835
Tiverton 1835-1865
Ministerial offices held as Prime Minister
First Lord of the Treasury
Leader of the House of Commons

Henry John Temple, 3rd Viscount Palmerston, (20 October 1784 – 18 October 1865) was a British Whig/Liberal statesman who served twice as Prime Minister in the mid-19th century and whose long political career, including many years as British Foreign Secretary (1830–34, 1835–41, and 1846–51).

Henry Temple was born on 20th October 1784, the eldest of five children *into a wealthy Irish branch of the Temple family in Westminster. His father was 2nd Viscount Palmerston, an Anglo-Irish peer, whilst his mother Mary was the daughter of a London merchant. Henry (known as Harry) was subsequently christened at the 'House of Commons church' of St Margaret in Westminster, which was most apt for someone destined to become a politician. In his youth he received a classic education based on French, Italian and some German, and after* accompanying his parents on an extended continental tour in 1792–4 *Temple then attended Harrow School 1795-1800. He then entered the University of Edinburgh 1800-1803 where he studied political economy.*

In April 1802 before he had turned eighteen, his father passed away, leaving behind his title and estates and therefore Temple became the 3rd Viscount Palmerston. He remained in education and attended the prestigious St John's College in Cambridge from 1803 until October 1806. Whilst he held the title of a nobleman he was no longer required to sit his exams in order to acquire his Masters, despite him requesting to do so. Temple was still an undergraduate when he was defeated as candidate in the contest for the vacancy in the University of Cambridge constituency, which had resulted from the death of William Pitt in January 1806. Lord Malmesbury, Temple's guardian, was instrumental in finding him a constituency and he was elected for Horsham in November 1806, but this was invalidated on petition on 20 January 1807.
Temple persevered and began his political career in earnest as a Tory MP for the borough of Newport on the Isle of Wight in June

1807 before switching parties, first to the Whigs and later to the Liberal party.

Only a year into serving as an MP, Temple spoke out on foreign policy, particularly with regards to the mission of capturing and destroying the Danish navy. This was a direct result of attempts from Russia and Napoleon to build a naval alliance against Britain, using the navy in Denmark. Temple held strong beliefs which would be a feature throughout his political life.

Temple was offered, but turn down the position of Chancellor of the Exchequer from the Prime Minister, Spencer Perceval in 1809, as he preferred the office of Secretary at War. It was during his time (on 1 April 1818) in the War Office, that Temple was shot by Lieutenant Davies, a retired officer who had a grievance with his pension. Temple escaped with only a minor injury, but when he found out that Davies had been diagnosed as insane, he paid for Davies' legal defence out of his own pocket and ensured that the man was well looked-after when he was sent to Bedlam.

However, in 1822 Charles Smith was not so fortunate, he was caught poaching on Temple's estates and was executed. Temple refused to intervene on the grounds that it was not right to use private influence to affect the due process of law.

George Canning the Tory Prime Minister put him into the cabinet in April 1827, where he remained, still Secretary at War, until 1828. He, along with other like-minded 'liberal Tory' colleagues, resigned the following year from Wellesley's new government, criticising him for his illiberal foreign and Irish policy.

In 1830, Wellesley opposed parliamentary reform and his government fell and Temple became Foreign Secretary, a post he held for 15 of the next 21 years. When Temple left office in 1841, relations with France were unnecessarily bad and he remained in opposition for 5 years, condemning Canning for appeasing France and the United States, a view that contributed to a feeling in the highest Whig circles that he ought not to return to the foreign office. Temple's reputation as an interventionist and his unpopularity with the Queen and other grandees was such that Lord John Russell's attempt in December 1845 to form a ministry failed because Lord Grey refused to join a government in which Temple would direct foreign affairs. A few months later, however, the Whigs returned to power and Temple returned to the Foreign Office in July 1846. On 2 December 1851 Prime Minister Russell forced Temple to resign. This ultimately led to the downfall of Russell's ministry as on 21 February 1852, Temple turned a vote on a militia bill into a vote of confidence on the Government which it lost. It was replaced by George Hamilton-Gordon's ministry in which Temple was made Home Secretary even though his forte was foreign affairs. In his new role, he was responsible for a Factory Act (This act related to the mills and required that the work of children aged 9 to 13 to be between the hours of 6am to 6pm in summer and 7am to 7pm in winter. Similarly the work of women and young persons was restricted to the hours between 6am and 6pm). In March 1854 the Crimean War broke out, it was deemed to be mishandled by Hamilton-Gordon, who was obliged to resign because of his government's shortcomings. The Queen (who regarded Temple as impetuous and brash) was forced to appoint Temple as Prime Minister after failing to find anyone who would accept the post. So in February 1855, aged seventy, Henry Temple became Prime Minister, the oldest person in British politics to have been appointed in this position for the first time. One of his first tasks included dealing with the mess of the Crimean War. Temple was able to secure his wish for a demilitarised Black Sea but could not achieve the Crimea being returned to the Ottomans. Nevertheless, peace was secured in a treaty signed in March 1856 and a month later Temple was appointed to the Order of the Garter by Queen Victoria. A considerable majority was achieved in the April 1857 General Election and was seen a personal triumph. Temple passed the Matrimonial Causes Act 1857, which for the first time made it possible for courts to grant a divorce and removed divorce from the jurisdiction of the ecclesiastical courts. The opponents in Parliament, who included Gladstone, were the first in British history to try to kill a bill by filibuster (an action such as prolonged speaking which obstructs progress in a legislative assembly in a way that does not technically contravene the required procedures). Temple persisted and got the bill passed. He resigned in February 1858, when he was defeated on a measure for removing conspiracies to murder abroad, from the class of misdemeanour to that of felony. The General Election of 1859 denied the Tories a majority so Temple resumed the premiership with Lord Russell and the Peelite, William Gladstone. Temple is often regarded as the first Liberal premier in 1859 and preceded Gladstone, who was his Chancellor, but the pair personally had a fractious relationship. In his last premiership Palmerston oversaw the passage of important legislation, The Offences against the Person Act 1861 codified and reformed the law, and was part of a wider process of consolidating criminal law. The Companies Act 1862 was the basis of modern company law. In 1865, following a vote of censure, Palmerston called a General Election in which he won with a convincing majority, however, he unfortunately did not see the new parliament convened because he died of a fever on 18 October 1865 aged 80 (two days before his 81st birthday).

Interesting Henry John Temple facts:

Laurence Fox portrays Lord Palmerston in series 3 of *Victoria* (2019), the series dramatizes his turbulent period as Foreign Secretary.

'Flashman in the Great Game' – Early in this historical novel, Lord Palmerston sends Flashman on a mission to India. It happens that the Indian rebellion of 1857 is about to break out.

Flying Colours – in this novel by CS Forester, Horatio Hornblower meets a young Lord Palmerston on returning to England.

Benjamin Disraeli (Earl of Beaconsfield)
29th British Prime Minister

Born
21 December 1804, London
Died
19 April 1881, age 76, London
Periods in office as Prime Minister 6 years 341
days (2 terms) from 27 February 1868 – 1 December 1868 (279 days) 20 February 1874 – 21 April 1880 (6 years 62 days)
Political party
Conservative
Constituencies Represented as MP
Maidstone 1837-1841
Shrewsbury 1841-1847
Buckinghamshire 1847-1876
Ministerial offices held as Prime Minister
First Lord of the Treasury
Leader of the House of Commons (1874-1876)
Leader of the House of Lords (1876-1880)
Lord Privy Seal (1876-1878)

Benjamin Disraeli, 1st Earl of Beaconsfield, (21 December 1804 – 19 April 1881) was a novelist and British politician of the Conservative Party who twice served as Prime Minister of the United Kingdom. He played a major role in the creation of the modern Conservative Party and the first mention of the term "Prime Minister" in an official government document occurred during the premiership of Benjamin Disraeli.

Disraeli was born in Bloomsbury of Italian-Jewish descent, the eldest son and second child of Isaac D'Israeli and Maria Basevi. An important event in Disraeli's boyhood was his father's quarrel in 1813 with the synagogue of Bevis Marks, which led to the decision in 1817 to have his children baptized as Anglicans, Disraeli being twelve when he was baptized. Until 1858, Jews by religion were excluded from Parliament, so without his father's decision, Disraeli's political career may never have taken the form it did.

Disraeli was educated at small private schools, first to a Nonconformist, and later to a Unitarian school. In November 1821, shortly before his seventeenth birthday, Disraeli was articled as a clerk by his father to a firm of solicitors for two years. In 1824, Disraeli wrote his first novel, the crude and jejune political satire *Aylmer Papillon.* The same year he started reading for the bar. Also in 1824 he speculated recklessly in South American mining shares, and, when he lost all a year later, he was left so badly in debt that he did not recover until well past middle age. Earlier he had persuaded the publisher John Murray, his father's friend, to launch a daily newspaper, the *Representative.* It was a complete failure. Disraeli, unable to pay his promised share of the capital, quarrelled with Murray and others. Moreover, in his novel *Vivian Grey* (1826–27), which was published anonymously in four volumes, it lampooned Murray while telling the story of the failure. When Disraeli was unmasked as the author he was widely criticised. In later editions Disraeli made many changes, softening his satire, but the damage to his reputation proved long-lasting. Disraeli had always been sensitive and moody but the criticism had now made him seriously depressed. He was still living with his parents in London, and on advice from his doctor he went in search of 'a change of air'. Along with his sister's fiancé, William Meredith, Disraeli travelled widely in southern Europe and beyond in 1830–31. The trip was financed partly by another high society novel, *The Young Duke*, written in 1829–30, but the tour was cut short suddenly by Meredith's death from smallpox in Cairo in July 1831. Disraeli wrote two novels in the aftermath of the tour, *Contarini Fleming* (1832) was avowedly a self-portrait and the following year and *The Wondrous Tale of Alroy* which portrayed the problems of a medieval Jew. After the two novels were published, Disraeli turned his attention to politics. As an independent radical, he stood for and lost High Wycombe twice in 1832, and once in 1835. Realising that he must attach himself to one of the political parties, in 1835 he unsuccessfully stood for Taunton as the official Conservative candidate. After failing in five elections in five years, finally in 1837, he was successfully returned as Conservative MP for Maidstone in Kent. In 1837 he also published the novels *Venetia* and *Henrietta Temple.* In 1839 he spoke on the Chartist petition and declared "the rights of labour" to be "as sacred as the rights of property" and in the same year he married Mrs. Wyndham Lewis, 12 years his senior.

In 1841 the Conservatives won the General Election and Robert Peel became Prime Minister, Disraeli was not given office in the cabinet, which he considered a rebuff and so became the inspiration of a group of young Tories, nicknamed 'Young England', led by George Smythe (later Lord Stangford). Disraeli wrote a novel in 1844 *Coningsby; or, The New Generation* in which the hero is patterned on Smythe. The cool, pragmatic, humdrum, middle-class Conservatism that Peel represented is contrasted to Young England's romantic, aristocratic, nostalgic, and escapist attitude. Disraeli wrote *Sybil* and *Tancred* in 1845 with Tancred being the last novel he wrote for 25 years. Also in 1845 when Peel repealed the Corn Laws, Disraeli found issue and Young England rallied against Peel, with not only their own members, but with the great mass of country squires who formed the backbone of the Conservative Party. Although Disraeli and his fellow protectionists could not stop the repeal of the Corn Laws (because the Whigs also backed the bill) the rebels put Peel in the minority, and on the issue of the Irish Coercion Bill forced him to resign in 1846. In the 1847 General Election, Disraeli stood, successfully, for the Buckinghamshire constituency. The new House of Commons had more Conservative members than Whig, but the depth of the Tory schism enabled Russell to continue to govern. The Conservatives were led by Bentinck in the Commons and by Stanley in the Lords. In 1848 Disraeli became leader of the Tories (Conservatives) in the House of Commons and in February 1851 Edward Smith Stanley offered Disraeli the position of Chancellor of the Exchequer, (a position he held within all Stanley's ministries). The Cabinet was known as the "Who? Who?" a term gained from the deaf old Duke of Wellesley's repeated questions to Stanley. Disraeli lowered the tax on tea in his 1852 budget and changed the income tax. In the December 1852 General Election, the government was beaten, and Stanley and his Cabinet resigned. With the fall of the government, Disraeli and the Conservatives returned to the opposition benches. Disraeli ended up spending three-quarters of his 44-year parliamentary career in opposition. During this period Disraeli met Queen Victoria who was said to be fascinated by him referring to him as 'Dizzy'. After Edward Stanley's resignation in February 1868, Queen Victoria invited Disraeli to become Prime Minister, on accepting Disraeli famously remarked 'I have reached the top of the greasy pole'. He immediately struck up an excellent rapport with Queen Victoria, who approved of his imperialist ambitions and his belief that Britain should be the most powerful nation in the world. In May 1868 the Capital Punishment Act received Royal Assent, which required that all prisoners sentenced to death for murder be executed within the walls of prison in which they were being held, bringing to an end the 'grotesque spectacle' of public executions. Disraeli's first term of 279 days ended within the same year, as there was a General Election victory for Gladstone's Liberals in December 1868. The following 12-year period, marked a change in politics from the chaotic collection of ill-defined groups that had been common from the beginning of Disraeli's career, to an emergence of two parties with coherent policies. Disraeli became Prime Minister again in February 1874 when he was 70 years of age. His second ministry was notable for many social developments, including the Artisan Dwelling Act (1875) which provided houses for the poor, the Public Health Act (1875) which provided water to housing along with refuse collection and the Trade Union Act (1876) which allowed picketing. There was also the abolition of using children as chimney sweeps and the Education Act (1880) which made attendance at school compulsory for children between the ages of four and ten. Queen Victoria rewarded Disraeli with the title of the Earl of Beaconsfield in 1876. Disraeli notable success on foreign policy was the success of his negotiation of the Congress of Berlin in 1878 where he secured 'Peace with Honour' in Europe. In April 1880 he was defeated in the General Election by Gladstone's Liberals and retired to the country. He died on 19 April 1881 aged 76 at his home in Curzon Street, London.

Interesting Benjamin Disraeli facts:

In 1870 Disraeli published his first novel for 25 years, *Lothair,* and in total he wrote 16 completed novels, his last one, Endymion was published the year before he died in 1880.

'There are three kinds of lies: lies, damn lies and statistics' is a quote often attributed to Disraeli, although no version of this is in any of his published works.

William Ewart Gladstone
30th British Prime Minister

Born
29 December 1809, Liverpool
Died
19 May 1898, age 88, Hawarden Castle, Flintshire
Periods in office as Prime Minister 12 years 120 days (4 terms) from 3 December 1868 – 17 February 1874 (5 years 77 days) 23 April 1880 – 9 June 1885 (5 years 48 days) 1 February 1886 – 20 July 1886 (170 days) 15 August 1892 – 2 March 1894 (1 year 110 days)
Political party
Liberal
Constituencies Represented as MP
Newark 1832-1845
Oxford University 1847-1865
South Lanchasire 1865-1868
Greenwich 1868-1880
Midlothian 1880-1885
Ministerial offices held as Prime Minister
Chancellor of the Exchequer (1873-1874 and 1880-1882)
First Lord of the Treasury
Leader of the House of Commons
Lord Privy Seal

William Ewart Gladstone 29 December 1809 – 19 May 1898)
was a British statesman of Scottish origin and a Liberal politician.
In a career lasting over 60 years, he served for 12 years as Prime
Minister of the United Kingdom, spread over four terms beginning
in 1868 and ending in 1894. He also served as Chancellor of the
Exchequer four times.

*Gladstone was born in Liverpool to Scottish parents on 29th
December, 1809, the fourth son of Sir John Gladstone MP
(originally Gladstones), who was also a successful merchant, their
fortune based on trading in corn with the United States and the
West Indies sugar plantations. William Gladstone was educated
from 1816–1821 at a preparatory school at the vicarage of St.
Thomas' Church at Seaforth, close to his family's
residence, Seaforth House. In 1821, William followed in the
footsteps of his elder brothers and attended Eton College
before enrolling at Christ Church, Oxford in 1828, where he
achieved a double first-class degree in December 1831 in
Mathematics and Classics.*

In the General Election of 1832, the Duke of Newcastle who was a
Conservative party activist, provided Gladstone with one of two
seats at Newark where the Duke controlled about a fourth of the
very small electorate. Initially a disciple of High Toryism,
Gladstone's maiden speech as a young Tory was a defence of the
rights of West Indian sugar plantation magnates (slave-owners)
of which his father was prominent. He immediately came under
attack from anti-slavery movement who demanded the
immediate abolition of slavery, but Gladstone opposed this and
said in 1832, that emancipation should come through the
adoption of an education among the slaves and when this is
achieved 'with the utmost speed that prudence will permit, we
shall arrive at that exceedingly desired consummation, the utter
extinction of slavery'. In June 1833, Gladstone concluded his
speech on the 'slavery question' by declaring that though he had

dwelt on 'the dark side' of the issue, he looked forward to 'a safe and gradual emancipation'. Parliament passed the Slavery Abolition Act in 1833. This act gave all slaves in the British Empire their freedom. Gladstone's was heavily involved with his father's claim for 2,508 slaves, and Gladstone senior eventually received £106,769 (modern equivalent £83m), in compensation. The British government paid out £20m to compensate some 3,000 families that owned slaves for the loss of their "property". This figure represented a staggering 40 per cent of the Treasury's annual spending budget and, in today's terms, calculated as wage values, equates to around £16.5bn.

Two years after he entered the House of Commons as an MP for Newark, Sir Robert Peel, the Prime Minister, appointed William Gladstone as his junior lord of the Treasury. The following year he was promoted to under-secretary for the colonies but Gladstone lost office when Peel resigned in 1835 and he then spent the next six years in opposition. Around this time Gladstone began his charitable work, (which at the time was open to a great deal of misinterpretation); the 'rescue and rehabilitation' of London's prostitutes. In later years even while serving as Prime Minister, he would walk the streets, trying to convince prostitutes to change their ways, spending large amount of his own money on this project, later in 1848 he founded the Church Penitentiary Association for the Reclamation of Fallen Women. When the Whigs were forced out of power in August, 1841, Gladstone returned to the government in Peel's second ministry and although his early parliamentary performances were strongly Tory, over time the effects of Tory policy forced him to take a more liberal view. His conversion from conservatism to liberalism took over a generation. In 1843 he entered the Cabinet as president of the Board of Trade. His Railway Act of 1844 set up minimum requirements for railroad companies (including limiting the cost to a penny a mile) and provided for eventual state purchase of railway lines. Gladstone also much improved the

working conditions for London dock workers. Early in 1845, when the Cabinet proposed to increase a state grant to the Irish Roman Catholic College at Maynooth, Gladstone resigned, not because he did not approve of the increase, but because it went against the views he had published seven years before. Later in 1845 he re-joined the Cabinet as Secretary of State for the Colonies until the government fell in 1846. At the July/August 1847 General Election, Gladstone was elected as the Conservative MP for Oxford University and although there were more Conservatives (325) than Whigs (292) in the house, the Tory schism enabled Lord Russell to continue to govern. After Peel's death in 1850, Gladstone emerged as the leader of the Peelites in the House of Commons, and at the end of 1852, a brilliant attack on Disraeli's budget brought the government down with Gladstone rising in the public's estimation. With the appointment of George Hamilton Gordon as Prime Minister as head of a coalition of Whigs and Peelites, Gladstone became Chancellor of the Exchequer. He defended the Crimean War as necessary for the defence of the public law of Europe, but its outbreak disrupted his financial plans. Determined to pay for it as far as possible by taxation, he doubled income tax in 1854.
He served as Chancellor until February 1855, but three weeks into Lord Palmerston's first premiership, he resigned along with the rest of the Peelites after a motion was passed to appoint a committee of inquiry into the conduct of the war. In 1859, Lord Palmerston formed a new mixed government with Radicals included, and Gladstone again joined the government as Chancellor of the Exchequer (with most of the other remaining Peelites) to become part of the new Liberal Party. In his second budget, Gladstone reduced considerably the number of articles subject to customs duty. The budget reduced the cost of living and his reputation as a financier grew and in 1861, the Post Office Savings Bank was established. This enabled people with small savings to open a bank account. Gladstone also committed himself to supporting a Bill to lower the franchise qualification.

This pleased the Radicals but horrified both Queen Victoria and Palmerston, because of his support of an extension of the franchise, Gladstone lost his Oxford University seat in the 1865 General Election, but he was returned as MP for Lancashire at a later poll in the same election. When Lord Russell retired in 1867 Gladstone became leader of the Liberal Party. In 1868 Gladstone was elected as MP for Greenwich following his defeat in Lancashire in the General Election.

More than a million votes were cast in the 1868 General Election. This was nearly three times the number of people who voted in the previous election. The Liberals won 387 seats against the Conservatives 271 and Gladstone became Prime Minister for the first time, announcing that his "mission was to pacify Ireland". When an Irish University Bill failed to pass the Commons in March 1873, Gladstone resigned but was forced back into office by Disraeli's refusal to form a government. In August he reshuffled his Cabinet and again took on the chancellorship of the Exchequer himself. He dissolved Parliament in January 1874, but his party was heavily defeated and his government resigned with Gladstone giving up the party leadership (though he remained MP for Greenwich). In March 1880 he gave up his Greenwich seat and was elected in Midlothian, and upon his return to Parliament, he overthrew a Conservative government securing a large Liberal majority. Gladstone again combined the duties of Prime Minister and Chancellor of the Exchequer for the next two and a half years. Troubles arose in Ireland in 1881 and he established the Irish Coercion Act, which permitted the Lord Lieutenant of Ireland to detain people for as "long as was thought necessary", also in 1881 the Irish Land Act which was largely Gladstone's own work, was intended to promote the prosperity of the Irish peasant, but it didn't stop violent crime continuing. In 1882 Lord Frederick Cavendish (the Chief Secretary for Ireland) and T.H. Burke (the Undersecretary) were murdered in Phoenix Park, Dublin. This led to an even more severe Coercion Bill being introduced as a result of the murders. Gladstone resigned as

Chancellor of the Exchequer and in 1885 the government was defeated on the budget by an alliance of Conservatives and Irish Nationalists. Gladstone resigned as Prime Minister and Robert Gascoyne-Cecil (Lord Salisbury) became was appointed.
Queen Victoria offered Gladstone an Earldom, which he declined. The Conservatives vowed to maintain the union of Great Britain and Ireland, but in late January 1886, Gladstone and the Irish Nationalists led by Charles Parnell, joined forces to defeat the government. Lord Salisbury resigned and Gladstone became Prime Minister for the third time, combining the office with that of Lord Privy Seal. In July 1886 Gladstone introduced a Home Rule Bill for Ireland which split the Liberal party and was defeated on the second reading. Gladstone again resigned after only 170 days into his third ministry. The Liberals were in opposition until 1892 when they won a minority administration at the General Election and Gladstone became Prime Minister for the fourth time, again combining the office with that of Lord Privy Seal. The Second Home Rule Bill for Ireland was introduced in 1893, and unlike the first attempt, which was defeated in the House of Commons, the second Bill was passed by the Commons only to be vetoed by the House of Lords. Gladstone resigned for the final time from the premiership on 2 March 1894. He died of cancer on 19 May 1898 at Hawarden Castle, Hawarden, aged 88, and his funeral was held at Westminster Abbey.

Interesting William Gladstone facts:

A statue of Gladstone erected in 1905, stands at Aldwych, London, near the Royal Courts of Justice.

Gladstone's burial in 1898 was commemorated in a poem by William McGonagall.

Ralph Richardson played Gladstone in the 1966 film *Khartoum*.

Robert Gascoyne-Cecil (3rd Marquess of Salisbury)
31st British Prime Minister

Born
3 February 1830, Hatfield House, Hertfordshire
Died
22 August 1903, age 76, Hatfield House, Hertfordshire
Periods in office as Prime Minister
13 years 255 days (3 terms) from 23 June 1885 – 28 January 1886 (220 days) 25 July 1886 – 11 August 1892 (6 years 18 days) 25 June 1895 – 11 July 1902 (7 years 17 days)
Political party
Conservative
Constituency Represented as MP
Stamford 1853-1868
Ministerial offices held as Prime Minister
First Lord of the Treasury
Secretary of State for Foreign Affairs
Leader of the House of Lords
Lord Privy Seal

Robert Arthur Talbot Gascoyne-Cecil, 3rd Marquess of Salisbury (3 February 1830 – 22 August 1903) was a British statesman. He was styled **Lord Robert Cecil** before the death of his elder brother in 1865, **Viscount Cranborne** from June 1865 until his father died in April 1868, and then the **Marquess of Salisbury**.

Robert Cecil was born at Hatfield House, the third son of the 2nd Marquess of Salisbury and Frances Mary, née Gascoyne. Robert Cecil's childhood was said to be unhappy and lonely. He was exceptionally clever but not especially strong, and he hated games. His father lacked warmth and his mother, died when he was only 10. He was sent to Eton, where he was perpetually bullied. The unhappy schooling shaped his pessimistic outlook on life and his negative views on democracy. He was taken out of school at 15 and was tutored privately. At 18 he entered Christ Church, Oxford where he gained an honorary degree through nobleman's privilege due to ill health. His doctor advised travel and so he set out on a long sea voyage in July 1851 to May 1853, visiting Australia and New Zealand. After almost two years he returned to England in better health and more self-assured.

Gascoyne-Cecil was still not sure of his future career as both the church and politics attracted him, but on 22 August 1853, aged 23, he was offered a seat in Parliament as a Conservative MP for Stamford in Lincolnshire and in doing so he chose politics. He retained this seat until he succeeded to his father's peerages in 1868 and it was not contested during his time as its representative. Cecil had also started writing political articles for journals, gaining him a reputation as a sharp and clever commentator. His first political post came in 1866, when he was appointed Secretary of State for India under Edward Smith-Stanley. At this time Cecil was deeply suspicious of the Conservative leader Benjamin Disraeli and resigned after only eight months as Secretary of State for India in disagreement over the Conservative government's adoption of parliamentary reform.

In 1868, on the death of his father, he inherited the title 3rd Marquess of Salisbury. In February 1874 Gascoyne-Cecil was persuaded to join Disraeli's ministry and once more became Secretary of State for India. During their seven years together in and out of office, Gascoyne-Cecil changed his perspective, and came to regard Disraeli with admiration and affection. In April 1878 he became Disraeli's Foreign Secretary and helped to lead Britain to 'peace and honour' at the Congress of Berlin (a meeting of the representatives of the era's great powers in Europe and the Ottoman Empire). Along with Disraeli, he was awarded the Order of the Garter from Queen Victoria for their success. After Disraeli's death in 1881, Gascoyne-Cecil led the Conservative opposition in the House of Lords and he became Prime Minister during the brief minority Conservative administration from June 1885 to January 1886, with Ireland and imperial problems being the chief issues. With Gladstone and the Liberals split on the issue of Irish Home Rule, Gladstone's ministry (from February to July 1886) was cut short, and although Cecil was without a Conservative majority (but aided by the Liberal Unionist's), on 25 July 1886, he once again became Prime Minister. His reforms in this period included the Local Government Act of 1888 which transferred the administration of counties to elected county councils, and the 1891 Free Education Act that abolished fees for primary education. Instead of the traditional role of First Lord of the Treasury, Lord Salisbury unusually combined the role of the Prime Minister with that of Foreign Secretary, a demanding double job, which he managed by adopting a hands off approach to home issues and focusing on the direction of foreign affairs especially British interests in Africa. Under his direction, the colony of Rhodesia (today's Zimbabwe) was established, with its capital city named Salisbury after him (later renamed Harare after Independence in 1982).

In 1889 Cecil set up the London County Council and in 1890 allowed it to build houses. Throughout its existence from 1889 to 1965, it was the first London-wide general municipal authority to be directly elected. It covered the area today known as Inner London and was replaced by the Greater London Council. In the 1892 United Kingdom General Election which was held from 4 July to 26 July 1892, it saw the Conservatives, led by Gascoyne-Cecil, win the greatest number of seats but no longer a majority as William Gladstone's Liberals won 80 more seats than in the 1886 General Election. The Liberal Unionists who had previously supported the Conservative government saw their vote and seat numbers go down and Cecil remained the Leader of the Opposition from 1892 until 1895. At the General Election in 1895 Cecil became Prime Minister for the third and final time again forming an alliance with the Liberal Unionist Party. Cecil's foreign policy ('Splendid Isolation') had left Britain with no allies, and tensions were high with Germany's Kaiser Wilhelm. In 1895 the Venezuelan crisis with the United States erupted and in October 1899 the Second Boer War started and didn't end until May 1902. At home Gascoyne-Cecil launched a land reform programme which helped hundreds of thousands of Irish peasants gain land ownership and largely ended complaints against English landlords. The Elementary School Teachers (Superannuation) Act of 1898 enabled teachers to secure an annuity via the payment of voluntary contributions. The Elementary Education (Defective and Epileptic Children) Act of 1899 permitted school boards to provide for the education of mentally and physically defective children as well as epileptic children. The Workmen's Compensation Act of 1897 was introduced making the employer liable for accidents at work. During the last two years of his ministry, from the autumn of 1900 until the summer of 1902, old age and ill health forced him to give up the Foreign Office though he continued as Prime Minister with Lord Landsdowne becoming the new Foreign Secretary. Gascoyne-Cecil was the last aristocratic statesman to head a British government while in the House of Lords and not the elected Commons. To try and improve his health in his last years he took to riding a tricycle, taking a footman along to push him up hills. His beloved wife (who he married in 1857 producing eight children) died in 1899, and as he approached seventy his health was failing. Queen Victoria died in 1901 and when the Boar war concluded in May 1902, Gascoyne-Cecil decided to resign in July of 1902, he recommended his nephew Arthur James Balfour to take over. Gascoyne-Cecil died at the age of 73 at Hatfield House on August 22, 1903, a little more than one year after retiring. Cecil was Queen Victoria's last Prime Minister and was buried at St. Etheldreda's Church in Hatfield, where William Lamb, 2nd Viscount Melbourne, Queen Victoria's first Prime Minister, is also buried.

Interesting Robert Cecil facts:

To date Cecil is the only British Prime Minister to sport a full beard.

At 6 feet, 4 inches (193 cm) tall, he was also the tallest Prime Minister.

The term *'Bob's your uncle'* is thought to originate from Gascoyne-Cecil after he ("Bob") appointed his nephew Arthur Balfour as Chief Secretary for Ireland in 1887, which was seen as an act of nepotism...and there you have it.

Cecil suffered from prosopagnosia, a cognitive disorder which makes it difficult to recognize familiar faces.

The 6th Marquess of Salisbury commissioned Andrew Roberts to write Cecil's authorised biography *'Salisbury: Victorian Titan'* which was published in 1999.

Archibald Primrose (5th Earl of Rosebery)
32nd British Prime Minister

Born
7 May 1847, London
Died
21 May 1929, age 82, Epsom, Surrey
Period in office as Prime Minister
1 year 110 days from 5 March 1894 until 22 June 1895
Political party
Liberal
Ministerial offices held as Prime Minister
First Lord of the Treasury
Leader of the House of Lords
Lord President of the Council

Archibald Philip Primrose, 5th Earl of Rosebery, 1st Earl of Midlothian, (7 May 1847 – 21 May 1929) was a British Liberal politician who served as Prime Minister of the United Kingdom in the reign of Queen Victoria, from March 1894 to June 1895. Between the death of his father, in 1851, and the death of his grandfather, the 4th Earl of Rosebery, in 1868 he was known by the courtesy title of **Lord Dalmeny**.

Archibald Primrose was born at his parents' house on Charles Street in Mayfair, London, he was the eldest of the two sons and the third of the four children of Archibald Primrose, Lord Dalmeny and Lady Wilhelmina Stanhope. Primrose attended preparatory schools in Hertfordshire and Brighton, and attended Eton College from 1860 – 1863. He then attended Brighton College between 1863 and 1865 before entering Christ Church, Oxford. When his grandfather died in 1868, Primrose was eligible to sit in the House of Lords as his grandfather had been created 1st Baron Rosebery in the Peerage of the United Kingdom.

In 1869 he bought his first racehorse, Ladas, which was against university rules. Primrose was offered a choice by the university authorities of either selling his horse or abandoning his studies...he chose the racehorse and continued a passion for horse racing for the next forty years. After leaving Oxford without a degree he travelled widely, visiting Italy and Russia. From 1868 into the early 1870s he visited America three times, and also visited Australia.

On March 20, 1878, Primrose married Hannah de Rothschild, the only child and sole heiress of Baron Mayer Amschel de Rothschild. Upon the death of her father in 1874, 23-year-old Hannah became the richest woman in the United Kingdom, inheriting Mentmore Towers which was a large country house in

Buckinghamshire, as well as a London mansion, a large art collection, and assets of more than two million pounds.

Primrose first stepped into politics when he managed Gladstone's successful Midlothian Campaign in 1879. In 1881 Gladstone convinced him to take up the post of Under Secretary at the Home Office, with special responsibility for Scotland. But as Gladstone was far too preoccupied with Irish affairs to take much notice of Primrose and Scottish affairs, Primrose resigned his post in June 1883. Shortly afterwards he left for a tour of the USA and Australia, where, on 18 January 1884, he made a speech in Adelaide in which he famously said: 'There is no need for any nation, however great, leaving the Empire, because the Empire is a Commonwealth of Nations'.

On his return to Britain, he found himself at odds with Gladstone's government over its Egyptian policy, but after the fall of Khartoum he took office as the Commissioner of the Board of Works and Lord Privy Seal. In February 1886 he became Foreign Secretary in Gladstone's third ministry, and in 1889 he served as the first chairman of the newly founded London County Council which was set up by the Conservatives, he was honoured by having the street 'Rosebery Avenue' in Clerkenwell named after him. The death of his wife, Hannah, in 1890 kept him out of politics for some time, but he was eventually persuaded by Queen Victoria and the Prince of Wales to return, and in 1892 he became Foreign Secretary again in Gladstone's last administration. On 2 March 1894, the 84-year-old Gladstone retired from active politics, almost blind and hard of hearing. Queen Victoria, who rejected the other leading Liberals, did not ask Gladstone who should succeed him but instead sent for Primrose, who reluctantly accepted the post of Prime Minister although regarding the position as a poisoned chalice.

Primrose did not enjoy the success in office of his Liberal predecessor Gladstone, and it was a short-lived administration. He inherited a divided Cabinet, faced an obstructive, Tory-dominated House of Lords and was heavily attacked in the Commons for opposing Irish Home Rule. On June 21, 1895, the Primrose Government lost a vote in committee on army supply by just seven votes. Primrose saw this as a vote of censure on his government and resigned as Prime Minister on 22 June 1895 and in October 1896, he resigned as leader of the Liberal Party. During the Boer War (1899-1902) Primrose became estranged from most of the Liberal Party because of his enthusiasm for the British Empire and although he was determined not to return to active politics he was drawn back in 1901, when the Liberal Imperial Council was formed by his supporters and in 1902 he became President of the Liberal League. Primrose's position made it impossible to join the Liberal government that returned to power in 1905 and he retired from politics altogether turning to writing which included biographies of Lord Chatham, Pitt the Younger, Napoleon, and Lord Randolph Churchill. Along with his passion for horse racing he had a great interest in collecting rare books. In 1911, Primrose made his last appearance in the House of Lords. On November 15, 1917, Primrose's youngest child 34-year-old Neil died from wounds received in action at Gezer, Palestine. Neil had followed his father into politics and was elected in 1910 as a Member of Parliament for Wisbech.

Rosebery died aged 82 at The Durdans, Epsom, Surrey, on 21 May 1929.

Interesting Archibald Primrose fact:

In 1881 the Scotland football team turned out in the primrose yellow and rose pink racing colours of Archibald Primrose, who became one of the Scottish FA's early patrons.

Arthur James Balfour (1st Earl of Balfour)
33rd British Prime Minister

Born
25 July 1848, Whittingehame, East Lothian
Died
19 March 1930, age 81, Fisher's Hill, Woking, Surrey
Period in office as Prime Minister
3 years 146 days from 12 July 1902 until 4 December 1905
Political party
Conservative
Constituencies Represented as MP
Hertford 1874-1885
Manchester East 1885-1906
City of London 1906-1922
Ministerial offices held as Prime Minister
First Lord of the Treasury
Leader of the House of Commons
Lord Privy (1902-1903)

Arthur James Balfour, 1st Earl of Balfour, 25 July 1848 – 19 March 1930) was a British Conservative statesman and philosopher, who maintained a position of power in the British Conservative Party for 50 years and served as Prime Minister of the United Kingdom from 1902 to 1905.

Balfour was born on 25 July 1848 at Whittingehame House, East Lothian, the third of eight children and eldest son of James Maitland Balfour, landowner and Scottish MP (1841–47), and his wife, Lady Blanche Mary Harriet. He inherited the estate of Whittingehame at the age of eight, when his father died in 1859. At the age of ten, Balfour went to the Revd C. G. Chittenden's Hoddesdon Grange preparatory school in Hertfordshire, where his short-sightedness and apparent delicate health initially proved a handicap. From 1861 until 1866 Balfour coasted calmly through Eton College, where he was denied the spectacles that could have corrected his myopia. He moved to Trinity College, Cambridge (1866–1869), where he started to wear spectacles and became an avid to tennis player and graduated with a second class honours degree.

After Balfour left Cambridge he inherited a comfortable fortune, together with Whittingehame and the Strathconan estates in Ross-shire, in 1870 he acquired a house in London at 4 Carlton Gardens which was conveniently close, to the Houses of Parliament and only a few doors away from William Gladstone at no. 11. In 1874 Balfour was elected Conservative Member of Parliament (MP) for Hertford until 1885. From 1885 to 1906 he served as the Member of Parliament for Manchester East. In spring 1878, he became Private Secretary to his uncle, Robert Gascoyne-Cecil (Lord Salisbury). He accompanied Gascoyne-Cecil (then Foreign Secretary) to the Congress of Berlin and gained his first experience in international politics in connection with the settlement of the Russo-Turkish conflict. Released from his duties as Private Secretary by the 1880 General Election, he began to take a bigger part in parliamentary affairs. He was for a time politically associated with Lord Randolph Churchill's 'Fourth Party' a group which was distinct from the Conservatives, Liberals and Irish Nationalists), and which brought down William Ewart Gladstone's government with a motion opposing the Home Rule for Ireland Bill. From 1885 Balfour's political career took off. He left Hertford and contested a new, popular constituency, East Manchester. Acting as his uncle's secretary, he entered upon a lengthy apprenticeship for the prime ministership. He served briefly as President of the Local Government Board (1885) and as Secretary of State for Scotland (1886), but Balfour really made his reputation as Chief Secretary for Ireland (1887–91). In that role Balfour adopted a two-fold strategy. First he ruthlessly suppressed rural violence, earning the epithet 'Bloody Balfour'. Second, he attempted to conciliate nationalist opinion by policies of social interventionism, including the sale of land to tenant farmers on easy terms and investment in light railways and seed potatoes. On the death of W. H. Smith in 1891 Gascoyne-Cecil promoted his nephew to leader of the House of Commons, and Balfour also became First Lord of the Treasury – the last time in British history that the position did not run concurrently with that of Prime Minister. After the fall of the government in 1892 he spent three years in opposition. When the Conservatives returned to power in coalition with the Liberal Unionists, in 1895, Balfour again became Leader of the House and First Lord of the Treasury.

When Gascoyne-Cecil resigned on 11 July 1902, Balfour succeeded him as Prime Minister, but straight away his cabinet was split on the free trade issue and his relations with the King were poor. Balfour's government did though make several important initiatives including the passage of the 1902 Education Act, the Anglo-French Entente of 1904, the establishment of the Committee of Imperial Defence and the Royal Commission on the Poor Laws.

Balfour went into the 1906 General Election hoping that success could be claimed in 'Ireland, Foreign Affairs, Colonial Policy, Education, National Defence', and even 'Social Reform'.
Balfour was, in fact, heading for a crushing electoral defeat. The Tories offered less to their working-class voters than at almost any election in their history, and working-class voters also felt less attracted to the Tories than at almost any time in their history. At the January/February 1906 General Election the Conservatives lost to the Liberals including more than half their seats, Balfour lost his own seat in Manchester East, and it left the party with its record fewest seats. The 1906 General Election became known as the 'Liberal landslide' and the Conservative Party's seat total of 156 MPs remains its worst result ever in a General Election. After the General Election Balfour remained as leader of the Conservatives and by 27 February 1906 a safe seat was found for him in the City of London. In 1909 he made no attempt to stop the Tory majority in the Lords from rejecting Lloyd George's 'Peoples Budget' budget which provoked the constitutional crisis that led to the Parliament Act 1911, which limited the Lords to delaying bills for up to two years. This proved to be a serious error, it resulted in Balfour having to lead his party through two unsuccessful elections in 1910, and as a result, in 1911 the development of a 'Balfour Must Go' campaign started. He resigned in November 1911, but despite stepping down, his career was far from over, at the outbreak of war in 1914 he became an unofficial adviser to the Liberal government, and not surprisingly, Asquith appointed him 1st lord of the Admiralty in the coalition of May 1915. Subsequently he served Lloyd George as Foreign Secretary (1916–19) in which capacity he produced the famous Balfour declaration committing the government to the establishment of a national homeland in Palestine for the Jews. His last role was as Lord President of the Council under Lloyd George (1919–1922) and under Stanley Baldwin (1925–1929). On 5 May 1922, Balfour was created Earl of Balfour and Viscount Traprain, of Whittingehame, in the County of Haddington. On 25

July 1928, his eightieth birthday, Balfour who had for long been a motoring enthusiast was presented a Rolls-Royce at Westminster as a tribute from both houses of parliament.

Apart from a number of colds and occasional flu, Balfour had enjoyed good health until the year 1928 and he had remained a regular tennis player. At the end of 1928 most of his teeth had to be removed and he began to suffer from the unremitting circulatory trouble which ended his life. Late in January 1929, Balfour was conveyed from Whittingehame to Fisher's Hill, which was his brother Gerald's home near Woking, Surrey. In the past he had suffered from occasional bouts of phlebitis and by the autumn of 1929 he was immobilised by it.

Balfour died at Fisher's Hill on 19 March 1930 aged 81. At his own request a public funeral was declined and he was buried on 22 March beside members of his family at Whittingehame.

Interesting Arthur Balfour facts:

As well as being a politician, Balfour was also an eminent theist and philosopher whose scintillating works and ideas caused animated comments in British literary circles at the end of the nineteenth and the beginning of the twentieth centuries.

As well as tennis, Balfour was a keen golfer and had a handicap of eight when he was Prime Minister.

Balfour wrote several books; *A Defence of Philosophic Doubt* (1879; republished, 1920), *Foundations of Belief* 1895 and *Theism and Humanism* (1915).

In 1919, he was elected Chancellor of his old university, Cambridge, in succession to his brother-in-law, Lord Rayleigh.

Sir Henry Campbell-Bannerman
34th British Prime Minister

Born
7 September 1836, Kelvinside House, Glasgow
Died
22 April 1908, age 71, 10 Downing Street
Period in office as Prime Minister
2 years 121 days from 5 December 1905 until 3 April 1908
Political party
Liberal
Constituency Represented as MP
Stirling Burghs 1868-1908
Ministerial offices held as Prime Minister
First Lord of the Treasury
Leader of the House of Commons

Sir Henry Campbell-Bannerman (7 September 1836 – 22 April 1908) was a British statesman and popular Liberal politician who served as Prime Minister of the United Kingdom from 1905 to 1908 and was Leader of the Liberal Party from 1899 to 1908. He also served as Secretary of State for War twice, in the Cabinets of Gladstone and Rosebery. He was the first, First Lord of the Treasury to be officially called "Prime Minister", the term only coming into official usage five days after he took office.

Sir Henry Campbell-Bannerman (known as CB) was born on 7 September 1836 at Kelvinside House in Glasgow as Henry Campbell, the second son and youngest of the six children born to Sir James Campbell of Stracathro (1790–1876) and his wife Janet Bannerman (1799–1873). Campbell-Bannerman was educated at the High School of Glasgow (1845–1847), the University of Glasgow (1851–1853), and Trinity College, Cambridge (1854–1858), where he achieved a Third-Class Degree in the Classical Tripos.

After graduating he was made a partner in the family firm, J.& W. Campbell & Co in Glasgow, and in April 1868, at the age of thirty-one, he stood as a Liberal candidate in a by-election for the Stirling Burghs constituency where he narrowly lost to fellow Liberal John Ramsay. However, at the General Election in November of 1868, Campbell-Bannerman turned the table defeating Ramsay and was elected to the House of Commons as the Liberal Member of Parliament for Stirling Burghs. Stirling Burghs was the constituency that he would go on to represent for almost forty years. In 1871, Henry Campbell became Henry Campbell-Bannerman, the addition of the surname Bannerman being a requirement of the will of his uncle, Henry Bannerman. Not liking the long name he invited friends to refer to him as C.B.

Campbell-Bannerman was appointed as Financial Secretary to the War Office in Gladstone's first government in November 1871, a position he held until 1874 when he became the Liberal government's chief spokesman on defence matters in the House of Commons. After serving as Parliamentary and Financial Secretary to the Admiralty between 1882 and 1884, Campbell-Bannerman was promoted to the Cabinet as Chief Secretary for Ireland in 1884.

In Gladstone's third and fourth governments, in 1886 and 1892 to 1894 and also in Archibald Primrose's government from 1894 to 1895, he served as Secretary of State for War. On June 21, 1895, Campbell-Bannerman induced the Duke of Cambridge, a cousin of Queen Victoria, to retire as commander in chief of the armed forces. During his 39-year tenure the Duke had blocked army reform, and the Queen, recognising the necessity of the change, rewarded Campbell-Bannerman with a knighthood. At the same time, however, a Commons vote, was taken (with few Liberals present), on a Conservative motion to reduce Campbell-Bannerman's salary, which unwittingly resulted in a defeat for the government and the resignation of the Archibald Primrose's ministry. The vote is the last time in the History of the British Parliament that a government has been defeated on a confidence motion when it had a workable majority.

On 6 February 1899 Campbell-Bannerman succeeded Sir William Vernon Harcourt as Leader of the Liberals in the House of Commons and as Leader of the Opposition. The Boer War of 1899 split the Liberal Party into Imperialist and Pro-Boer camps. Campbell-Bannerman faced the difficult task of holding together a strongly divided party, which was subsequently and unsurprisingly defeated in the "khaki election" of 1900. Campbell-Bannerman caused particular friction within his own party when in a speech to the National Reform Union in June 1901, he described the concentration camps set up by the British in the Boer War as "methods of barbarism". This also caused a public uproar when he refused to take back his remarks about Kitchener's methods being used to win the war. By the end of the war, party tensions eased, as did Campbell-Bannerman's "step by step" approach to the divisive issue of Irish Home Rule.

Following Arthur James Balfour's resignation in 1905, Edward VII invited Sir Henry Campbell-Bannerman, as leader of the next largest party, to form a government. Campbell-Bannerman accepted the King's offer and his new cabinet included two future Prime Ministers, Herbert Henry Asquith who had been a Liberal imperialist, and David Lloyd George, who had been "pro-Boer". Also included in the cabinet was the first person from the working class to to attain cabinet rank in Great Britain, John Elliot Burns.

In 1905 the title "Prime Minister" was noted in a royal warrant that placed the Prime Minister, mentioned as such, in the order of precedence in Britain immediately after the Archbishop of York.

The General Election of January 1906 produced a large Liberal majority in the Commons, but much of the Campbell-Bannerman legislative program was nullified by the House of Lords.

The government of Campbell-Bannerman allowed local authorities to provide free school meals (though this was not compulsory) and strengthened the power of the trade unions with their Trade Disputes Act 1906 which gave labour unions considerable freedom to strike. The Workmen's Compensation Act 1906 gave some workers the right against their employer to a certain amount of compensation if they suffered an accident at work. The Probation of Offenders Act 1907 was passed, which established supervision within the community for young offenders as an alternative to prison and laid the foundation of the modern Probation Service. Campbeli-Bannerman's government also granted the Boer states, the Transvaal and the Orange River Colony, self-government within the British Empire through an Order in Council so as to bypass the House of Lords. This led to the Union of South Africa in 1910, giving South African its first Prime Minister, General Louis Botha.

Not long after Campbell-Bannerman became Father of the House in 1907, his health took a turn for the worse. Following a series of heart attacks, the most serious in November 1907, he began to fear that he would not be able to survive to the end of his term. He eventually resigned as Prime Minister on 3 April 1908. Campbell-Bannerman remained both a Member of Parliament and Leader of the Liberal Party, and continued to live at 10 Downing Street immediately after his resignation, as he intending to make other arrangements in due course. However, his health began to decline at an even quicker pace than before, and he died on 22 April 1908 aged 71, nineteen days after his resignation.Campbell-Bannerman was buried in the churchyard of Meigle Parish Church, Perthshire, near Belmont Castle, his home since 1887.

Interesting Henry Campbell-Bannerman facts:

There is a blue plaque outside Campbell-Bannerman's house at 6 Grosvenor Place in London, unveiled in 2008.

Campbell-Bannerman spoke French, German and Italian fluently.

A bronze bust of Campbell-Bannerman, which was sculpted by Paul Raphael Montford, is housed in Westminster Abbey.

Campbell Bannerman's brother was a Conservative MP from 1888 to 1906 and was opposed to the policies of his Liberal Prime Minister brother.

Herbert Henry Asquith
35th British Prime Minister

Born
12 September 1852, Morley, City of Leeds, West Yorkshire
Died
15 February 1928, age 75, The Wharf, Sutton Courtenay, Oxfordshire
Period in office as Prime Minister
8 years 243 days from 8 April 1908 until 5 December 1916
Political party
Liberal
Constituencies Represented as MP
East Fife 1886-1918
Paisley 1920-1924
Ministerial offices held as Prime Minister
First Lord of the Treasury
Leader of the House of Commons
Sec. State of War (1914)

Herbert Henry Asquith, 1st Earl of Oxford and Asquith, (12 September 1852 – 15 February 1928), generally known as H. H. Asquith, was a British statesman and Liberal politician who introduced significant domestic reform and took Britain into World War One. He was the last Prime Minister to lead a majority Liberal government.

Asquith was born in Morley, in the West Riding of Yorkshire, the younger son of Joseph Dixon Asquith (1825–1860) and his wife Emily, née Willans (1828–1888), in his younger days he was called Herbert ("Bertie" as a child). After the death of his father, a wool merchant, in 1860, Asquith and his family moved to Huddersfield, where Herbert and his brother, went to day school, later they attended a Moravian boarding school in Fulneck near Leeds. In 1863 at the age of 11 Herbert was sent to London with his brother to live with relatives and to attend the City of London School. In 1870, Asquith won a scholarship to attend Balliol College, part of the University of Oxford, where he studied the classics, he was elected a fellow of Balliol and served as President of the Oxford Union. While still at Oxford Asquith had already entered Lincoln's Inn to train as a barrister and was admitted to the bar in 1876.

Between 1876 and 1884 Asquith supplemented his income by writing regularly for *The Spectator*, which at that time had a broadly Liberal outlook. Also with his law firm flourishing, Asquith began to pursue his political ambitions and in the General Election of June 1886 he became the Liberal member for East Fife the constituency he represented for the next 32 years.

In September 1891 Asquith wife of 14 years died of typhoid fever following a few days' illness while the family were on holiday in Scotland, Asquith was left widowed with five young children (he remarried three years later). When William Gladstone and the Liberals returned to power in 1892, Asquith, was given

Cabinet office as Home Secretary. In a government sharply divided over fundamental issues. Asquith himself was a strong believer in free trade, Home Rule for Ireland, and social reform, which were all vital issues of the day. Asquith remained at the Home Office until the government fell to the Conservatives in 1895, and with no government post, Asquith divided his time between politics and the bar.

After the Liberal landslide at the General Election of 1906 Asquith was appointed Chancellor of the Exchequer, a post he held for over two years, producing three budgets. Although the first budget was restrained by what he had inherited, Asquith was able, in his second and third budgets, to lay the foundations for limited redistribution of wealth and welfare provisions for the poor. Through taxation, he used the increased revenues to fund old-age pensions, which was the first time a British government had provided them.

In June 1906 three suffragettes, Annie Kenney, Adelaide Knight, and Mrs Sparborough were arrested when they tried to obtain an audience with the then Chancellor Asquith who refused a delegation. Asquith at that point was a known advocate of denying woman the vote (in later years he came around to support woman's suffrage). When offered the choice of six weeks in prison or giving up campaigning for one year, the suffragettes chose prison.

When Campbell-Bannerman became seriously ill and resigned from office in April 1908, Asquith was appointed by King Edward VII as the new Prime Minister.

In his first cabinet reshuffle David Lloyd George was promoted to be Asquith's replacement as Chancellor and Winston Churchill succeeded Lloyd George as President of the Board of Trade, entering the Cabinet despite being only 33 and the fact that he had crossed the floor to become a Liberal only four years previously.

Asquith had decided to take on the House of Lords, which often blocked reforming Liberal bills, preventing them becoming law.

The Lords had unwisely rejected Chancellor Lloyd George's
'People's budget' of 1909 leading to a General Election in
December 1910. The 1910 election was billed as a referendum on
a Lords v Commons issue. Asquith had no overall majority after
the election, but it gave him the public support he needed.
He introduced the Parliament Bill which became law in 1911, and
the Lords were forced into passing it by the threat that hundreds
of new Liberal peers would be created if they did not.
The Parliament Act of 1911 drastically changed the way the
British government operated. The act prevented the Lords
from vetoing any financial legislation, and also reduced the
duration of any Parliament term from seven years to five
years. In addition, the act provided that MP's were to be
paid to enable 'ordinary' people who were not in possession
of an independent income to enter politics. The 1911 act
ultimately reduced the power that the House of Lords
wielded in Britain.
Although it was successful in implementing significant reforms,
Asquith's government faced additional challenges in the years
between 1911 and 1914. Most pressing was the growing crisis in
Ireland. In 1912Asquith renewed attempts to introduce home rule
in Ireland, but Unionists, comprised largely of Conservatives and
the military, wanted Ireland to remain as part of the British
Union. The situation deteriorated to such an extent that in 1914 it
appeared civil war would result. Asquith was successful in getting
the Home Rule Law passed, but it was delayed by the outbreak of
World War I, postponed further and never enacted. The
assassination of Archduke Franz Ferdinand of Austria (and his
wife) in Sarajevo on 28 June 1914 initiated a month of
unsuccessful diplomatic attempts to avoid war. The First World
War broke out in July 1914 but a dearth of munitions in 1915
resulted in Asquith having to form a new coalition government
(elections were suspended for the duration of the war). The
pressure continued on Asquith with the ongoing stalemate on the
western front. In 1916 the Easter Rising in Dublin and the Battle

of the Somme with its massive casualties led to Asquith being blamed in the press for the military failures. The long-awaited introduction of conscription was insufficient to quell dissent and In December he resigned on 5 December 1916 and was replaced by David Lloyd George. After resigning, Asquith continued in his post as Liberal leader even after losing his seat in the 1918 elections in East Fife to the Unionist's by 8,996 to 6,996 votes. He eventually regained a seat by standing in, and winning a by-election in Paisley in 1920. In 1925 Asquith was granted the title of Earl of Oxford and elevated to the House of Lords, and in 1926 finally resigned as Liberal leader.

Asquith died, aged 75, after having two strokes in two years, at The Wharf on the morning of 15 February 1928.

Interesting H.H Asquith facts:

The actress Helena Bonham-Carter is Asquith's great-granddaughter.

Asquith's eldest son Raymond, was killed at the Somme in 1916.

Asquith is the only Prime Minister to have taken office on foreign soil. King Edward VII was in Biarritz so Asquith travelled there for the official 'kissing hands' with the monarch.

Asquith had five children by his first wife, Helen, and two surviving children (three others died at birth or in infancy) by his second wife, Margot.

In the last years of his life he wrote a number of novels, the best known being *The Genesis of the War* (1923), *Fifty Years of Parliament* (1926), and *Memories and Reflections* (1928).

David Lloyd George
36th British Prime Minister

Born
17 January 1863, Chorlton-on-Medlock, Manchester

Died
26 March 1945, age 82, Ty Newydd, Llanystumdwy, Caernarvonshire

Period in office as Prime Minister
5 years 318 days from 6 December 1916 until 19 October 1922

Political party
Liberal

Constituency Represented as MP
Caernarvon Boroughs 1890-1945

Ministerial offices held as Prime Minister
First Lord of the Treasury

David Lloyd George, 1st Earl Lloyd-George of Dwyfor, (17 January 1863 – 26 March 1945) was a Welsh statesman who served as Prime Minister of the United Kingdom from 1916 to 1922. He was the last Liberal to hold the post of Prime Minister and the first and only Welshman up to date to hold the office of Prime Minister.

Lloyd George was born on 17 January 1863 in Chorlton-on-Medlock, Manchester, to Welsh parents and was brought up as a Welsh-speaker. His father, William George, had been a teacher in both London and Liverpool. On his father's death in Pembrokeshire in 1864 his mother moved with her children to Llanystumdwy, to live with her brother, Richard Lloyd (1834 - 1917). Lloyd George was educated at the Llanystumdwy National School and passed the Preliminary Law Examination in 1877, taking his final with honours in 1884. In 1885 he began to practice as a solicitor in Cricieth and gained a reputation as a fearless advocate and eloquent speaker.

In April 1890 he was elected Liberal MP at a by-election for Caernarvon, aged 27. It was a seat he was to retain for 55 years. As backbench members of the House of Commons were not paid at that time, he supported himself and his growing family by continuing to practise as a solicitor. During the 10 years of Liberal opposition that followed the election of 1895, he became a leading figure in the radical wing of the party. He bitterly and courageously opposed the Boer war (1899-1902) and while attempting to address a Liberal meeting in Birmingham in December 1901, his life was threatened by an angry mob. In 1905 Lloyd George entered the new Liberal Cabinet of Sir Henry Campbell-Bannerman as President of the Board of Trade. Their first priority on taking office was repeal of the 1902 Education Act. Lloyd George took the lead, and the bill was introduced in the Commons on 9 April 1906, the bill passed the House of Commons greatly amended, but was completely mangled by the House of Lords, for the rest of the year, Lloyd George made numerous public speeches attacking the House of Lords for mutilating the bill with wrecking amendments, but was rebuked by King Edward VII for these speeches.

In 1908 Lloyd George succeeded H.H Asquith as Chancellor of the Exchequer. His first task was the 1908 budget, which had been prepared by Asquith and which introduced old-age pensions through the House of Commons. By 1909, when his own first budget was due, the Liberal government was in trouble. Much of its reforming legislation had been blocked by the House of Lords and Lloyd George feared that the fledgling Labour Party might steal its thunder. At the same time, the need for more battleships to counter the looming threat from Germany made it harder to find the money for further reforms. The new chancellor's response was what became known as the 'People's Budget', it was supported in Cabinet by both Asquith and Winston Churchill and was introduced with a four hour speech in the House of Commons by Lloyd George on April 29th 1909. Income tax and death duties were both raised and a new supertax at sixpence in the pound levied on the amount by which incomes above £5,000 a year (equivalent to more than £350,000 today). The most controversial proposals, however, were for a capital gains tax on the 'unearned increment' in the value of land created not by the landowner but by the community at large and duty on the capital value of undeveloped land. The budget raised fierce opposition from rich landowners, in the City and in the House of Lords. The budget finally passed the Commons on November 3rd and went to the Lords. It was decisively voted down on November 30th by 350 votes to 75. The inevitable result was a General Election in January 1910. The Liberals remained in power, but only with the support of Labour and the budget passed the Commons again and this time was accepted by the upper house. The key consequence, however, was the Parliament Act of 1911, which severely reduced the powers of the House of Lords.

His next major reform was the 1911 National Insurance Act. This provided British workers with insurance against illness and unemployment. All wage-earners had to join his health scheme in which each worker made a weekly contribution, with both the employer and state adding an amount. In return for these payments, free medical attention and medicines were made available, as well as a guaranteed 7-shillings per week unemployment benefit.

Towards the end of July 1914, it became clear that the country was on the verge of war with Germany. Despite his initial reluctance to sanction Britain's entry into the First World War, Lloyd George served in Asquith's coalition war cabinet as Minister for Munitions and as Secretary for War. Unhappy with Asquith's conduct of the war and with ambitions of his own, he conspired with the Conservatives to oust Asquith, succeeding him as Prime Minister on 7 December 1916. This episode caused a split in the party from which it never entirely recovered. Asquith and several other prominent Liberals resigned from the government.

Throughout the war, although Lloyd George argued constantly with military leaders of how to conduct the battles, his leadership was a huge reason the war was won. One of Lloyd George's great contributions to the war was formulating the need for convoys that travelled the ocean as a possible antidote to the U-boat attacks. In late April 1917 the War Cabinet discussed the 'convoy controversy' and although not a popular avenue with certain members of the Admiralty, his idea became the standard for shipping. Just weeks before the end of the conflict, on 11 September 1918, the Lloyd George was cheered by crowds that lined the streets to greet his arrival in Manchester. But within hours, he was confined to bed having collapsed with a fever. (The 'Spanish Flu' pandemic of 1918-1920)

Lloyd George spent the next 10 days immobile, with a respirator to aid his breathing. His plight was hushed up for fear that the news would sap public morale and hand the German enemy a propaganda coup.

The war finally ended when Germany was forced to seek an armistice (truce) on November 11, 1918.

Lloyd George as Prime Minister was acclaimed as the man who had won the war, and in the December 1918 General Election the coalition won a huge majority. It was also the first election in which women were allowed to vote.

In 1918 the Representation of the People Act was passed which allowed women over the age of 30 who met a property qualification to vote. Although 8.5 million women met this criteria, it was only about two-thirds of the total population of women in the UK. The same Act abolished property and other restrictions for men, and extended the vote to virtually all men over the age of 21. Additionally, men in the armed forces could vote from the age of 19. The electorate increased from eight to 21 million, but although it was a start there was still huge inequality between women and men.

The 1918 Education Act was drawn up by Lloyd George's President of the Board of Education, Herbert Fisher. This raised the school leaving age to fourteen and included the provision of ancillary services (medical inspection, nursery schools, special needs provision, etc.)

In 1919 Lloyd George signed the Treaty of Versailles, which established the League of Nations and the war reparations settlement.

At home though, Lloyd George was troubled by domestic problems. In December 1921 his agreement to the independence of the South of Ireland (Irish Treaty) was reluctant after prolonged negotiations, and he presided over a period of depression, unemployment, strikes and serious allegations that he had sold honours. As a result his popularity faded.

After a famous meeting at the Carlton Club, The Conservative Party sealed Lloyd George's fate on 19 October 1922 by voting in favour of the motion to end the coalition and fight the election 'as an independent party with its own leader and its own programme'. Lloyd George submitted his resignation to the King that afternoon. Although he remained politically active for some years, he never again held office. In 1926 he set in train the Liberal Industrial Enquiry. From 1933 to 1936 he wrote his *War Memoirs* and '*The truth about the peace treaties*' was published in 1938. In August 1936, he visited Germany and met Hitler stating "Chancellor Adolf Hitler is one of the greatest of the many great men I have ever met". When war came in 1939 he took no part in its direction but remained a member of the House of Commons until January 1945, when he resigned his seat and was granted an earldom, taking as his titles Earl Lloyd-George of Dwyfor and Viscount Gwynedd. He died aged 82 on 26 March 1945. He was buried according to his own wishes in the wooded slope above the river Dwyfor near his home.

Interesting David Lloyd George facts:

He is the only Prime Minister to speak Welsh as his first language.

Although Wales has been part of the United Kingdom since the Middle Ages, Lloyd George is the only Welshman (to date) to be the country's Prime Minister.

He was the last Liberal leader to hold the post of Prime Minister.

Andrew Bonar Law
37th British Prime Minister

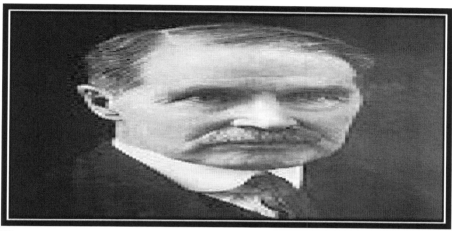

Born
16 September 1858, Rexton, New Brunswick, Canada
Died
30 October 1923, age 65, London
Period in office as Prime Minister
209 days from 23 October 1922 until 20 May 1923
Political party
Conservative
Constituencies Represented as MP
Glasgow Blackfriars 1900-1906
Dulwich 1906-1910
Bootle 1911-1918
Glasgow Central 1918-1923
Ministerial offices held as Prime Minister
First Lord of the Treasury
Leader of the House of Commons

Andrew Bonar Law 16 September 1858 – 30 October 1923)
was a British Conservative politician who served as Prime Minister
of the United Kingdom from 1922 to 1923.

*Andrew Bonar Law (he disliked the name Andrew and never used
it) so his family and close friends called him Bonar (rhyming with
honour) was born in Rexton, on the east coast of Canada. The son
of the Rev. James Law (1822 - 1882), who was pastor of St.
Andrew's Presbyterian Church for 32 years from 1845 to 1877.
James Law had five children, four boys and a girl. Only one of the
family, Robert, remained in Rexton until his death. Bonar Law's
first three years of public schooling were spent in Rexton, but
after the death of his mother, an aunt took him to Scotland to live
with her where he completed high school in Glasgow. It was only
formal education he ever received as he finished school aged
sixteen. His first job was that of a bookkeeper for an iron firm and
when he retired in business to enter politics, he was head of the
largest iron company in Scotland.*

At the 'Khaki' General Election of 1900 (named khaki due to it
being heavily influenced by post- Boar war sentiment) Bonar Law
was elected to the House of Commons as a Conservative
for Glasgow Blackfriars and Hutchesontown. On 11 August 1902
with Bonar Law's proven experience in business matters and his
skill as an economic spokesman for the government, Arthur
Balfour offered him the position of Parliamentary Secretary to the
Board of Trade which he accepted.
Bonar Law married Annie Pitcairn Robley on 24 March 1891 and
they had six children, four boys and two girls. Sadly Annie died
on 31 October 1909, and although devastated he continued his
political career, deciding to work even harder as a strategy to
cope with his loneliness. He stood for, and won the Conservative
party leadership in 1911. The Conservative party had bitter
divisions over tariffs at this time and as a result Bonar Law
encouraged his own extremists to pursue their attack on Irish

Home Rule in the belief that this was a calculated way to restore party unity. The outbreak of First World War in August 1914 resolved the Irish dilemma but it created a new one. Bonar Law found himself under pressure both to maintain the party truce and to follow his backbenchers and the press in attacking the Liberals' conduct of the war and in May 1915 he made a private agreement with H.H Asquith to join a coalition. In December 1916 in collaboration with David Lloyd George, they presented Asquith with proposals for the reorganisation of the machinery of war which led to Asquith's resignation. Bonar Law then served under Lloyd George as Chancellor and member of the war cabinet enabling a smooth period of joint co-operation. Bonar Law, as Chancellor, had to find the funds to pay for the war, and 1917 he raised the enormous sum of £600 million via a War Loan campaign, overruling his officials, and the governor of the Bank of England by setting interest rates at 5 rather than 6 per cent, thus securing a significant saving to the nation. He borrowed huge sums, but in total he found 26 per cent of wartime expenditure from taxation, and he astutely managed war-loan and war-bond programs. When the war ended on 11 November 1918 Bonar Law judged that the Conservatives' best interests lay in keeping the coalition and fighting the election under Lloyd George's leadership. At the 'Coupon Election' on December 14, 1918, the 'Coupon Election' was so-called as candidates for the Liberal Party who had supported the coalition government of Lloyd George during World War One were issued with a letter of support signed by both Lloyd George and Bonar Law. Asquith, the official leader of the Liberals, referred to the letter as a 'Coupon'. Where a 'Coupon' Liberal stood for election, no Conservative challenged him. Where a Conservative stood, no 'Coupon' Liberal challenged him. Therefore there was no chance of coalition candidate competing against another. The coalition was re-elected by a landslide, and the 1918 General Election was also the first election when everyone in the UK voted on the same day (14 December 1918). However, the count did not begin until

December 28. 10,786,818 people voted which was over double the voters of December 1910, when 5,235,238 voted. Lloyd George and Bonar Law formed an unlikely, but highly successful partnership but Bonar Law's resignation from the government, (but not from the Commons) on 17 March 1921, due to dangerously high blood pressure, signalled the beginning of the end of the coalition government. Bonar Law's health improved after six months in the south of France, and on his return he became critical of the policies of the government. At the Carlton Club on 19 October 1922 Bonar Law along with Stanley Baldwin was instrumental in the Tories voting by 187 against 88 to fight the next election on their own. The Conservative withdrawal from the coalition forced Lloyd George to resign. The King then invited Bonar Law to form a new administration on 23 October 1922. For the first time since 1910 a single party with a parliamentary majority governed Britain, the wartime coalition government had ended and so on the 15 November 1922 a General Election was held. Bonar Law's Conservative Party won 344 seats and formed the next government. The Labour Party who had promised to nationalise the mines and railways, along with a massive house building programme while revising the peace treaties, saw them rise from 57 to 142 seats. The Liberal Party increased their vote and went from 36 to 62 seats. Sadly, Bonar Law had just ten short months (209 days) as Prime Minister before throat cancer forced his retirement in May 1923.
Bonar Law died six months later on 30 October 1923 aged 65.

Interesting Andrew Bonar Law facts:

In the 1981 TV series *The Life and Times of David Lloyd George* Bonar Law appears in two episodes and is played by Fulton Mackay.

Bonar Law was the shortest-serving Prime Minister of the 20th century.

Stanley Baldwin (1st Earl Baldwin of Bewdley) 38th British Prime Minister

Born
3 August 1867, Bewdley, Worcestershire
Died
14 December 1947, age 80, Stourport-on-Severn, Worcestershire
Periods in office as Prime Minister
7 years 85 days (3 terms) from 22 May 1923 – 22 January 1924
(246 days) 4 November 1924 – 4 June 1929 (4 years 213 days) 7
June 1935 – 28 May 1937 (1 year 356 days)
Political party
Conservative
Constituency Represented as MP
Bewdley 1908-1937
Ministerial offices held as Prime Minister
Chancellor of the Exchequer (1923)
First Lord of the Treasury
Leader of the House of Commons

Stanley Baldwin, 1st Earl Baldwin of Bewdley, (3 August 1867 – 14 December 1947) was a British Conservative statesman who dominated the government of the United Kingdom between the world wars serving as Prime Minister on three occasions (between 1923 to 1937).

Baldwin was the only son of Alfred Baldwin, chairman of the Great Western Railway and head of a large concern that included iron and steel manufactories and collieries. Born in 1867 at Lower Park House (Lower Park, Bewdley) in Worcestershire, Baldwin went to St Michael's School, at the time located in Slough, Berkshire, followed by Harrow School, he then went on to the University of Cambridge, where he studied history at Trinity College. Baldwin studies deteriorated by year, he got a First at the end of his first year, a Second at the end of his second, and a Third at the end of his third, and so graduating from Cambridge University with a third class degree.

After leaving Cambridge Baldwin worked for his father's business, and in 1898 he oversaw the company's flotation on the Stock Market. In 1902 he saw the rationalisation of the various parts of the business amalgamated into Baldwins Ltd, together with other steelworks and collieries in south Wales. In 1904 Baldwin was selected for the Conservative safe seat of Kidderminster. However, in the 1906 General Election, the Liberal Party achieved a landslide victory and Baldwin lost out to Edmund Broughton Barnard by 2,354 votes to 2,083. In 1908 Baldwin's father died and he inherited nearly £200,000 (over £20 million in today's money) and was also offered his father's parliamentary seat of Bewdley. After an unopposed return in the by-election he was introduced into the House of Commons on 3rd March 1908. On the outbreak of the First World War he was forty-seven, and too old for military service but he encouraged his own workers to join the armed forces by paying out of his own pocket, the Friendly Society subscriptions. Bonar Law, appointed Baldwin as his parliamentary private secretary, and by late 1916 he gave his support to David Lloyd George in his plot to overthrow H. H. Asquith, the Prime Minister. He became Secretary of the Treasury in 1917 in David Lloyd George's wartime coalition government and in 1921 he entered the Cabinet as President of the Board of Trade. In October 1922 he made the key speech at the Carlton Club meeting of Conservative backbenchers that brought about Lloyd George's resignation. In Bonar Law's following Conservative government Baldwin became Chancellor of the Exchequer and the following year in 1923, he became Prime Minister when ill health forced Andrew Bonar Law to retire. He called a General Election on 6 December 1923 to seek approval for the government's plans to introduce protective tariffs, but failed to gain a majority resulting in first Labour government under Ramsay MacDonald with the support of the Liberal's. Labour's first government was short-lived. By November 1924, the Conservatives were back in power with a landslide majority and Baldwin as Prime Minister. In the General Strike of 1926 that lasted nine days, from 4th to 12th May 1926, Baldwin proclaimed a state of emergency and refused to negotiate further until the strike was over. The following year he passed the Trade Disputes Act, which declared general strikes to be revolutionary and illegal. Baldwin wanted to change the image of the Conservative Party to make it appear a less right-wing organisation and so in March 1927, he suggested to his Cabinet that the government should propose legislation for the enfranchisement of nearly five million women between the ages of twenty-one and thirty. This measure meant that women would constitute almost 53% of the British electorate. There was little opposition in Parliament to the bill and it became law on 2nd July 1928 and as a result, all women over the age of 21 could now vote in elections. The Conservatives lost the General Election of May 1929 when Labour came back to power. Baldwin considered leaving politics, and spent much of the next two years fighting elements within his own party. With the Great Depression, the world financial crisis began to overwhelm Britain in 1931, Baldwin returned to government as Lord President of the Council in the National Coalition, although the Labour Party was virtually destroyed, leaving MacDonald as Prime Minister for a largely Conservative coalition. In February 1934, the Defence Requirements Committee (DRC), reported to Cabinet that upon Adolf Hitler's rise to power in Germany in 1933, Nazism first became recognized as an international threat and Germany was now Britain's 'ultimate potential enemy'. It was decided that Neville Chamberlain should be put in charge of the defence expenditure. In June 1935 Baldwin became Prime Minister for the third time when MacDonald resigned. Baldwin called for a General Election on 14th November, which resulted in a large, albeit reduced, majority for the National Government, with the greatest number of members being Conservatives. In December 1936 with King Edward VIII's proposed marriage to the twice-divorced Mrs Wallis Simpson, and consequent abdication, Baldwin took the lead in making it plain that if the King persisted he should give up the throne and his management of the abdication crisis was highly praised. Baldwin was aware that most opposition MPs had difficulty living on their pay of £200 a year. One of his final acts as Prime Minister was to double their pay and to introduce a salary for the Leader of the Opposition so that he would not need to indulge in what he felt was potentially corrupting work outside Parliament. Baldwin resigned from office on 28th May, 1937, following the successful coronation celebrations of George VI and was ennobled as Earl Baldwin of Bewdley. He died in his sleep at Astley Hall, near Stourport-on-Severn, Worcestershire, on 14 December 1947, aged 80.

Interesting Stanley Baldwin facts:

Baldwin was (through his Scottish mother) a first cousin of the writer and poet Rudyard Kipling.

In 1956, Baldwin's son A. W. Baldwin published a biography entitled *My Father: The True Story.*

James Ramsay MacDonald
39th British Prime Minister

Born
12 October 1866, Lossiemouth, Scotland
Died
9 November 1937, age 71, Aboard the liner Rinea Del Pacific whilst in the Atlantic Ocean
Periods in office as Prime Minister
6 years 291 days (2 terms) from 22 January 1924 – 4 November 1924 (288 days) 5 June 1929 – 7 June 1935 (6 years 3 days)
Political party
Labour
Constituencies Represented as MP
Leicester 1906-1918
Aberavon 1922-1929
Seaham 1929-1935
Combined Scottish Universities 1936-1937
Ministerial offices held as Prime Minister
First Lord of the Treasury
Leader of the House of Commons
Secretary of State for Foreign Affairs

James Ramsay MacDonald (12 October 1866 – 9 November 1937) was first Labour Party Prime Minister of the United Kingdom, in the Labour governments of 1924 and 1929–31 and in the national coalition government of 1931–35.

James Ramsay MacDonald (known as Ramsay MacDonald) was born on 12 October 1866 in Lossiemouth, Morayshire, the son of John MacDonald, a farm labourer, and Anne Ramsay, housemaid. MacDonald received an elementary education at the Free Church of Scotland school in Lossiemouth from 1872 to 1875, and then at Drainie parish school. In 1881 at the age of 15, he left school at the end of the summer term, and after a few months working on a nearby farm, MacDonald was appointed as a pupil teacher at Drainie. In 1885 at 18 MacDonald left Scotland to take up a position as an assistant to a Bristol clergyman where the activities of the Social Democratic Federation acquainted him with left-wing ideas.

In 1886 MacDonald moved to London and obtained a job as an invoice clerk in a city warehouse. He lived in cheap lodgings in Kentish Town and attended evening classes where he studied for a science scholarship in the Birkbeck Institute and the City of London College. Over time he did a variety of jobs, and became actively involved in the Socialist Union. On 6 March 1888 he set up the London General Committee of Scottish Home Rule Association. Meanwhile, he studied science at evening classes but collapsed from exhaustion just before the exams. Later in 1888 MacDonald became private secretary to Thomas Lough, a merchant and a radical politician. Lough became a Liberal MP in 1892, and MacDonald gained access to the world of Liberal politics in London. Later that year he became a journalist, and joined the Fabian Society. In May 1894 MacDonald joined Keir Hardie's newly formed Independent Labour Party, and was adopted as an ILP Parliamentary candidate for a seat in Southampton which he heavily lost in the 1895 General Election. He lost again in the 1900 General Election, and in that year became Secretary of the Labour Representation Committee, the forerunner of the Labour Party (the name was changed to 'The Labour Party' in February 1906). Here he led negotiations with Gladstone and the Liberal party that allowed Labour candidates a clear run at a number of seats in working class areas which led to a breakthrough for Labour in the 1906 General Election. At the 1906 General Election, MacDonald was one of 29 Labour MPs elected representing the Leicester Constituency. In 1911, MacDonald became Leader of the Labour Party, but resigned in 1914 when the party did not support his strongly anti-war stance, a stance that led to public accusations of treason and cowardice, and which in 1915 led the journal *John Bull* to mount a campaign for MacDonald's removal from Parliament on the grounds he was elected under a false name. It emerged that MacDonald was simply unaware that his birth had been registered under the surname Ramsay. MacDonald stood for Parliament in the 1921 Woolwich East by-election and lost, but he returned in 1922 and was elected MP for Aberavon in Wales with a 2,100 majority and was subsequently re-elected leader of the Labour Party. At this point the Labour Party had displaced the Liberals as the main opposition to the Conservative Government. After the December 1923 election the Conservatives found themselves without a majority in the House of Commons, and when they lost a vote of confidence in January 1924, King George V asked Ramsay MacDonald to form a government. With support from the Liberals, he did so, and therefore became the first Labour Prime Minister. He was also the first Prime Minister from a working class background, and one of very few without a university education. Besides himself, ten other members of his cabinet came from working class origins, a dramatic breakthrough in British history. Although his minority Government lasted only nine months it was still able to support the unemployed with the extension of benefits and amendments to the Insurance Acts, and the 1924 (Wheatley) Housing Act was passed, which greatly expanded municipal housing for low paid workers. MacDonald had achieved his main ambition of demonstrating that Labour could govern responsibly and effectively. In the first-ever Labour government, the survival of MacDonald's small Commons majority had depended on the good will of opposition parties. In August 1924, the government dropped the prosecution of the Communist newspaper editor J.R. Campbell under the Incitement to Mutiny Act (for calling on members of the armed forces to refuse certain orders), Conservative and Liberal Members of Parliament then combined to pass a motion of no confidence in the Labour government and a new General Election was called for 29 October 1924. Four days before the election, the Daily Mail published a letter allegedly to be from Grigory Zinoviev, head of the Communist International, which it argued revealed 'a great Bolshevik plot to paralyse the British Army and Navy and to plunge the country into civil war' and the Communist Party as 'masters of Mr. Ramsay MacDonald's Government'. The letter was later confirmed as a forgery but the Conservatives went on to decisively win the October 1924 election. During the next five years the inability of the Baldwin government to tackle unemployment helped Labour to further advance. At the General Election of May 1929, Labour emerged as the biggest party, but with the Liberals holding the balance of power. MacDonald, now representing the seat of Seaham in County Durham, became Prime Minister of a minority government. In 1930 his government passed a revised Old Age Pensions Act, a more generous Unemployment Insurance Act, and an act to improve wages and conditions in the coal industry, tackling the main cause of the General Strike. By August 1931 the balance of payments deficit obliged the cabinet to attempt to restore confidence by balancing its budget, but it split over proposed cuts in unemployment benefit. MacDonald astonished his colleagues by accepting the King's invitation to lead a National Government with the Liberals and Tories. Originally seen as a temporary expedient, the National Government rapidly assumed a permanent form by holding a General Election. The election was held on Tuesday 27

October 1931 and saw a landslide election victory for the National Government which had been formed two months previously after the collapse of the second Labour government. Collectively, the parties forming the National Government won 67% of the votes and 554 seats out of 615. The bulk of the National Government's support came from the Conservative Party, with the Conservatives winning 470 seats. MacDonald retained the premiership but he was aware of his fading powers, and in 1935 he agreed to a timetable with Baldwin to stand down as Prime Minister, after King George V's Silver Jubilee celebrations in May 1935. He resigned on 7 June in favour of Baldwin, and remained in the cabinet, taking the largely honorary post of Lord President vacated by Baldwin. At the 1935 election MacDonald standing as National Labour, was defeated at Seaham by Emanuel Shinwell (Labour) losing his 5,951 majority with a 23.8% swing (new majority 20,498). Shortly after though he was elected at a by-election in January 1936 for the Combined Scottish Universities seat. By 1936 his physical and mental health had started to deteriorate and after being advised by his doctor to take a sea voyage to aid his health, MacDonald took a holiday to South America aboard the liner *Reina del Pacifico* but died during the cruise on 9 November 1937, aged 71.

Interesting Ramsay MacDonald facts:

In his second minority government in 1929, MacDonald set an historic precedent by appointing Margaret Bondfield as the first female minister.

MacDonald's wife, Margaret was involved in social work in East London. She played an active part in the Women's Labour league. The couple had six children.

All members (including MacDonald) or associates of the National Government were expelled by the Labour party.

Neville Chamberlain
40th British Prime Minister

Born
18 March 1869, Birmingham
Died
9 November 1940, age 71, Heckfield, Hampshire
Period in office as Prime Minister
2 years 349 days from 28 May 1937 until 10 May 1940
Political party
Conservative
Constituencies Represented as MP
Birmingham Ladywood 1918-1929
Birmingham Edgbaston 1929-1940
Ministerial offices held as Prime Minister
First Lord of the Treasury
Leader of the House of Commons

Arthur Neville Chamberlain 18 March 1869 – 9 November 1940) was the Conservative Prime Minister of the United Kingdom from May 28, 1937, to May 10, 1940, whose name is identified with the policy of 'appeasement' toward Adolf Hitler's Germany in the period immediately preceding World War II.

Arthur Neville Chamberlain was born into a political family at Southbourne House in the Edgbaston district of Birmingham, on 18 March 1869. His father, Joseph, was an influential politician of the late 19th century and Neville's older half-brother Austen held many Conservative cabinet positions in the early 20th century and won the Nobel Peace Prize. His mother was Florence Kenrick, cousin to William Kenrick MP, she died when he was only six. Chamberlain was educated at home by his elder sister Beatrice, and he and later he went to school at Rugby where he did well academically. Chamberlain left Rugby in 1886 and attended Mason College in Birmingham, where he studied science and engineering design.

Chamberlain was working in an accounting firm when, in 1890, his father announced that the family was going to start a business growing and processing sisal (a plant with strong fibres that can be used to make rope and other products) in the Bahamas. Neville and his brother Austen were put in charge of the operation and moved to the Bahamas establishing the Andros Fibre Company. Austen soon returned to England, while Neville became the company's managing director. Although the 20,000 acre plantation seemed promising at first, it eventually failed. Chamberlain returned to England, extremely disappointed but he had gained experience and a reputation for being a hands-on manager, taking a strong interest in the day-to-day running of affairs. On his return he became a leading manufacturer in Birmingham, where he was elected a councillor in 1911. Chamberlain was in his early forties when he met and fell in love with Anne Cole, and the two were married in January 1911. Their daughter Dorothy was born that December, and son Frank two years later. Chamberlain served as Lord Mayor of Birmingham for a year in 1915 and in 1916 David Lloyd George appointed him Director General of the Department of National Service. However, the pair had a fraught relationship and Chamberlain resigned within the year. In 1918 he was elected as the Conservative MP for Ladywood but refused to serve under Lloyd George in the coalition government. In 1922 he became Postmaster General and was made Minister of Health within months. In August 1923 he was appointed Chancellor of the Exchequer in the Stanley Baldwin government, a position he only held for five months due to the 1923 General Election defeat to Labour.

When the Labour government was defeated on a motion of no confidence a third General Election in less than two years was held in October 1924, Chamberlain narrowly defeated the Labour candidate, Oswald Mosley (who later led the British Union of Fascists), by less than 100 votes. Chamberlain served as Minister of Health once again, a position he held until June 1929. His Local Government Act of 1929 reformed the Poor Law, effectively laying the foundations of the welfare state, and he reorganised local government finance. Labour won the 1929 election, but after the 1931 election, Ramsay MacDonald made him Chancellor of the Exchequer in his national government and Stanley Baldwin retained him in turn. During the economic crisis, he achieved his father's protectionist ambitions by passing the Import Duties Bill in 1932. After the abdication of the King, Stanley Baldwin announced that he would remain until shortly after the coronation of King George VI and Queen Elizabeth. On 28 May, two weeks after the Coronation, Baldwin resigned, advising the King to send for Chamberlain. Unfortunately his brother, Austen did not live to see Neville become Prime Minister having died two months earlier. Some of Chamberlain's early efforts as Prime Minister focused on improving the lives of workers. The Factories Act of 1937 restricted the number of hours that children and women worked. The following year, Chamberlain supported the Holiday with Pay Act, which gave workers a week off with pay. However, his work on the domestic front was quickly overshadowed by growing foreign relations issues. Rather than challenge acts of aggression by Nazi Germany, Chamberlain sought ways to pacify Hitler. In an attempt to sway Fascist Italy away from German influence, he agreed on April 16, 1938 to recognize Italian supremacy in Ethiopia and kept Great Britain out of the Spanish Civil War (1936–39). On three occasions in September 1938, Chamberlain went to Germany in efforts to prevent the outbreak of a general European war over Hitler's demand that Czechoslovakia cede the Sudetenland to Germany. Hitler agreed to meet in Munich with Chamberlain, Benito Mussolini the Italian leader and French premier Edouard Daladier to discuss a diplomatic resolution to the crisis. The four leaders, without any input from Czechoslovakia in the negotiation, agreed to cede the Sudetenland to Hitler. Chamberlain also separately drafted a non-aggression pact between Britain and Germany that Hitler signed. On Chamberlain's return to London's Heston Aerodrome, a thankful crowd cheered wildly as the door to his airplane opened. As the rain fell, he stepped onto the airport tarmac, holding aloft the nonaggression pact that had been inked by him and Hitler only hours before. The Prime Minister read to the nation the brief agreement that reaffirmed '*the desire of our two peoples never to go to war with one another again*'. After a royal audience, Chamberlain returned to his official residence at No.10 Downing Street and from a second-floor window, Chamberlain addressed the crowd and invoked Prime Minister Benjamin Disraeli's famous statement upon returning home from the Berlin Congress of 1878, '*My good friends, this is the second time in our history that there has come back from Germany to Downing Street peace with honour. I believe it is peace for our time*'. Nonetheless, he immediately ordered the acceleration of the British rearmament program. Chamberlain seemed to have underestimated Hitler's ambitions as in March 1939, Hitler violated the Munich Pact by invading Czechoslovakia. Britain and France agreed to protect Poland later that month, but after Hitler's forces entered Poland that September, Chamberlain officially declared war on Germany. The declaration came shortly after the invasion, but his attempted appeasement of Hitler and the delay in making the announcement had negatively impacted on Chamberlain's popularity. Plans for limited conscription applying to single men aged between 20 and 22 were given parliamentary approval in the Military Training Act in May 1939, and on the day Britain declared war on Germany, 3 September 1939, Parliament immediately passed a more wide-reaching measure. The National Service (Armed Forces) Act imposed conscription on all males aged between 18 and 41 who had to register for service. Those medically unfit were exempted, as were others in key industries and jobs such as baking, farming, medicine, and engineering. Chamberlain remained Prime Minister during a period of sporadic military action and admitted into his war cabinet, Winston Churchill, as first Lord of the Admiralty. After the failure of a British expedition to Norway in April 1940, Chamberlain lost the support of many Conservatives in the House of Commons. He resigned on May 10 1940, the day of the German invasion of the Low Countries. In Churchill's coalition government he served loyally as Lord President of the Council until September 30, 1940, when ill health forced him to resign along with the Conservative Party leadership. Chamberlain died of bowel cancer on 9 November 1940 at the age of 71.

Interesting Neville Chamberlain fact:

Chamberlain's cousins, Wilfred Byng Kenrick and Sir Wilfrid Martineau, like Chamberlain, were Lord Mayors of Birmingham.

Sir Winston Churchill
41st British Prime Minister

Born
30 November 1874, Blenheim Palace, Oxfordshire
Died
24 January 1965, age 90, London
Periods in office as Prime Minister
8 years 240 days (2 terms) from 10 May 1940 - 26 July 1945 (5 years 78 days) and 26 October 1951 - 5 April 1955 (5 years 78 days)
Political party
Conservative
Constituencies Represented as MP
Oldham 1900-1906
Manchester North West 1906-1908
Dundee 1908-1922
Epping 1924-1945
Woodford 1945-1960
Ministerial offices held as Prime Minister
First Lord of the Treasury
Leader of the House of Commons (1940-42)
Minister of Defence

Sir Winston Leonard Spencer Churchill (30 November 1874 – 24 January 1965) was a British statesman, army officer, and writer. He was Prime Minister of the United Kingdom from 1940 to 1945, when he led the country to victory in the Second World War, and again from 1951 to 1955. Apart from two years between 1922 and 1924, Churchill was a Member of Parliament from 1900 to 1964 and represented a total of five constituencies. Ideologically an economic liberal and imperialist, he was for the largest part of his career a member of the Conservative Party, leading the party from 1940 to 1955. He was a member of the Liberal Party from 1904 to 1924.

From an early age, young Churchill displayed the traits of his father, Lord Randolph Churchill, a British statesman from an established English family, and his mother, Jeanette "Jennie" Jerome, an independent-minded New York socialite. Churchill grew up in Dublin, Ireland, where his father was employed by his grandfather, the 7th Duke of Marlborough, John Spencer-Churchill. At 13 he scraped into the lowest class at Harrow, and Randolph, believing that his son was academically unsuited for politics or law, had him placed in the army class. Churchill enrolled at Sandhurst as an officer cadet in September 1893, though it took him three attempts to pass the entrance exam. He took to Sandhurst well, but the death of his father aged 45 had a profound impact on him, convincing him of the need to make his mark early in life.

Churchill obtained his commission as a cavalry officer in the 4th (Queen's Own) Hussars in February 1895 and was also employed as a war reporter, spending his 21st birthday in Cuba, he acquired two lifelong habits – siestas and Havana cigars. The following year Churchill sailed with his regiment for India and in 1898 fought in Sudan. While in the Army, he wrote military reports for the *Pioneer Mail* and the *Daily Telegraph*, and two books on his experiences, *The Story of the Malakand Field*

Force (1898) and *The River War* (1899). On 6 July 1899 Churchill
stood for the Conservatives at the Oldham by-election but lost
narrowly to the Liberals. The Boer Republics declared war on
Britain on 11 October 1899, and Churchill travelled to South
Africa to cover the conflict as a war correspondent. On 15
November, he was on an armoured train in Natal when it was
ambushed. The legend has it that after a heroic defence in which
he helped most of the train to escape, Churchill was captured and
taken to a makeshift prison. Not to be held long, he soon took his
opportunity to escape and clambered over a prison wall into the
night, jumping on a passing train and hiding among sacks. The
Boer authorities issued a reward for his capture and Churchill was
alone and on the run in Africa. While on the run he ironically met
a mining engineer from Oldham called Dan Dewsnap who hid him
in a coal mine for three days. Churchill's escape made him a
national hero and, although he stayed in South Africa until the
following summer, the incident was enough to ensure his celebrity
status. Upon his return to Britain, he wrote about his experiences
in the book *London to Ladysmith via Pretoria* (1900). Churchill
again stood for the Conservative Party for Oldham in the October
General Election and this time he was successfully returned as
MP. A wing of the Conservative Party, had wanted to introduce
tariffs or taxes on imported foods and goods, while others like
Churchill defended the Victorian policy of Free Trade. This led to
the Oldham Conservative Party formally passing a motion of no-
confidence in Churchill. This was ratified by the Executive
Committee in January 1904 and Churchill ceased to be the official
Conservative candidate. Churchill still remained as MP for the
borough until the General Election of 1906 but on 31 May 1904
he completed his break with the Conservative Party, crossing the
floor of the House of Commons to take up a seat on the Liberal
opposition benches alongside Lloyd George. In the General
Election of 1906 Churchill stood as a Liberal candidate for North-
West Manchester where he swept to victory and became a junior
minister in the Liberal Government. He rose rapidly within the

Liberal government, and in 1908, he entered the Cabinet as President of the Board of Trade (aged 33, he was the youngest Cabinet member since 1866). He was obliged to submit to re-election after his appointment as the Ministers of the Crown Act required newly appointed Cabinet ministers to re-contest their seats. He lost the North-West Manchester seat by 429 votes but On 9 May 1908, the Liberals stood him in the by-election for Dundee where he won with a majority of 2,709. In February 1910, Churchill was promoted to Home Secretary, giving him control over the police and prison services, where he implemented a prison reform programme. In March 1911, Churchill introduced the second reading of the Coal Mines Bill in Parliament, which imposed stricter safety standards at coal mines. In October 1911, Asquith appointed Churchill as First Lord of the Admiralty, and he took up official residence at Admiralty House. Over the next two and a half years he focused on naval preparation, visiting naval stations and dockyards, seeking to improve morale and scrutinising German naval developments. Churchill oversaw the naval effort when World War I started in 1914. On 18 March 1915 Churchill planned to sail through the Dardanelles and force Germany's ally, Turkey, out of the war. An attack was launched and troops landed on Gallipoli on 25 April. It was a disaster, they were pinned down and losses were heavy. Churchill was held by many MPs, particularly Conservatives, to be personally responsible. In May 1915, Asquith agreed under parliamentary pressure to form an all-party coalition government, but the Conservatives' one condition of entry was that Churchill must be removed from the Admiralty. Churchill had to accept demotion and became Chancellor of the Duchy of Lancaster. On 25 November 1915, Churchill resigned from the government (although he remained an MP) and joined the Army, stating that he wanted to take an active part in the war and fight on the Western Front. When his battalion was amalgamated with another, rendering his command redundant, he returned to London and was able give his colleagues in the House of

Commons a soldier's view of the conflict. By the end of the First World War, Churchill was back into office but Gallipoli was still a stain on his reputation. In the following years Churchill had a number of positions including: Minister of Munitions 1917–1919, Secretary of State for War and Air 1919–1921 and Secretary of State for the Colonies 1921–1922. In October 1922, he underwent an operation for appendicitis, and while he was in hospital the Conservatives withdrew from Lloyd George's coalition government. This precipitated the November 1922 General Election in which Churchill lost his Dundee seat. He spent much of the next six months in France, where he devoted himself to painting and writing his memoirs. He wrote an autobiographical history of the war, *'The World Crisis'* and had the first volume published in April 1923 with the rest being published over the next ten years. At the 1923 General Election Churchill stood as the Liberal candidate at Leicester West, but lost to Labour by 4,398 votes. In a by-election On 19 March 1924 he stood as an independent candidate in the Westminster Abbey constituency, and stood under the label of 'Constitutionalist', he was narrowly defeated by 43 votes, it was his third election defeat in less than two years. His political affinities now lay increasingly to the right of his Liberal colleagues. When his chief detractor Andrew Bonar Law was replaced by Stanley Baldwin as Conservative leader, Churchill seized the opportunity and in the 1924 General Election he again stood as a 'Constitutionalist' independent candidate this time in Epping. This Conservative's didn't stand a candidate and gave him backing and he was elected with a majority of 9,763. He formally re-joined the Conservative Party and under Stanley Baldwin in November he 1924 was made Chancellor of the Exchequer. It was during this time that he made one of his worst political decisions (an opinion which he reflected on himself) when he brought about Britain's restoration to the Gold Standard. The Gold Standard was a widely used monetary system in the 19th and early part of the 20th century and the consequences of its return were many. Although initially welcomed by the Bank of

England it damaged Britain's exports and resulted in high
unemployment, deflation and the General Strike of 1926.
Churchill in total presented five budgets as Chancellor, among his
measures were reduction of the state pension age from 70 to 65,
immediate provision of widow's pensions, reduction of military
expenditure, income tax reductions and the imposition of taxes
on luxury items. In the 1929 General Election, Churchill retained
his Epping seat with a majority of 4,967, but the Conservatives
were defeated and Ramsay MacDonald formed his second Labour
government. For the next eleven years Churchill was mainly
writing and making speeches and was prone to 'dark moods' for
which he used the phrase 'Black Dog'. During the 1930's Churchill
wrote *Marlborough: His Life and Times* a biography about John
Churchill, 1st Duke of Marlborough, who was a lineal descendant
of Churchill's. The book comprises four volumes, the first of which
appeared in October 1933 (557 pages, 200,000 words) with
subsequent volumes in 1934, 1936 and 1938. On 3 September
1939, the day Britain declared war on Germany, Chamberlain
reappointed Churchill as First Lord of the Admiralty and he joined
Chamberlain's war cabinet. As First Lord, Churchill was one of the
highest-profile ministers during the so-called 'Phoney War', when
the only significant action by British forces was at sea. After
the Allies failed to prevent the German occupation of Norway, the
Commons held an open debate from 7 to 9 May 1940 on the
government's conduct of the war. This has come to be known as
the Norway Debate, and is renowned as one of the most
significant events in parliamentary history. In the early hours of
10 May, German forces invaded Belgium, Luxembourg and the
Netherlands as a prelude to their assault on France. After a
division vote which was in effect a vote of no confidence in
Chamberlain's government, Labour declared that they would not
serve under his leadership although they would accept another
Conservative. Chamberlain advised the King to send for Churchill,
who became Prime Minister of an all-party war-time coalition
government on 10 May 1940. At sixty-five Churchill belied his age

with evocative speeches that boosted morale and included the iconic phrase 'we shall fight on the beaches' when the Germans were over-running territory and forcing the evacuation from Dunkirk, Churchill showed that Britain was prepared to stand strong. In his 'finest hour' speech he told Parliament that he expected the Battle of Britain to occur very soon, refusing the armistice and uniting the British behind the resistance movement while strengthening unity and resolve across the British Empire. The 8th May 1945 was Victory in Europe Day (VE Day) when Churchill broadcast to the nation that Germany had surrendered and that a final ceasefire on all fronts in Europe would come into effect at one minute past midnight that night (i.e., on the 9th). In the evening, Churchill made another broadcast to the nation asserting that the defeat of Japan would follow in the coming months (the Japanese surrendered on 15 August 1945). Churchill resigned as Prime Minister on 23 May 1945 and later that day, he accepted the King's invitation to form a new government. The new government was known officially as the National Government, which stayed in place until the General Election in July 1945. Polling day was 5 July, but the results of the election did not become known until 26 July. Having lost the election, Churchill, despite enjoying much personal support amongst the British population, resigned as Prime Minister and was succeeded by Clement Attlee who formed the first majority Labour government. Churchill continued to lead the Conservative Party and for six years served as Leader of the Opposition, making his famous 'Iron Curtain' speech in America alongside American President Harry S. Truman, in which he warned against the expansionistic policies of the Soviet Union. In addition to the 'iron curtain' that had descended across Eastern Europe, Churchill's 'iron curtain' phrase immediately entered the official vocabulary of the Cold War. In February 1950, Labour won the General Election, but with a much-reduced majority. Twenty months later The Labour government called a snap election for Thursday 25 October 1951 in the hope of increasing their 5 seat parliamentary majority. Although Labour got the most votes (13,948,883 against 13,717,850) Churchill at the age of 76, was returned as Conservative Prime Minister once again with a 17 seat majority (26 above Labour). Churchill's second ministry was concerned with the mass construction of new housing, the end of food rationing in 1954, the Mining and Quarries Act 1954 and the housing repairs and rent act 1955. Churchill himself suffered a serious stroke on the evening of 23 June 1953, and became partially paralysed down one side. Although he recovered and carried on through 1954 his declining health forced him to retire as Prime Minister on 5 April 1955 and he was succeeded by Anthony Eden. In June 1962, when he was 87, Churchill had a fall in Monte Carlo and broke his hip. He was flown home to a London hospital where he remained for three weeks. Churchill suffered his final stroke on 12 January 1965 and he died nearly two weeks later on the 24th aged 90. He was given a state funeral six days later on 30 January 1965.

Interesting Winston Churchill facts:

Churchill was a prolific writer, writing forty-three books that filled seventy-two volumes, he was awarded the Nobel Prize in Literature in 1953 for his many published works.

Churchill was married to Clementine Hozier for 57 years, they married in September 1908 and had five children.

The Imperial War Museum in London houses the Churchill War Rooms, a historic underground complex that housed a British government command centre throughout the Second World War.

Numerous films have been made about Churchill including 'Darkest Hour' in 2017 in which Gary Oldman won an Academy Award for Best Actor playing Winston Churchill. Churchill himself had the luxury of having a fully-equipped cinema in his home at Chartwell and visited Charlie Chaplin in Hollywood 1929.

Clement Atlee
42nd British Prime Minister

Born
3 January 1883, Rushyford, London
Died
8 October 1967, age 84, London
Period in office as Prime Minister
6 years 93 days from 26 July 1945 until 26 October 1951
Political party
Labour
Constituencies Represented as MP
Limehouse 1922-1950
Walthamstow West 1950-1955
Ministerial offices held as Prime Minister
First Lord of the Treasury
Minister of Defence (1945-1946)

Clement Richard Attlee, 1st Earl Attlee, (3 January 1883 – 8 October 1967) was a British politician who served as Prime Minister of the United Kingdom from 1945 to 1951 and Leader of the Labour Party from 1935 to 1955. He was three times Leader of the Opposition (1935–1940, 1945, 1951–1955).

Clement Atlee was born in Putney and was the fourth son (he had three sisters) of Henry Attlee, a prosperous London solicitor and Ellen Watson. He was educated at Northaw Place, a boys' preparatory school in Hertfordshire, before moving onto Haileybury College and University College, Oxford. He graduated in 1904 as a Bachelor of Arts with second-class honours in modern history. Attlee then trained as a barrister at the Inner Temple and was called to the bar in March 1906. He worked for a time at his father's law firm Druces but he abandoned plans of a career in law which he found boring. On 13th March 1906, Attlee took a commission in the Territorial Army and became a second lieutenant. Around this time he began regular visits to the impoverished East End of London, where he volunteered at a charitable club for working-class boys in Stepney. The charity was supported by Haileybury College and his visits to the house influenced his whole political future. The harsh poverty he saw in East London undermined his faith in the existing order.
Attlee joined the Fabian Society in 1907 (a British socialist organisation) and in the autumn of that year, when the manager of Haileybury House resigned, Attlee took on the job. It was a residential position with an annual salary of £50. He joined the Independent Labour Party in 1908 and spent four evenings a week at Haileybury, one night at an ILP branch meeting and he refereed football matches on Saturday's. In 1909, he stood unsuccessfully at his first election as an Independent Labour Party candidate for Stepney Borough Council. Also in 1909 he became secretary at Toynbee Hall (a charitable institution) but after a year he left because the atmosphere there did not agree with his socialism. He later said the trustees of Toynbee regarded him as

a "bit of a bolshie". In 1911, Attlee did some lecturing at Ruskin College and after that he was employed by the UK Government as an 'official explainer', touring the country to explain the Chancellor of the Exchequer's (David Lloyd George's) National Insurance Act. In 1913 he was appointed a lecturer in the social service department at the London School of Economics (LSE). At the outbreak of the First World War Attlee applied to join the British Army but initially his application was turned down, as at the age of 31 he was seen as being too old; however, he was finally allowed to join in September, and was commissioned in the rank of Captain. His decision to fight caused a rift between him and his older brother Tom, who, as a conscientious objector was jailed for his beliefs in 1917. Attlee himself fought in the Gallipoli Campaign in Turkey and later served in the Mesopotamian Campaign in what is now Iraq, where, in April 1916, he was badly wounded, after being hit in the leg by shrapnel while storming an enemy trench during the Battle of Hanna. He was sent to India first, and then back to the UK to recover. In February 1917, he was promoted to the rank of Major. After fully recovering from his injuries, he was sent to France in June 1918 to serve on the Western Front for the final months of the war. After being discharged from the Army in January 1919, he returned to Stepney, and returned to his old job lecturing part-time at the London School of Economics. After the war, Attlee moved into politics, becoming Mayor of Stepney in 1919, during his time as Mayor, the council undertook action to tackle slum landlords who charged high rents but refused to spend money on keeping their property in habitable condition. The council served and enforced legal orders on homeowners to repair their property. It also appointed health visitors and sanitary inspectors, reducing the infant mortality rate, and took action to find work for returning unemployed ex-servicemen. In 1920, while mayor, he published his first book, *The Social Worker*, describing his time as a social worker and social work lecturer, which set out many of the principles that informed his political philosophy and that were to underpin the actions of his government in later years. In the November 1922 General Election, Attlee was elected Labour MP for Stepney Limehouse in the East End of London with a majority of 1,899 and formally resigned as a lecturer in January 1923. He was again returned as Labour MP in the December 1923 General Election with a larger majority of 6,185, and he served as Undersecretary of State for War in the first Labour government. The third General Election in two years saw the Labour Party defeated in October 1924 (Attlee's majority 6,021). Attlee spent six years in opposition until Labour came to power in a hung parliament at the May 1929 General Election. In May 1930, Labour MP Oswald Mosley left the party after its rejection of his proposals for solving the unemployment problem, and Attlee was given Mosley's post of Chancellor of the Duchy of Lancaster. In March 1931, he became Postmaster General, a post he held for five months until August, when the Labour government fell after failing to agree on how to tackle the financial crisis of the Great Depression. On Tuesday 27 October 1931 there was a landslide election victory for the National Government after which the leader Ramsay MacDonald offered Attlee a job in the National Government, but he turned down the offer and opted to stay loyal to the main Labour party. Attlee had become increasingly disillusioned with MacDonald, a man he had previously looked up to as a great leader, but who he now thought of as a betrayer of the rank-and-file. After George Lansbury resigned as Labour leader in October 1935 Attlee served as interim leader taking Labour through the November 1935 General Election, which saw the party stage a partial comeback from its disastrous 1931 performance. Labour won 38 per cent of the vote, the highest share Labour had won up to that point, and gaining over one hundred seats. After the election Attlee stood in a leadership election in which he won both ballots, formally being elected Leader of the Labour Party on 3 December 1935. In 1937, Attlee wrote a book entitled *The Labour Party in Perspective* that sold fairly well in which he set out some of his views. He argued that there was no point in Labour compromising on its socialist principles in the belief that this would achieve electoral success. Attlee remained as Leader of the Opposition when the Second World War broke out in September 1939, and after Neville Chamberlain resigned, Labour and the Conservatives entered a coalition government led by Winston Churchill on 10 May 1940. Only Attlee and Churchill remained in the War Cabinet from the formation of the Government of National Unity in May 1940 through to the election in May 1945. Attlee was initially the Lord Privy Seal, before becoming Britain's first ever Deputy Prime Minister in 1942, as well as becoming the Dominions Secretary and the Lord President of the Council.

In 1945, following the end of the War and the defeat of Nazi Germany, Churchill tendered his resignation as Prime Minister and called an immediate General Election. Attlee and the Labour Party campaigned on the theme of 'Let Us Face the Future', positioning themselves as the party best placed to rebuild Britain after the war. The 1945 General Election was held on 5 July 1945, and the results of the election were announced on 26 July. Labour won power by a huge landslide holding 393 seats in the House of Commons, with a working majority of 146, the first time in history that the Labour Party had won a majority in Parliament. The Attlee government proved itself to be a radical, reforming government. From 1945 to 1948, over 200 public Acts of Parliament were passed. The New Towns Act of 1946 set up development corporations to construct new towns. The National Insurance Act 1946, required people to pay a flat rate of national insurance and return, they (and the wives of male contributors) were eligible for a wide range of benefits, including pensions, sickness benefit, unemployment benefit, and funeral benefit. Various other pieces of legislation provided for child benefit and support for people with no other source of income, it became known as the 'cradle to grave' welfare state.

On the 5th July 1948 an historic moment occurred in British history, a culmination of a bold and pioneering plan to make healthcare no longer exclusive to those who could afford it but to make it accessible to everyone. The National Health Service was born. Attlee's Minister of Health, Aneurin Bevan, created three core principles: 1. that it meet the needs of everyone 2. that it be free at the point of delivery, and 3. that it be based on clinical need, not ability to pay. On foreign issues Attlee's government was a key architect of the North Atlantic Treaty Organization (NATO) of 1949 and in 1950 he readily accepted the need for Allied entry in the Korean War and for a new rearmament program. Additionally, Attlee oversaw the beginning of the dismantling of the British Empire, granting independence to India in 1947. Attlee's government also carried out their manifesto commitment for nationalisation of basic industries and public utilities. The Bank of England and civil aviation were nationalised in 1946 with coal mining, the railways, road haulage, canals and Cable and Wireless being nationalised in 1947. Electricity and gas followed in 1948. The February 1950 General Election gave Labour a massively reduced majority of five seats compared to the 146 majority of 1945. Although re-elected, the result was seen by Attlee as very disappointing, and was widely attributed to the effects of post-war austerity denting Labour's appeal to middle-class voters. Attlee's second term was much tamer than his first. Some major reforms were nevertheless passed, the steel industry was nationalised and about 20 per cent of the British economy had been taken into public ownership. With such a small majority and splits in the Labour Party, Attlee was finding it increasingly impossible to govern, he thought his only chance was to call a snap election in October 1951, in the hope of achieving a more workable majority and to regain authority. Labour narrowly lost to the Conservative Party, despite winning considerably more votes (achieving the largest Labour vote in electoral history). Attlee tendered his resignation as Prime Minister the following day after six years and three months in office. Attlee remained leader of the opposition endeavouring to preserve the unity of his party following the infighting between the left-wing (Bevanites) and the right-wing (Gaitskellites). Attlee, now aged 72, contested the May 1955 General Election but with the Conservatives winning a 60 seat majority he retired as Leader of the Labour Party on 7 December 1955, having led the party for twenty years. On 14 December Hugh Gaitskell was elected as his replacement. After retiring from the House of Commons Attlee was elevated to the peerage to take his seat in the House of Lords as Earl Attlee and Viscount Prestwood on 16 December 1955. Attlee died peacefully in his sleep of pneumonia, at the age of 84 at Westminster Hospital on 8 October 1967.

Interesting Clement Attlee facts:

In 1979 a statue of Clement Attlee was erected in the Houses of Parliament.

Clement Attlee published his memoirs, '*As it Happened*', in 1954.

On 30 November 1988, a bronze statue of Clement Attlee was unveiled by Harold Wilson outside Limehouse Library in Attlee's former constituency.

A blue plaque unveiled in 1979 commemorates Attlee at 17 Monkhams Avenue (where he had lived), in Woodford Green in the London borough of Redbridge.

In 2004, he was voted the most successful British Prime Minister of the 20th century by a poll of 139 academics organised by Ipsos MORI.

Attlee married Violet Millar on 10 January 1922 and they later had four children.

Sir Anthony Eden
43rd British Prime Minister

Born
12 June 1897, Rushyford, County Durham
Died
14 January 1977, age 79, Alvediston, Wiltshire
Period in office as Prime Minister
1 year 279 days from 6 April 1955 until 9 January 1957
Political party
Conservative
Constituency Represented as MP
Warwick and Leamington 1923-1957
Ministerial offices held as Prime Minister
First Lord of the Treasury

Robert Anthony Eden, 1st Earl of Avon (12 June 1897 – 14 January 1977), was a British Conservative politician who served in three different decades as Foreign Secretary and then as Prime Minister from 1955 to 1957.

Eden was born on 12 June 1897 at Windlestone Hall, County Durham, into a conservative family. He was the youngest son of Sir William Eden, 7th and 5th Baronet, a former colonel and local magistrate. Eden's mother, Sybil Frances Grey, was a member of the prominent Grey family of Northumberland. After private tuition at Windlestone, Eden was educated at two independent schools. One was Sandroyd School in Cobham from 1907 to 1910 (where he excelled in languages) before moving on to Eton College in January 1911, where he was proficient at cricket, rugby and rowing.

After leaving Eton, on 29 September 1915, Eden enlisted with the 21st battalion, the Yeoman rifles, of the King's Royal Rifle Corps. He saw active service for the first time at Ploegsteert Wood in May 1916. Shortly after arriving in France, Eden heard the devastating news that his youngest brother, Nicholas, who at the age of sixteen was a midshipman on HMS *Indefatigable*, and had been killed at the battle of Jutland. Eden himself experienced some of the most hostile fighting in the trenches of the Western Front, and in June 1917 he was awarded the Military Cross for his selfless rescue of his wounded Sergeant under fire at Ploegsteert. His last posting was in the British lines at La Fère on the River Oise in March 1918 at the time of the Ludendorff spring offensive. On 26 May 1918 he was promoted to Brigade Major in the 198th infantry brigade, and at the age of twenty he was the youngest Brigade Major in the British army.

After demobilisation with the rank of Captain on 13 June 1919, the day after his twenty-second birthday, Eden returned to Windlestone to contemplate his future career. In the autumn of

1919 he entered Christ Church, Oxford, to read oriental languages, specialising in Persian and Arabic and he obtained first-class honours in 1922. At the General Election of November 1922 Eden stood in the Conservative interest in the Labour stronghold of Spennymoor in his home county which he lost but gained valuable experience. Eden entered parliament the following year in the December 1923 General Election at Warwick and Leamington with a majority of 5,203, (a majority he got up to 29,323 in 1931), and he was to retain the seat in Leamington for the next thirty-four years. In the lead up to the General Election Eden married Beatrice Helen Beckett on 5 November 1923, and they had three sons, Simon (1924), Robert (1928) who survived for only fifteen minutes, and Nicholas (1930), named in memory of Eden's younger brother.

Eden's interests in politics was mainly in defence and foreign policy, and in July 1926 he was appointed parliamentary private secretary to Sir Austen Chamberlain, the then Foreign Secretary. At the 1929 General Election which the Conservatives lost, Eden received less than 50% of the vote at Warwick for the one and only time, but still had an increased majority of 6,609. In 1931 Eden was appointed under-secretary of state at the Foreign Office and he swiftly became established as a respected British presence on the international scene. On 31 December 1933 Eden was promoted to the post of Lord Privy Seal and had now become a roving ambassador for the Foreign Office. In the next fourteen months he was to become the first Western politician to meet Hitler, Mussolini, and Stalin. He described Mussolini, as a 'complete gangster with dreadful table manners', Stalin as having an intensely cruel face and Hitler as having an easy charm which he could switch on at will.

In the National Government reshuffle in June 1935 following Ramsay MacDonald's retirement, Eden entered the cabinet for the first time as minister for League of Nations affairs (without portfolio). On 22 December 1935 he became Foreign Secretary for the first time, becoming Foreign Secretary at a critical time in international relations. Mussolini was established in Abyssinia, Hitler was shortly to tighten his grip on the demilitarized Rhineland, and in the Far East the Japanese planned further advances through China and all three countries were potential enemies of Great Britain. Also on the agenda was the Spanish Civil War, which had broken out in July 1936 and was to continue until March 1939.

When Neville Chamberlain succeeded Stanley Baldwin as Prime Minister in May 1937, Eden initially welcomed the prospect of a more pro-active Downing Street involvement in foreign affairs, especially as Chamberlain shared his view that war with Germany could be avoided through rearmament and collective security backed by the League of Nations. But growing dissatisfaction and disagreements with Chamberlain led to his resignation as Foreign Secretary on 20 February 1938, as a public protest he stated that 'There are occasions when strong political convictions must override all other considerations'. Eden's resignation brought him international recognition and he visited America in December 1938, where he was treated more like visiting royalty and was received at the White House by U.S President Franklin D. Roosevelt. As war became ever more inevitable during 1939, Eden (at the age of forty-two) joined the London rangers, a motor battalion of the King's Royal Rifle Corps. On 3 September, when war was declared, Eden accepted office in the National Government as Dominions Secretary. In May 1940 Chamberlain fell from power and was replaced by Churchill as Prime Minister. Churchill's arrival in Downing Street proved to be the turning point of Eden's career. As the new war secretary, Eden moved closer to the executive decision-making process, although still not a member of the war cabinet. On 22 December, Eden joined Churchill's war cabinet after being made Foreign Secretary, and only Clement Attlee, served longer in the central councils of the war with Churchill. On 22 November 1942 Eden was made leader of the House of Commons, in addition to his duties in the war cabinet, on the defence committee, and in running the Foreign Office. In June 1945 Eden heard that his eldest son, Simon, a pilot officer with the RAF in Burma, was missing, presumed dead. Simon's death hit Eden hard and it was the last act of Eden's increasingly fragile marriage to Beatrice. Their separation had an air of inevitability about it, and the marriage was dissolved in 1950. Apart from brief interludes, Eden had been in office for the greater part of two decades. The enforced spell of opposition due to the Labour landslide at the 1945 General Election gave him a much needed chance to recharge his political and personal batteries.

When Attlee called a General Election for 25 October 1951, Eden made history during the campaign by appearing in the first televised election broadcast in Britain. The Conservatives won the election with a majority of seventeen seats and Eden became Foreign Secretary for the third time.

In August 1952 Eden he married Clarissa Anne Spencer-Churchill, the daughter of Major John Strange Spencer-Churchill, and the niece of the Prime Minister, Winston. In April 1953 he nearly lost his life after a failed operation to remove gallstones, when his bile duct was accidentally cut. A life-saving operation followed in Boston in May 1953 and he spent the rest of the summer recuperating. The following year in October 1954 Eden accepted the Order of the Garter, which he had declined in 1945, the honour being conferred upon him by the Queen at Windsor. Although he turned 80 in November 1954 there was still no indication of when Churchill might retire, and it wasn't until 5 April 1955, amid a newspaper strike, that Churchill finally relinquished power, with Eden becoming Prime Minister the next day. Although the Conservatives had a lead of only 4 per cent in the opinion polls, Eden believed that he should take an early opportunity of seeking a fresh mandate from the electorate, and nine days after becoming Prime Minister he announced a General Election for 26 May 1955. This was an act of considerable political bravery, but Eden's decision was vindicated when the Conservatives, after a quiet campaign during which Eden emphasized the theme of the 'property-owning democracy', won by sixty seats, the first peacetime occasion on which an incumbent administration had increased its majority since 1900. The spring budget on 19 April with £135 million of tax reliefs had contributed to the Conservatives' electoral victory, but economic problems now filled the domestic agenda. A major strike on the railways led Eden to declare a state of emergency and there was also concern over the effect the prolonged dock strike was having on the balance of payments deficit. An increase in purchase tax, which took back most of the earlier reliefs in the so-called 'pots and pans' Budget on 26 October, also caused further damage to the government. Despite the industrial unrest in the early part of 1955, Eden's premiership was dominated by foreign affairs. The Suez Crisis precipitated on July 26, 1956, when the Egyptian president, Gamal Abdel Nasser, nationalised the Suez Canal (Britain and France feared that Nasser might close the canal and cut off shipments of petroleum flowing from the Persian Gulf to western Europe). When diplomatic efforts to settle the crisis failed, Britain and France secretly prepared military action to regain control of the canal and, if possible, to depose Nasser. On 5 November 1956, British and French paratroopers landed at Port Said, and the next day the main amphibious forces succeeded in capturing 23 miles of the canal. This move was soon met by growing opposition at home and by U.S. sponsored resolutions in the UN, which quickly put a stop to the Anglo-French action. Eden was forced into a humiliating retreat. On December 22 the UN evacuated British and French troops. Nasser emerged from the Suez Crisis a victor, while Britain and France lost most of their influence in the Middle East as a result of the episode. Public opinion polls, though narrowly in favour of Eden's action, showed a divided Britain. On 19 November Downing Street announced that Eden was cancelling his engagements owing to ill health and two days later it was announced that, on medical advice due to recurrent fevers, Eden would be travelling to Jamaica to recuperate. Eden returned on 14 December but further medical advice left him no option but to resign. Eden therefore resigned as Prime Minister on 9 January 1957 and also resigned from the House of Commons. Eden lived for twenty years after leaving Downing Street and spent a lot of his time preparing his memoirs which appeared in three volumes between 1960 and 1965. In December 1976, while holidaying in Florida, he fell seriously ill and the Prime Minister, James Callaghan, arranged that he should be flown home to Wiltshire in an RAF plane. Eden died aged 77 at his home at Alvediston Manor, Wiltshire, on 14 January 1977.

Interesting Anthony Eden facts:

Eden learned French and German at an early age, and was later able to converse fluently with his political counterparts in private, but always negotiated through an interpreter.

Eden favoured a silk-brimmed, black felt Homburg hat which became known as the 'Eden hat', and so along with the Duke of Wellington, he was one of only two British Prime Ministers to have given his name eponymously to an article of clothing or footwear.

On 14 May 1940 Eden made a broadcast calling for men between the ages of 17 and 65 to enrol in a new force, the Local Defence Volunteers (LDV). By July nearly 1.5 million men had enrolled and the name was changed to the Home Guard.

Eden had honorary degrees from thirteen different universities.

Eden was the last surviving member of Churchill's War Cabinet.

The resignation document written by Eden for release to the cabinet on 9 January 1957 admitted his dependence on stimulants due to "bad abdominal operations".

Harold Macmillan
44th British Prime Minister

Born
12 February 1894, London
Died
29 December 1986, age 92, Chelwood Gate, Sussex
Period in office as Prime Minister
6 years 282 days from 10 January 1957 until 18 October 1963
Political party
Conservative
Constituencies Represented as MP
Stockton on Tees 1924-1929 and 1931-1945
Bromley 1945-1964
Ministerial offices held as Prime Minister
First Lord of the Treasury

Maurice Harold Macmillan, 1st Earl of Stockton (10 February 1894 – 29 December 1986) was one of the outstanding Conservative leaders of the 20th century in terms of achieving both unity in his party and electoral success.

Macmillan was born at 52 Cadogan Place in Chelsea, London, to Maurice Crawford Macmillan, a publisher, and his wife, American-born Helen (Nellie) Artie Tarleton Belles He was the grandson of a founder of the London publishing house of Macmillan & Co. Macmillan received an intensive early education, he learned French at home every morning and from an early age he received introductory lessons in classical Latin and Greek. Macmillan attended Summer Fields School, Oxford (1903–06) and in 1906 he won a scholarship to Eton. However, over the next three years he suffered poor health contracting pneumonia, from which he only just survived. Once recovered Macmillan won a place at Balliol College in 1912, where his personal tutor was Ronald Knox who was an English Catholic priest, theologian, radio broadcaster and author of detective stories. Knox became an important influence on Macmillan's intellectual development. While at university Macmillan became involved in politics and he joined the Canning Club (Conservative), the Russell Club (Liberal) and the Fabian Society (Socialist) and in meetings of the Oxford Union he supported progressive causes such as women's suffrage.

On the outbreak of the First World War Macmillan was suffering from appendicitis but as soon as he recovered he joined the Grenadier Guards. He was commissioned as a second lieutenant and was sent to a training battalion at Southend-on-Sea and left for France on 15th August, 1915. His battalion arrived to fight on the Western Front where on 27th September 1915, Macmillan took part in the offensive at Loos when towards the end of the battle he was shot through his right hand. He was evacuated to hospital and although it was not a serious wound he never recovered the strength of that hand. The wound consequently affected the standard of his handwriting and was also responsible for what became known as the 'limp handshake'. After receiving treatment in London Macmillan was sent back to the Western Front, where in April 1916 he took part in the offensive at the Somme. In July 1916, Macmillan was wounded while leading a patrol in No Man's Land and after being hit by a bomb on the back and face, he was hospitalised for a couple of days but by the end of the month he moved with his battalion to Beaumont-Hamel. On 15th September 1916 Macmillan was wounded again during an attack on the German trenches, after being shot in the leg he took refuge in a shell-hole until he was found by members of the Sherwood Foresters regiment. He had received serious wounds and the surgeons decided it would be too risky to attempt to remove the bullet fragments from his pelvis, and so he was returned to England where for a while his life was in danger. His mother arranged for him to be transferred to a private hospital in Belgrave Square where he spent the final two years of the war undergoing a long series of operations. He was still on crutches on Armistice Day on 11 November 1918, with the hip wound eventually taking four years to completely heal and still leaving him with a slight shuffle when he walked. In 1919 after the war Macmillan then served in Ottawa, Ontario, Canada, as an *aide-de-camp (French expression meaning helper)* to Victor Cavendish, 9th Duke of Devonshire, the then Governor General of Canada and his future father-in-law. He returned to London in 1920 where he joined the family publishing firm Macmillan Publishers as a junior partner. Macmillan married Lady Dorothy Cavendish, the daughter of the 9th Duke of Devonshire, on 21 April 1920 and although they had four children and 46 years of marriage together it wasn't a traditional marriage. His wife Dorothy carried on a lifelong affair with Tory backbencher Robert Boothby (an open secret in political and journalistic circles) but was unable to pursue a divorce that was most likely to end his political career, and so Macmillan and Dorothy lived largely separate lives. Although tempted to join

the Liberal Party, Macmillan, calculated that the party was in decline and decided instead to join the Conservative Party. In the 1924 General Election he became the Conservative MP for Stockton-On-Tees but in the face of high regional unemployment he was defeated in the 1929 General Election by a majority of 2,389. He did return to the House of Commons again as MP for Stockton in the October 1931 General Election with a majority of 11,031. Macmillan spent the 1930s on the backbenches and in March 1932 he published 'The State and Industry' following on from an earlier pamphlet named 'Industry and the State' (co-produced with Robert Boothby).
Macmillan was a strong believer in social reform and his left-wing views were unpopular with the Conservative Party leadership. Macmillan was also highly critical of the foreign policies of Stanley Baldwin and Neville Chamberlain and remained a backbencher until 1940 when Winston Churchill invited him to join the government as Parliamentary Secretary to the Ministry of Supply. In 1942 Macmillan went to North Africa where he filled the new cabinet post as Minister at Allied Headquarters and on 14 September 1944, Macmillan was appointed Chief Commissioner of the Allied Central Commission for Italy. He returned to England after the European war, and was Secretary of State for Air for two months in Churchill's caretaker government. Macmillan lost his seat in Stockton in the landslide Labour post-war General Election victory of July 1945 (majority 8,664) but he returned to Parliament in the November of 1945 in a by-election victory in Bromley with a 5,557 majority. In 1946 Winston Churchill asked Macmillan to join a committee to look into reshaping the Conservative Party. On 3rd October, Macmillan published an article in the *Daily Telegraph* where he suggested that the name should be changed to the "New Democratic Party" which was never implemented. In the article he called for the Liberal Party to join Conservatives in an anti-socialist alliance. With the Conservative victory at the General Election in October 1951 Macmillan retained his Bromley seat with a majority of 12,125

and became Minister of Housing & Local Government under Churchill, who entrusted him with fulfilling the pledge to build 300,000 houses per year (which was achieved a year ahead of schedule at the end of 1953). Macmillan was then made Minister of Defence from October 1954, with the major theme of his tenure at Defence was the ministry's growing reliance on the nuclear deterrent resulting in 'The Defence White Paper' of February 1955, which announced the decision to produce the hydrogen bomb. Macmillan was briefly Foreign Secretary from April to December 1955 and immediately after was appointed Chancellor of the Exchequer. One of Macmillan's innovations at the Treasury was the introduction of Premium Bonds which he announced in his budget of 17 April 1956. Although the Labour Opposition initially disparaged them as a 'squalid raffle', they proved an immediate hit with the public and £1,000 was won in the first prize draw in June 1957.

With the Suez Crisis of November 1956, Macmillan was accused by the Labour Shadow Chancellor Harold Wilson of being 'first in, first out' by being at first, very supportive of the invasion, then instigating Britain's humiliating withdrawal. Britain's humiliation at the hands of the US caused deep anger among Conservative MPs and with Prime Minister Eden's political standing destroyed he resigned on grounds of ill health on 9 January 1957. At that time the Conservative Party had no formal mechanism for selecting a new leader, and so on 10 January 1957, after taking advice from Churchill, the Queen appointed Macmillan as Prime Minister. Macmillan set out his premiership with an image of calm and style, although initially he was accused of cronyism when he appointed seven former Etonians to his Cabinet. Macmillan was the first Conservative Prime Minister to accept that countries within the British Empire should be given their freedom and in 1957 the Gold Coast, Ghana, Malaya and North Borneo were granted their independence. In January 1958, Macmillan refused to introduce strict controls on money and his economic policies resulted in an economic boom and a reduction in unemployment.

This resulted in the Conservatives winning the 1959 General Election, increasing their majority from 67 to 107 seats.
In February 1959 Macmillan became the first British Prime Minister to visit the Soviet Union since the Second World War and held talks with Soviet leader Khrushchev to ease tensions in East-West relations over West Berlin. During his time as Prime Minister, average living standards steadily increased while numerous social reforms were carried out including, the 1957 Housing Act, the 1960 Offices Act, the 1960 Noise Abatement Act and the Factories Act 1961. He also introduced of a graduated pension scheme to provide an additional income to retirees, the establishment of a Child's Special Allowance for the orphaned children of divorced parents and a reduction in the standard work week from 48 to 42 hours. But as the sixties progressed, Macmillan began to fear his Conservative party was in decline, and with the defeat in a by-election in April 1962 of a safe Tory seat in Orpington, (a majority of 14,760 was lost with a swing of 26.3%), he became convinced of the need to act. Macmillan had lost faith in several members of his cabinet, including his high-profile colleague and friend, Chancellor Selwyn Lloyd. On the evening 12 July 1962 he sacked Lloyd, and the following day (Friday 13th) six other cabinet members were sacked. Macmillan called them into his office one by one to confirm the news, and with one third of his 21 cabinet ministers being sacked, the press dubbed it the 'night of the long knives'. The report *The Reshaping of British Railways* (Beeching report) was published on 27 March 1963 with Macmillan's premise that the railways should be run as a profitable business, it led to the notorious Beeching Axe, destroying many miles of permanent way and severing towns from the railway network. On 27 July 1960 Macmillan had appointed John Profumo as British Secretary of State for War, an appointment which was later to cause scandal. At the country estate of Lord Astor on July 8, 1961, Profumo was introduced to 19-year-old London dancer Christine Keeler by Stephen Ward, an osteopath with contacts in both the aristocracy and the

underworld. Also present at this gathering was a Russian military attaché, Eugene Ivanov, who was Keeler's lover. Profumo began an affair with Keeler, and rumours of their involvement soon began to spread. In March 1963 Profumo lied about the affair to Parliament, stating that there was "no impropriety whatsoever" in his relationship with Keeler. Evidence to the contrary quickly became too great to hide however, and 10 weeks later in June 1963 Profumo resigned admitting "with deep remorse" that he had deceived the House of Commons. The whole episode damaged the credibility of Macmillan's government and the affair became an attack not only on Profumo, but on the morality of Macmillan's government. Although Macmillan's reputation was partly rehabilitated by the successful negotiations in July 1963, between Great Britain, the United States, and the Soviet Union for the Nuclear Test-Ban Treaty, the Profumo affair directly contributed to Macmillan's departure from 10 Downing Street. A full report by Judge Alfred Denning into the Profumo Scandal was published on 26 September 1963, this combined with Macmillan suffering prostate problems that required surgery on 10 October, led to Macmillan resigning as Prime Minister on 18 October 1963, and retiring from politics in September 1964. Macmillan died at Birch Grove, the Macmillan family mansion on the edge of Ashdown Forest near Chelwood Gate in East Sussex, four days after Christmas in 1986 aged 92 years and 322 days.

Interesting Harold Macmillan facts:

During his early years as Prime Minister, Macmillan had been nicknamed 'Supermac', but after 'the night of the long knives' he acquired a new nickname...'Mac the knife'.

Macmillan's memoirs include: *Winds of Change, 1914–1939* (1966); *The Blast of War, 1939–1945* (1967); *Tides of Fortune, 1945–1955* (1969); *Riding the Storm, 1956–1959* (1971); *Pointing the Way, 1959–1961* (1972); *At the End of the Day, 1961–63* (1973); and *The Past Masters: Politics and Politicians, 1906–1939* (1975).

Sir Alec Douglas-Home
45th British Prime Minister

Born
2 July 1903, London
Died
9 October 1995, age 92, Berwickshire
Period in office as Prime Minister
363 days from 19 October 1963 until 16 October 1964
Political party
Conservative
Constituencies Represented as MP
Lanark 1931-1945 and 1950-1951
Kinross and Western Perthshire 1963-1974
Ministerial offices held as Prime Minister
First Lord of the Treasury

Alexander Frederick Douglas-Home, also called (1951–63) Alexander Frederick Douglas-Home, 14th Earl of Home, or (from 1974) Alexander Frederick Douglas-Home, Baron Home of the Hirsel of Coldstream, 2 July 1903 – 9 October 1995, was a British Conservative politician who served as Prime Minister from October 1963 to October 1964.

Sir Alec Douglas-Home was born at 28 South Street Mayfair, London, into an aristocratic family. The eldest child of seven, his father was Charles Douglas-Home, Lord Dunglass. He was educated at Ludgrove School, followed by Eton College. After Eton, Douglas-Home went to Christ Church, Oxford, where he graduated with a third-class honours BA degree in Modern History in 1925. He was a talented sportsman and he represented the Oxford University Cricket Club, Middlesex County Cricket Club and Marylebone Cricket Club (MCC), at first-class level. Between 1924 and 1927 he played ten first-class matches, scoring 147 runs at an average of 16.33 with a best score of 37 not out. As a bowler he took 12 wickets at an average of 30.25 with a best of 3 for 43. Three of his first-class games were internationals against Argentina on the MCC "representative" tour of South America in 1926–27.

Douglas-Home had shown little interest in politics while at Eton or Oxford but became interested in politics due to the widespread unemployment and poverty in the Scottish lowlands where his family lived. His political thinking was influenced by that of Noel Skelton, a member of the Unionist party (as the Conservatives were called in Scotland between 1912 and 1965). Skelton advocated "a property-owning democracy", based on share-options for workers and industrial democracy.
Douglas-Home's first taste of election politics was in the 1929 General Election where he stood as a Unionist candidacy at Coatbridge, which was a safe Labour seat. He lost with 9,210 votes to Labour's 16,879 but gained valuable experience.

Although he was not a natural orator, he began to learn how to deal with hostile audiences and get his message across. When a coalition "National Government" was formed in 1931 to deal with a financial crisis, Douglas-Home was adopted as the pro-coalition Unionist candidate for Lanark. At the 1929 election Labour had captured Lanark from the Unionists, but with the backing of the pro-coalition Liberal party which supported him rather than fielding its own candidate, he won the seat in the October 1931 General Election with 63.3% of the vote (majority 8,860).

In 1936 Douglas-Home married Elizabeth Alington and they had four children (3 daughters and a son).

Douglas-Home was Parliamentary Private Secretary to Prime Minister Neville Chamberlain from 1937 to 1939 and he went to Munich with Chamberlain to meet Adolf Hitler in 1938. As private secretary he was present at the main meetings between Chamberlain and Hitler.

Douglas-Home had volunteered for active military service, seeking to join the Lanarkshire Yeomanry shortly after Chamberlain left Downing Street. The consequent medical examination revealed that he had a hole in his spine surrounded by tuberculosis in the bone. Without surgery he would have been unable to walk within a matter of months. A hazardous operation was performed in September 1940, the operation lasted six hours, in which the diseased bone in the spine was scraped away and replaced with healthy bone from Douglas-Home's shin. He was encased in plaster and kept flat on his back for two years. Towards the end of 1942 he was released from his plaster jacket and fitted with a spinal brace, and in early 1943 he was mobile for the first time since the operation. In July 1943 Douglas-Home returned to the House of Commons and into Churchill's caretaker Conservative government. He was appointed to his first ministerial post, in the Foreign Office, and with Anthony Eden as Foreign Secretary, Douglas-Home was appointed as one of his two Under-secretaries of State. At the July 1945 General Election Douglas-Home lost his Parliamentary seat in a landslide

Labour victory. The Lanark seat was a close fought seat with Labour winning with 17,784 votes as opposed to Douglas-Home's 15,900 (majority 1884). Douglas-Home was then appointed a director of the Bank of Scotland in 1946.

When Clement Attlee, the Labour Prime Minister, called a General Election for 23 February 1950, Douglas-Home once again stood as Unionist candidate for Lanark. With the Cold War at its height, Tom Steele, Douglas-Home's Labour opposition's association with the communists was a crucial electoral liability. Douglas-Home regained the seat with one of the smallest majorities (685) with 19,890 votes to Labour's 19,205.

In July 1951 his father, the 13th Earl of Home died and Douglas-Home succeeded him, inheriting the title of Earl of Home together with the extensive family estates, the new Lord Home took his seat in the House of Lords. Douglas-Home was appointed to the new post of Minister of State at the Scottish Office, which was a middle-ranking position, senior to Under-secretary but junior to James Stuart, the Secretary of State who was a member of the cabinet. In addition to his ministerial position Douglas-Home was appointed to membership of the Privy Council, which was an honour granted selectively to ministers below cabinet rank. When Anthony Eden succeeded Churchill as Prime Minister in 1955, he promoted Douglas-Home to the cabinet as Secretary of State for Commonwealth Relations which gave Douglas-Home the chance to visit to visit Australia, New Zealand, Singapore, India, Pakistan and Ceylon (Sri Lanka). During the Suez Crisis in 1956 Douglas-Home had to try and maintain Commonwealth unity and he was firmly in support of the invasion. When the invasion was abandoned under pressure from the US in November 1956, Douglas-Home had to work with the dissenting members of the Commonwealth to build the organisation into 'a modern multiracial Commonwealth'. In 1960 Harold Macmillan took the unprecedented step of appointing two Foreign Office cabinet ministers, Douglas-Home, as Foreign Secretary, in the Lords, and Edward Heath, as Lord Privy Seal and deputy Foreign Secretary in

the Commons. With British application for admission to
the European Economic Community (EEC) pending, Heath was
given particular responsibility for the EEC negotiations as well as
for speaking in the Commons on foreign affairs in general.
Douglas-Home's attention was mainly concentrated on the Cold
War, where his forcefully expressed anti-communist beliefs were
tempered by a pragmatic approach to dealing with the Soviet
Union. His first major problem in this area was in 1961 when on
the orders of the Soviet leader, Nikita Khrushchev, the Berlin
Wall was erected to stop East Germans escaping to West
Germany via West Berlin. The following year the Cuban Missile
Crisis threatened to turn the Cold War into a nuclear one when
Soviet nuclear missiles were sent to Cuba provocatively close to
the US. During the missile crisis, Douglas-Home, stayed calm and
strengthened Prime Minister Macmillan's resolve, encouraging him
to back up President Kennedy's defiance of Soviet threats of
nuclear attack. In October 1963 when Macmillan resigned due to
ill health, Douglas-Home became leader of the Conservative
Party, knowing it would be difficult to lead a government from
the House of Lords, he renounced his title, becoming Sir Alec
Douglas-Home. After the title was renounced, the safe
Conservative seat of Kinross and Western Perthshire was vacant
and Douglas-Home was adopted as his party's candidate.
Parliament was due to meet on 24 October after the summer
recess, but its return was postponed until 12 November pending
the by-election. For twenty days Douglas-Home was Prime
Minister while a member of neither house of Parliament, a
situation without modern precedent. He won the by-election
comfortably with a majority of 9,328.
A month after becoming Prime Minister, international affairs the
most dramatic event with the assassination of American President
John F. Kennedy on 22 November 1963. Douglas-Home who had
previously worked with Kennedy, broadcast a tribute on television
and later attended Kennedy's state funeral in Washington. By the
time he took over as Prime Minister, the Conservative Party had

been in office for 12 years and had contested 3 elections, Douglas-Home was the fourth party leader during the period. In contrast, Harold Wilson had become a fearful leader of the Labour Party. On 15 October 1964 the Conservatives, although doing better than predicted, lost the General Election to Wilson's Labour Party. Labour won 317 seats, the Conservatives 304 and the Liberals 9, giving Labour a small 5 seat majority. Douglas-Home announced his resignation as Conservative leader on 22 July 1965. Edward Heath took over as leader of the Conservative party and Douglas-Home accepted the foreign affairs portfolio in Heath's shadow cabinet. Sir Alec Douglas-Home was an unexpected Prime Minister who served for only 363 days, the second shortest premiership in the 20th century. Douglas-Home remained as an MP and Wilson's small majority after the 1964 General Election had made the transaction of government business difficult, and so in 1966 Wilson called another election in which Labour gained a stronger working majority of 96. As the 1970 General Election approached there was concern within the Conservative party that they would lose again, but to the surprise of many, the Conservatives won the election with a majority of 31 seats. Edward Heath invited Douglas-Home to join the cabinet and he took charge of Foreign and Commonwealth Affairs and he remained as Foreign Secretary until the 1974 General Election defeat, when aged 70, he retired. He died at the age of 92 in October 1995.

Interesting Alec Douglas-Home fact:

In retirement Douglas-Home published three books: *The Way the Wind Blows* (1976), *Border Reflections* (1979), and his correspondence with his grandson Matthew Darby, *Letters to a Grandson* (1983).

Douglas-Home became president of the Marylebone Cricket Club (MCC) in 1966

Harold Wilson
46th British Prime Minister

Born
11 March 1916, Huddersfield, Yorkshire
Died
23 May 1995, age 79, London
Periods in office as Prime Minister
7 years 280 days (2 terms) from 16 October 1964 - 19 June 1970 (5 years 247 days) and 4 March 1974 - 5 April 1976 (2 years 33 days)
Political party
Labour
Constituencies Represented as MP
Ormskirk 1945-1950
Huyton 1950-1983
Ministerial offices held as Prime Minister
First Lord of the Treasury
Minister for the Civil Service

James Harold Wilson, Baron Wilson of Rievaulx, was
a Labour politician who served as Prime Minister from 1964 to
1970 and 1974 to 1976.

*Wilson was born at Warneford Road, Huddersfield, in the West
Riding of Yorkshire, England. The son of Herbert Wilson (1882–
1971) and his wife, Ethel Seddon (1882–1957). His mother was a
former school teacher and his father was a chemist who had been
a supporter of the Liberal Party, but after the First World War he
changed his allegiance to the Labour Party. Wilson was educated
at New Street Elementary School (1920-1927), Royds Hall School
(1927-1932) and Bebington Grammar School (1932-1934). He
did well at school and, although he missed getting a scholarship,
he won a history exhibition, which was topped up by a county
grant enabling him to study Modern History at Jesus College,
Oxford. Wilson was a very hard-working student and his first
academic triumph was to win the Gladstone Memorial Prize for a
long essay on 'The state and the railways in Great Britain 1823–
63' with the essay reflecting his keen interest in the British
Railway System, along with a keen interest in the American Civil
War. The following year he won the George Webb Medley Senior
Scholarship, which gave him £300 a year, enabling him to
graduate from Oxford with a first class Bachelor of Arts degree.*

He continued in academia, becoming one of the youngest Oxford
dons of the century at the age of 21. He was a lecturer
in Economic History at New College from 1937 and a
research fellow at University College.
He married Mary Baldwin on New Year's Day 1940 and they had
two sons.
On the outbreak of World War II, Wilson was drafted into the Civil
Service and became a statistician and economist for the coal
industry. He was Director of Economics and Statistics at
the Ministry of Fuel and Power in 1943–44 and received
an OBE for his services. In 1945 he published a book '***New Deal***

for Coal ' which was the basis of the Labour Party's plans for nationalising the coal mines. As the war drew to a close, Wilson searched for a seat in an upcoming General Election. He was selected for the constituency of Ormskirk (a market town in Lancashire) and he resigned from the Civil Service. On 5 July 1945 Wilson won the Ormskirk seat in a Labour landslide with a majority of 7,022. On 29 September 1947, the then Prime Minister Clement Attlee made Wilson President of the Board of Trade and aged only 31, he had become the youngest member of the Cabinet in the 20th century. He was also the youngest cabinet minister since William Pitt the Younger in 1792. The boundaries of Wilson's Ormskirk constituency were significantly altered before the General Election of 1950 and he stood instead for the new seat of Huyton near Liverpool, being narrowly elected with a majority of 834 (this rose to over 20,000 by the 1970's). He continued to serve the constituency of Huyton for a further 33 years until he retired in 1983. Wilson was becoming known in the Labour Party as a left-winger, and joined Aneurin Bevan and John Freeman in resigning from the government in April 1951. The resignations were in protest at the introduction of National Health Service (NHS) medical charges which was to meet the financial costs imposed by the Korean War. After Labour lost the 1951 General Election, Wilson became involved in the Labour 'Keep Left' movement, Nye Bevan's political group. Despite his association with Bevan, in 1955 Wilson backed Hugh Gaitskell, the right-wing Labour candidate, against Bevan for the party leadership. In December 1955, Hugh Gaitskell was appointed Labour leader and he appointed Wilson as Shadow Chancellor of the Exchequer. From 1959 to 1963 Wilson combined the job of Chairman of the House of Commons' Public Accounts Committee with that of Shadow Chancellor. Wilson established himself as a leader within Labour and made a challenge to Gaitskell's leadership in November 1960, but was comfortably defeated by 166 votes to 81. Gaitskell died on 18 January 1963 and was succeeded (on a temporary basis) by deputy leader

George Brown. The first leadership election was held on 7 February 1963 and James Callaghan was eliminated. The second ballot was held on 14 February 1963 when Wilson defeated George Brown by 144 votes to 103, and so at the age of 46, Wilson became Labour's youngest ever leader.

At the October 1964 General Election the Profumo scandal had wounded Harold Macmillan and hurt the Conservatives, enabling Labour to win with a 3% swing for a slim majority of four seats. Wilson at 48 became Prime Minister, the youngest person to hold office since Archibald Primrose 70 years earlier.

With an unworkable small majority Wilson took the gamble of a snap General Election on 31 March 1966. Labour won 364 seats and the gamble paid off with a healthy 98 seat majority.

As Prime Minister Wilson's main plan was to modernise, and he believed that he would be aided by the "white heat of the technological revolution". In his time as Prime Minister the House of Commons passed the 1965 Race Relations Act (outlawing discrimination on the "grounds of colour, race, or ethnic or national origins" in public places). The 1965 Abolition of Death Penalty Act (replaced the penalty of death with a mandatory sentence of imprisonment for life). The 1967 Sexual Offences Act (decriminalised homosexual acts in private between two men, both of whom had to have attained the age of 21). The 1967 Abortion Act (legalising abortions by registered practitioners, and regulating the free provision of such medical practices through the National Health Service). The 1968 Theatres Act (abolished censorship of the stage) and the 1969 Divorce Reform Act (allowing couples to divorce after a separation of two years). In Comprehensive Education, from 1966 to 1970, the proportion of children in comprehensive schools increased from about 10% to over 30%. Housing was increased with 1.3 million new homes being built between 1965 and 1970. Family Allowances from April 1964 to April 1970, increased as a percentage for male manual workers aged 21 and above from 8% to 11.3%. and Wilson's government also created the Open University. However, Wilson

had inherited an overstretched military and a £400 million balance of payments deficit, which caused successive sterling crises. To try and counter balance this, Wilson created the Department for Economic Affairs, which sought to implement an ambitious National Plan. In November, 1967, Wilson's Chancellor of the Exchequer, James Callaghan, was forced to devalue the pound and by the end of the 1960s, with unemployment and inflation increasing, Wilson's popularity had declined and there was a surprise 31 seat victory in the June 1970 General Election for Edward Heath and the Conservative Party. This was the first General Election in which people could vote from the age of 18, after the passing of the Representation of the People Act the previous year. Wilson held onto the Labour leadership and remained in opposition until the next General Election which was held on 28 February 1974, where Labour gained 14 seats (301 total), but was still seventeen short of an overall majority.
The Conservative Party, led by incumbent Prime Minister Edward Heath, lost 28 seats, but achieved a higher share of the vote than Labour, resulting in the first hung parliament since 1929. Heath was unable to form a coalition and resigned, allowing Wilson (with a minority government) to became Prime Minister for a second time. Because Labour was unable to form a majority coalition with another party, Wilson called another early election to be held in October 1974, the first year that two General Elections were held in the same year since 1910. Wilson and Labour secured a small majority of 3 buy winning 319 seats (out of 635). In 1975 Wilson held a referendum on membership of the European Economic Community, and allowed his Cabinet to support both the Yes and No campaigns. This led to a bitter split in the party and his government was again having trouble with the economy. Faced with the prospect of having to get a loan from the IMC (International Monetary Fund), Wilson came under increasing attack from all sections of the Labour Party. On March 16, 1976, with the pound floundering and a crucial budget soon to be presented, Wilson announced his resignation. In April 1976 the

Queen appointed Wilson a Knight of the Garter, and in 1983 he was created a life peer. Wilson still sat in the House of Lords and made his final appearance in April 1994. He died from colon cancer and Alzheimer's disease in May 1995, aged 79, with a memorial service held in Westminster Abbey on 13 July 1995. It was attended by the Prince of Wales, former Prime Ministers Edward Heath, James Callaghan, and Margaret Thatcher.

Interesting Harold Wilson facts:

Wilson stood in 10 General Elections in Huyton, winning them all before the constituency was dissolved under the 1983 boundary changes. Therefore Wilson was the only MP to ever directly represent Huyton (1950-1983)

Wilson appeared on the *Morecambe and Wise* Christmas Specials in 1978 and 1980

Wilson won four of five General Elections, more than any other post-war British leader of any party.

His own version of politics in his time may be found in his books *The Labour Government, 1964–1970*: A Personal Record (1971), *The Governance of Britain* (1976), and *Final Term: The Labour Government 1974–76* (1979).

Two statues of Harold Wilson stand in prominent places. The first, unveiled by the then Prime Minister Tony Blair in July 1999, stands outside Huddersfield railway station in St George's Square, Huddersfield. A second bronze statue of Wilson, also unveiled by Tony Blair in 2006 is in Wilson's former constituency of Huyton, near Liverpool.

In 1963, Soviet defector Anatoliy Golitsyn is said to have secretly claimed that Wilson was a KGB agent.

Edward Heath
47th British Prime Minister

Born
9 July 1916, Broadstairs, Kent
Died
17 July 2005, age 89, Salisbury, Wiltshire
Period in office as Prime Minister
3 years 259 days from 19 June 1970 until 4 March 1974
Political party
Conservative
Constituencies Represented as MP
Bexley 1950-1974
Sidcup 1974-1983
Old Bexley and Sidcup 1983-2001
Ministerial offices held as Prime Minister
First Lord of the Treasury
Minister for the Civil Service

Sir Edward Richard George Heath, (9 July 1916 – 17 July 2005), often known as **Ted Heath**, was a British politician who served as Prime Minister of the United Kingdom from 1970 to 1974 and Leader of the Conservative Party from 1965 to 1975. Heath served 51 years as a Member of Parliament from 1950 to 2001.

Heath was born in July 1916, his father (William) was a carpenter and his mother (Edith) a maid. He was known as "Teddy" as a young man. He was educated at Chatham House Grammar School in Ramsgate, and in 1935 with the aid of a county scholarship he went up to study at Balliol College, Oxford. In June 1937 he was elected President of the Oxford University Conservative Association, and in 1937–38 Heath was chairman of the national Federation of University Conservative Associations. In 1938 (his third at university) he was Secretary and then Librarian of the Oxford Union. Heath was also a talented musician and won the college's organ scholarship in his first term which enabled him to stay at the university for a fourth year. He eventually graduated from Oxford with a Second Class Honours BA in Philosophy, Politics and Economics in 1939.

As an undergraduate, Heath travelled widely in Europe. He was in opposition to the appeasement toward Nazi Germany which the Conservative Prime Minister Neville Chamberlain favoured, after witnessing first-hand a Nuremberg Rally in 1937. Heath spent late 1939 and early 1940 on a debating tour of the United States before being called up to the Army on 22 March 1941. He received an emergency commission as a second lieutenant in the Royal Artillery and participated as an adjutant (a principal aide to a commanding officer) in the Normandy landings. As a temporary major he commanded a battery of his own, and he provided artillery support during the Allied campaigns in France and Germany in 1944–45. For his service he was appointed a Member of the Order of the British Empire (MBE), Military

Division on 24 January 1946. He was demobilised in August 1946 and promoted to the substantive rank of lieutenant-colonel on 1 May 1947.

His pre-war visit to Nazi Germany and his experience of the war shaped his belief in the benefits of what later became the European Union.

Heath worked in the Ministry of Civil Aviation in 1946–47, and was editor of the *Church Times* from January 1948 to October 1949, before becoming a member of a merchant banking firm in the City of London. In 1950, Heath was elected to Parliament as a Conservative member for Bexley in south-east London, a previously held Labour seat, winning the seat with a majority of 155. Bexley was a seat he went on to represent (taking into account changes in boundary and title) for 50 years.

He rose quickly in the government, serving as Chief Whip under Prime Minister Anthony Eden. In 1960 the then Prime Minister Harold Macmillan appointed Heath Lord Privy Seal with responsibility for the negotiations to secure the UK's first attempt to join the European Communities (or Common Market as it was then more widely known). After Macmillan's retirement in October 1963, under new Prime Minister Sir Alec Douglas-Home, Heath was President of the Board of Trade and Secretary of State for Industry Trade and Regional Development, and oversaw the abolition of retail price maintenance. After Douglas-Home resigned following the 1964 General Election defeat, Heath won the party's leadership contest in July 1965, gaining 150 votes to Reginald Maudling's 133 and Enoch Powell's 15. He was the first Tory to be elected leader by his fellow MPs. After only eight months as Conservative leader, Heath faced a snap General Election which was held on 31 March 1966 (the last General Election where the voting age was 21). The Conservatives lost 51 seats in a Labour landslide, but Heath continued as leader and worked hard to prepare his party for future power, emphasizing personal initiative and a reduction of the role of the central government as elements of modern conservatism. In April 1968,

Enoch Powell made his controversial "Rivers of Blood" speech, which criticised immigration to the United Kingdom. Heath sacked Powell, appearing on the BBC *Panorama* programme, on 22 April 1968, stating "I dismissed Mr Powell because I believed his speech was inflammatory and liable to damage race relations. I am determined to do everything I can to prevent racial problems developing into civil strife ... I don't believe the great majority of the British people share Mr Powell's way of putting his views in his speech."

At the General Election in June 1970, Heath's Conservatives surprisingly (opinion polls had predicted a Labour win) defeated the governing Labour Party under Harold Wilson, with a majority of 31. Heath's new cabinet included Margaret Thatcher (Education and Science), William Whitelaw (Leader of the House of Commons) and the former Prime Minister Alec Douglas-Home (Foreign and Commonwealth Affairs). In his ministry a long-term capital investment programme in school building was launched. A Family Fund was set up to provide assistance to families with children who had congenital conditions, while new benefits were introduced which helped hundreds of thousands of disabled people whose disabilities had been caused neither by war nor by industrial injury. An Attendance Allowance was introduced for those needing care at home, together with Invalidity Benefit for the long-term sick, while a higher Child Allowance was made available where invalidity allowance was paid. Widow's Benefits were introduced for those aged between forty and fifty years of age, improved subsidies for slum clearance were made available, while Rent Allowances were introduced for private tenants. In April 1971, the right to education was given to all children with Down's syndrome for the first time. The school leaving age was raised to 16, while Family Income Supplement was introduced to boost the incomes of low-income earners. Heath had taken office promising to be tough on pay and tough on trade unions, and it was battles with the unions that characterised his four years in Downing Street. There were widespread strikes including the miners' strikes of 1972 and 1974, power cuts were frequent, no rubbish was collected for six weeks, a three-day working week was introduced and there was a pay freeze. After having fulfilled his long-held ambition of taking Britain into the European Community, in 1973, he called a General Election in February 1974, with the question, "who governs Britain - the unions or the government?" the answer was ambiguous and the first hung parliament since 1929 ensued. After failed talks with Liberal leader Jeremy Thorpe, Heath resigned as Prime Minister on 4 March 1974, and was replaced by Wilson's minority Labour government. On Thursday 10 October a second General Election was held that year, the first year that two General Elections were held in the same year since 1910. The Conservative Party, still led by Heath, released a manifesto promoting national unity, but lost 20 seats, with Labour winning an extra 18 seats, meaning Labour won with the narrowest majority recorded of 3 seats. Even after the defeat Heath resolved to remain Conservative leader but on 4 February 1975 in a Conservative leadership contest, Margaret Thatcher defeated Heath in the first ballot by 130 votes to 119, with Hugh Fraser coming in a distant third with 16 votes. This was not a big enough margin to give Thatcher the 15% majority necessary to win on the first ballot, but having finished in second place Heath immediately resigned and did not contest the next ballot. Subsequently Heath became highly critical of Thatcher and of the Conservative Party's movement to the political right and its opposition to European integration. He never forgave Thatcher for ousting him as leader and it became known in political circles as 'The Incredible Sulk' after he refused a position in Thatcher's Shadow Cabinet. Heath continued as a central figure on the left of the Conservative Party and continued to serve as a backbench MP for the London constituency of Old Bexley and Sidcup and he chaired important governmental committees which determined national policy. During the 1990-1991 war in the Persian Gulf, Heath was the British government's negotiator with Saddam Hussein of Iraq, and succeeded in gaining the release of many

British hostages. In 1992, after forty two years as an MP, he became the longest-serving MP ('Father of the House') and the oldest British MP.

Heath retired from Parliament at the 2001 General Election.

In August 2003, at the age of 87, Heath suffered a pulmonary embolism while on holiday in Salzburg, Austria. He never fully recovered, and owing to his declining health and mobility made very few public appearances in the last two years of his life.

Sir Edward Heath, who never married, died at his home from pneumonia at 7.30pm on 17 July 2005, at the age of 89.

Interesting Edward Heath facts:

Heath was an accomplished organist, and in 1971 he conducted the London Symphony Orchestra, the first of several orchestras he was to conduct.

He wrote several books, including *Music: A Joy for Life* (1976); *Sailing: A Course of My Life* (1975), an account of his sailing adventures; and the autobiography *The Course of My Life* (1998).

Heath was created a Knight of the Garter on 23 April 1992.

He was a keen yachtsman and he captained Britain's winning team for the Admiral's Cup in 1971, while still Prime Minister.

Heath was a supporter of Burnley Football Club.

Heath was the founding President of the European Community Youth Orchestra (in 1976), now the European Union Youth Orchestra.

Heath's Wiltshire home, Arundells, in Salisbury is now open to the public as a museum to his career.

James Callaghan
48th British Prime Minister

Born
27 March 1912, Portsmouth, Hampshire
Died
26 March 2005, age 92, Ringmer, East Sussex
Period in office as Prime Minister
3 years 30 days from 5 April 1976 until 4 May 1979
Political party
Labour
Constituencies Represented as MP
Cardiff South 1945-1950
Cardiff South East 1950-1983
Cardiff South and Penarth 1983-1987
Ministerial offices held as Prime Minister
First Lord of the Treasury
Minister for the Civil Service

Leonard James Callaghan, Baron Callaghan of Cardiff, 27 March 1912 – 26 March 2005), known as **Jim Callaghan**, was a Prime Minister from 1976 to 1979 and Leader of the Labour Party from 1976 to 1980.

Callaghan was born in Portsmouth, England, on March 12, 1912. His father, James Callaghan, was a chief petty officer in the Royal Navy. In 1921 when Callaghan was nine his father died of a heart attack aged only 44 plunging the family into poverty and forcing them to rely on charity. Their financial situation was improved in 1924 when the first Labour government was elected and introduced changes which allowed Mrs Callaghan to be granted a widow's pension of ten shillings a week. This was granted on the basis that her husband's death was partly due to his war service. Callaghan attended Portsmouth Northern Grammar School (now Mayfield School) and gained the Senior Oxford Certificate in 1929. Unfortunately the family could not afford the entrance to university and so instead he sat the Civil Service entrance exam.

At the age of 17, Callaghan left to work as a clerk for the Inland Revenue at Maidstone in Kent. While working as a tax inspector, Callaghan joined the Maidstone branch of the Labour Party and the Association of the Officers of Taxes (AOT) a trade union for those in his profession, and within a year, he became the office secretary of the union. In 1932 he passed a Civil Service exam which enabled him to become a senior tax inspector, as well as becoming the Kent branch secretary of the AOT. In 1933 he was elected to the AOT's national executive council and in 1934, he was transferred to Inland Revenue offices in London. Following a merger of unions in 1936, Callaghan was appointed a full-time union official and to the post of Assistant Secretary of the Inland Revenue Staff Federation (IRSF) resigning from his Civil Service duties. With the outbreak of World War II Callaghan applied to join the Royal Navy in 1940, but was initially turned down on the basis that a Trade Union official was deemed to be a reserved occupation. He was finally allowed to join the Royal Navy Volunteer Reserve as an Ordinary Seaman in 1942. While he trained for his promotion his medical examination revealed that he was suffering from tuberculosis (an infectious disease usually caused by bacteria), so he was admitted to the Royal Naval Hospital Haslar which was in Gosport, near Portsmouth. After he recovered, he was discharged and assigned to duties with the Admiralty in Whitehall. He was assigned to the Japanese section and wrote a service manual for the Royal Navy '*The Enemy: Japan*'. He then served in the East Indies Fleet on board the escort carrier HMS *Activity* and was promoted to the rank of Lieutenant in April 1944.

Whilst on leave from the Navy, Callaghan was selected as a Parliamentary candidate for Cardiff South and in 1945 he served on HMS *Queen Elizabeth* in the Indian Ocean. After VE Day, he returned to the UK to stand in the July 1945 General Election and was returned as a Labour MP with a majority of 5,944. In 1947 he was appointed Parliamentary Secretary to the Ministry of Transport and he moved to be Parliamentary and Financial Secretary to the Admiralty in 1950 where he was a delegate to the Council of Europe resisting plans for a European army. Callaghan was elected to the Shadow Cabinet every year while the Labour Party was in opposition from 1951–1964. He was Parliamentary Adviser to the Police Federation from 1955–1960 when he negotiated an increase in police pay and in November 1961, he became Shadow Chancellor. When Labour leader Hugh Gaitskell died in January 1963, Callaghan ran to succeed him, but only came third in the leadership contest behind Harold Wilson and George Brown. At the General Election in October 1964, Callaghan was returned with a majority of 10,837 and the new Prime Minister, Harold Wilson, appointed him as Chancellor of the Exchequer. The new Labour government was immediately faced with a deficit of £800 million, which contributed to a series of sterling crises. A possible solution was to devalue the pound against other currencies to make imports more expensive (which meant more inflation), but exports cheaper. On 11 November 1964, when Callaghan gave his first budget he announced increases in income tax, petrol tax and the introduction of a new capital gains tax. The budget also contained social measures to increase the state pension and the widow's pension. By the summer of 1966, the pressure on sterling was acute but Wilson and Callaghan were still determined to resist devaluation. On 12 July 1966 the Cabinet rejected the devaluation option and agreed to a tough package of deflation and austerity instead. However, due to several factors including international crises and dock strikes, by November 1967 the financial pressures had become overwhelming. On 16 November Callaghan, with Wilson's backing, recommended to the Cabinet that sterling should be devalued by just under 15 per cent. This was agreed and then implemented, at 14 per cent on 18 November. A package of measures including defence cuts, restrictions on hire purchase (credit) and higher interest rates was also agreed. Callaghan immediately resigned as Chancellor and became the new Home Secretary on 30 November 1967.

In 1968 Callaghan presented to Parliament the Race Relations Act making it illegal to refuse employment, housing or education on the basis of ethnic background. The Act extended the powers of the Race Relations Board at the time, to deal with complaints of discrimination and unfair attitudes. On 12 August 1969, the Battle of the Bogside erupted in Derry, Northern Ireland, resulting in three days of fierce clashes in the Bogside district between the RUC and thousands of Catholic/nationalist residents. On 14 August 1969, Callaghan as Home Secretary was responsible for sending troops to Northern Ireland after a request from the Ulster Unionist Government. After Edward Heath failed to get a majority at the 'who rules' General Election in 1974, Harold Wilson and the Labour Party were returned to power and Callaghan was appointed Foreign Secretary. In this post he had responsibility for renegotiating Britain's terms of membership of the European Economic Community (ECC). When Harold

Wilson resigned in 1976, Callaghan defeated Michael Foot for the leadership of the Labour Party by 176 votes to 137 (a 39 vote majority) and consequently became the Prime Minister. Callaghan's government lost its majority of seats in Parliament on his first day in office, forcing him to rely upon the support of the Liberal Party through 1977 to 1978 and then the Scottish National Party for the remainder of the government. It is for this reason that the 1979 referendum on the devolution of powers to Scotland was produced, which was narrowly defeated by the Scottish voters. In 1977 Callaghan, and his Chancellor of the Exchequer, Denis Healey, controversially began imposing tight monetary controls. This included deep cuts in public spending on education and health. His time as Prime Minister also saw the introduction of the Police Act of 1976, which formalised Police complaints procedures, the Housing (Homeless Persons) Act of 1977, which established the responsibility of local authorities to provide housing to homeless people and the Education Act of 1976, which limited the number of independent and grant-maintained schools in any one area.

With Britain's economy performing badly, wage restrictions for public sector workers caused a wave of strikes across the winter of 1978 to 1979, which become known as the 'Winter of Discontent' and saw Labour's performance in the opinion polls slump dramatically. On 28 March 1979, the House of Commons passed a motion of no-confidence brought about by Conservative leader Margaret Thatcher by one vote, 311–310, which forced Callaghan to call a General Election that was held on 3 May 1979. The Conservatives ran a campaign on the slogan 'Labour Isn't Working' and saw a 5.2% swing from Labour to the Conservatives (the largest swing since the 1945 election), which resulted in a parliamentary majority for the Conservatives of 43 seats. Callaghan continued as Labour leader until 15 October 1980 when he resigned and in 1983 he became Father of the House as the longest continually-serving member of the Commons.

In 1987, he was made a Knight of the Garter and stood down at the 1987 General Election after 42 years as an MP. Shortly afterwards, he was elevated to the House of Lords on 5 November 1987 as a life peer with the title Baron Callaghan of Cardiff.

Callaghan died on 26 March 2005 at Ringmer, East Sussex one day before his 93 birthday. He died as the longest-lived former UK Prime Minister, having beaten Harold Macmillan's record 39 days earlier. He died just 11 days after his wife (Audrey) of 67 years and was survived by his son and two daughters.

Interesting James Callaghan facts:

Callaghan is the only Parliamentarian to have the honour of holding the offices of Chancellor of the Exchequer, Home Secretary, Foreign Secretary and Prime Minister.

On 5 April 1976, at the age of 64 years and 9 days, Callaghan became Prime Minister—the oldest Prime Minister at time of appointment since Winston Churchill.

Callaghan would become the last British Prime Minister to be an armed forces veteran and the only one ever to have served in the Royal Navy.

Callaghan published his autobiography 'Time and Chance' in 1987.

Callaghan played rugby union before the Second World War for Streatham RFC in the position of lock.

Callaghan's daughter, Margaret Jay, Baroness Jay of Paddington was a Labour MP and Leader of the House of Lords.

Baroness Margaret Thatcher
49th British Prime Minister

Born
13 October 1925, Grantham, Lincolnshire
Died
8 April 2013, age 87, London
Period in office as Prime Minister
11 years 209 days from 4 May 1979 until 28 November 1990
Political party
Conservative
Constituencies Represented as MP
Finchley 1959-1992
Ministerial offices held as Prime Minister
First Lord of the Treasury
Minister for the Civil Service

Margaret Hilda Thatcher, Baroness Thatcher, (née **Roberts**, 13 October 1925 – 8 April 2013) was a British stateswoman who served as Prime Minister from 1979 to 1990 and Leader of the Conservative Party from 1975 to 1990. She was the longest-serving British prime minister of the 20th century and the first woman to hold that office.

Thatcher (until marriage known as Margaret Roberts) spent her childhood in Grantham where her father (Alfred), and mother (Beatrice), owned a tobacconist's and a grocery shop. She attended Huntingtower Road Primary School and won a scholarship to Kesteven and Grantham Girls' School, a grammar school where she was head girl in 1942–43.
She was accepted for a scholarship to study chemistry at a women's college - Somerville College, Oxford. She arrived at Oxford in 1943 and graduated in 1947 with Second-Class Honours specialising in X-ray crystallography, in the four-year Chemistry Bachelor of Science degree.

After graduating, Thatcher moved to Colchester in Essex to work as a research chemist for a plastics company. She joined the local Dartford Conservative Association and in January 1950 (aged 24) she was selected as their prospective parliamentary candidate. She stood in the 1950 and 1951 General Elections but lost out on both occasions in what was considered a safe Labour seat. She did though gain national publicity as the youngest woman candidate in the country. In December 1951 she married her husband, Denis, and she qualified as a barrister in 1953 specialising in taxation. In August 1953 Denis and Margaret had twins (Carol and Mark) who were six weeks premature.
In 1954 Thatcher was defeated when she sought selection to be the Conservative party candidate for the Orpington by-election, and didn't stand in the May 1955 General Election as she considered her two children were too young to leave at two year old.

As her children got older Thatcher began looking for a safe Conservative seat and was selected as the candidate for Finchley in April 1958. She was elected to Parliament at the October 1959 General Election with a majority of 16,260 and into a Conservative government led by Harold Macmillan. In October 1961 she was promoted to the frontbench as parliamentary undersecretary at the Ministry of Pensions and National Insurance (1961–64) by Macmillan. After the Conservatives lost the 1964 election (Thatcher was returned as MP for Finchley with an 8,802 majority) she became spokeswoman on Housing and Land, in which position she advocated her party's policy of giving tenants the 'Right to Buy' their council houses.

She moved to the Shadow Treasury team in 1966 and, as Treasury spokeswoman, opposed Labour's mandatory price and income controls, arguing they would unintentionally produce effects that would distort the economy. Edward Heath appointed Thatcher as the Fuel and Power spokeswoman, and prior to the 1970 General Election, she was promoted to Shadow Transport spokeswoman and later to Education (1969–70). When the Conservatives returned to office in 1970, under the premiership of Heath, she achieved cabinet rank as Secretary of State for Education and Science (1970–74). In August 1970, she had to respond to a Treasury demand for education cuts in four areas: further education fees, library book borrowing charges, school meal charges and free school milk. Due to the latter, it resulted with the British press famously dubbing the future Prime Minister "Thatcher, Thatcher, milk snatcher". This came about with her sponsoring legislation to eliminate the free milk program for students over the age of seven. The decision provoked a storm of protest from Labour and the press but the row just hardened her determination, stating that she had learned a valuable lesson from the experience. The Conservatives lost the February 1974 General Election when Labour formed a minority government and then went on to win a narrow majority in the October 1974 General Election. The defeats for the Conservatives put Heath's leadership of the Conservative Party increasingly in doubt, and although Thatcher wasn't initially seen as the obvious replacement, on 4 February 1975 she defeated Heath by 130 votes to 119 in the first leadership ballot. Heath subsequently resigned as Conservative leader. In the second ballot on 11 February 1975, Thatcher beat William Whitelaw by 146 votes to 79 to become the new Conservative Leader. She appointed Whitelaw as her deputy but there was never any future harmony with Heath. In 1976, Thatcher gave her 'Britain Awake' foreign policy speech after which is was reported in the Russian Red Star (the official newspaper of the Soviet and later Russian Ministry of Defence) in which she was described as 'The Iron Lady', a title that followed her throughout her political career. In the mid to late 1970's England was in a time of economic and political turmoil, with the government nearly bankrupt, employment on the rise and conflicts with the unions leading to the 'Winter of Discontent'. On 28 March 1979 Thatcher brought about a motion of no confidence in James Callaghan's ministry and the Labour government lost by one vote (311 to 310). At the following General Election in May 1979, the Conservatives under Thatcher, came to power with a parliamentary majority of 43 seats (Conservatives 339 seats, Labour 269 and Liberals 11 seats). Thatcher had made history as she was appointed Britain's first female Prime Minister. Thatcher's new government pledged to check and reverse Britain's economic decline and she knew that in the short-term, painful measures were required. In her speech to the Conservative Party Conference on 10 October 1980 she used the phrase "you turn if you want to, the lady's not for turning" in response to opposition to her liberalisation of the economy. The phrase was considered a defining speech in Thatcher's political development and received a 5 minute standing ovation. The economy was already entering a recession so indirect taxes were increased (direct taxes were cut), interest rates were raised to deal with rising inflation and expenditure reduced on social services such as education and housing. By the end of Thatcher's first term, unemployment in Britain was more than three million and didn't begin to fall until near the end of her second term in 1986. Thatcher's actions led to vital long-term gains being made, inflation was checked and the government created the expectation that it would do whatever was necessary to keep it low. In the budget of spring 1981, increasing taxes at the lowest point of the recession, made it possible to cut interest rates and economic recovery started in the same quarter followed by eight years of growth.

On 2 April 1982, after many years of sovereignty dispute between Argentina and Britain, Argentina invaded and occupied the Falkland Islands. Following the invasion Thatcher had an emergency meeting with the cabinet and approval was given to form a task force to retake the islands. This was backed in an emergency session of the House of Commons the next day. On 5 April 1982 Thatcher's government dispatched a naval task force to engage the Argentine Navy and Air Force before making an amphibious assault on the islands. The conflict lasted 74 days and ended with an Argentine surrender on 14 June 1982, which returned the islands to British control. In total, 649 Argentine military personnel, 255 British military personnel, and three Falkland Islanders died during the hostilities. In the early 1980's Thatcher's approval rating had fallen to 23%, lower than recorded for any previous Prime Minister, but after her handling of the Falklands war the electorate was impressed. At the General Election in June 1983, Thatcher's government was re-elected with a landslide victory and it's Parliamentary majority more than trebled to 144 seats (the biggest victory since Labour's success in 1945). In Thatcher's second term as Prime Minister she was committed to reducing the power of the unions, and in response to legislation introduced to limit their power several unions launched strikes. In March 1984, the National Coal Board (NCB) proposed to close 20 of the 174 state-owned mines and cut

20,000 jobs out of 187,000. Two-thirds of the country's miners, led by the National Union of Mineworkers (NUM) under Arthur Scargill, downed tools in protest. However the strike was declared illegal by the High Court of Justice when Scargill refused to hold a ballot on the strike. Thatcher refused to meet the union's demands and after a year out on strike, in March 1985 the NUM leadership conceded without a deal. The cost to the economy was estimated to be at least £1.5 billion, and the strike was blamed for much of the pound's fall against the US dollar. Thatcher's privatisation policies raised more than £29 billion from the sale of nationalised industries, and another £18 billion from the sale of council houses.

On the 12 October 1984 Margaret Thatcher along with her cabinet were staying in the Grand Brighton Hotel in Brighton for the Conservative Party conference. At approximately 2:54 am a long-delay time-bomb which had been planted by the Irish Republican Army (IRA) exploded. The blast brought down a five-ton chimney stack, which crashed down through the floors into the basement. The bomb killed five people, and several more were permanently disabled, along with another thirty-four people who were taken to hospital later recovering from their injuries. The blast badly damaged Thatcher's bathroom but she and her husband, Denis, escaped injury. Thatcher insisted that the Conservative conference would go on as usual the next day. At the conference she declared in her speech, that although shocked, the fact that the conference went ahead was a sign that not only had the attack failed, but that all attempts to destroy democracy by terrorism would fail.

At the June 1987 General Election Thatcher ran a campaign focusing on lower taxes, a strong economy, strong defence and that inflation was standing at 4%, its lowest level for some twenty years. The Conservatives were returned to government, having suffered a net loss of only 21 seats, leaving them with 376 MPs and a second landslide majority of 102. Thatcher became the first Prime Minister since the Earl of Liverpool in 1820 to lead a party into three consecutive electoral victories. The implementation of a Community Charge (known as the Poll Tax) which was introduced in Scotland in 1989 and in England and Wales the following year. This proved to be among the most unpopular policies of Thatcher's premiership. The new tax produced outbreaks of street violence and a demonstration in March 1990 around Trafalgar Square in London deteriorated into riots. The reaction to the tax alarmed the Conservative rank-and-file, who feared that Thatcher could not lead the party to a fourth consecutive term. On 1 November 1990, Geoffrey Howe, by then the last remaining member of Thatcher's original 1979 cabinet, resigned from his position as Deputy Prime Minister, mainly over Thatcher's open hostility to moves towards European Monetary Union. In Howe's resignation speech he used a cricket metaphor by stating the position for European negotiations was 'like sending your opening batsmen to the crease only for them to find, the moment the first balls are bowled, that their bats have been broken before the game by the team captain'. Howe's resignation speech led to a challenge on Thatcher's leadership of the Conservative Party on 14 November 1990 by Michael Heseltine. Thatcher won the first ballot, with votes of 204 Conservative MPs (54.8%) to 152 votes (40.9%) for Heseltine and 16 abstentions, but her total fell four votes short of the necessary majority plus 15 percent. Thatcher initially declared to fight on and win in the second ballot, but when many colleagues in her cabinet deserted her leadership she felt she had no choice but to withdraw.

After never losing a General Election as leader, and 11 years 209 days as Prime Minister, she resigned on November 28 1990 and returned to the backbenches as a constituency parliamentarian. At the 1992 General Election, aged 66, she retired from the House of Commons and was given a life peerage as Baroness Thatcher (of Kesteven in the County of Lincolnshire) which entitled her to sit in the House of Lords.

After retiring from the Commons, Lady Thatcher (as she became known) remained a potent political figure. And for the next decade she toured the world as a lecturer. In March 2002, following several small strokes, she announced an end to her career in public speaking. Denis Thatcher, her husband of more than fifty years, died in June 2003. After his death her own health deteriorated further and faster, causing progressive memory loss, and she died aged 87 at the Ritz hotel in London on 8 April 2013. She was honoured at a ceremonial funeral in St Paul's Cathedral nine days later. More than 2,000 guests from around the world paid their last respects and thousands of members of the public and the armed forces lined the funeral procession route through London. In total, two current heads of state, 11 serving prime ministers and 17 serving foreign ministers from around the world attended.

Interesting Margaret Thatcher facts:

She wrote two best-selling volumes of memoirs - *The Downing Street Years* (1993) and *The Path to Power* (1995) and also a book of reflections on international politics - *Statecraft* - which was published in 2002.

She became the first woman ever to lead a Western political party and to serve as Leader of the Opposition in the House of Commons.

The term 'Thatcherism' became a well-known phrase to represents a belief in free markets and a small state.

She was the longest-serving British Prime Minister of the 20th century and the first woman to hold that office.

John Major
50th British Prime Minister

Born
29 March 1943, St Helier, Carshalton, Surrey
Period in office as Prime Minister
6 years 156 days from 28 November 1990 until 2 May 1997
Political party
Conservative
Constituency Represented as MP
Huntingdon, Cambridgeshire, 1979 to 2001
Ministerial offices held as Prime Minister
First Lord of the Treasury
Minister for the Civil Service

Sir John Major (born 29 March 1943) served as Prime
Minister and Leader of the Conservative Party from 1990 to 1997.

*John Major was born on 29 March 1943 at St Helier Hospital and
Queen Mary's Hospital for Children in St Helier, Surrey, the son of
former music hall performer Tom Major-Ball and Gwen Major (née
Coates). He began attending primary school at Cheam Common
School from 1948, and in 1954 he passed the 11+ exam which
enabled him to go to Rutlish Grammar School, in Wimbledon. He
left school on the eve of his sixteenth birthday in 1959 with three
O-levels and joined the Brixton Young Conservatives.*

After leaving school Major had a variety of jobs including working
as a clerk in insurance and working in the garden ornaments
business. In 1962 after caring for his ill mother, he was
unemployed for a short while, a situation which he described as
'degrading'. He found work in December 1962 working at the
London Electricity Board, and at the age of 21, Major stood as a
Conservative Councillor in the Larkhall ward at the Lambeth
London Borough Council election in May 1964, losing out to
Labour. In 1965, he moved jobs and went into banking, and
through his work he was sent for a long secondment in Jos,
Nigeria in December 1966 where he cultivated his hatred for
racism. While in Nigeria in 1967 he was involved in a serious car
accident, damaging his leg leading to him being flown home. After
finally recovering Major stood again as Councillor in the May 1968
Lambeth London Borough Council election, this time for the
Ferndale ward. Although a Labour stronghold Major took the third
seat available winning by 70 votes (991 to 921) and after being
elected he took a big interest in housing matters. In February
1970 Major became Chairman of the Lambeth Housing Committee
but at the 1971 Lambeth London Borough Council election, he
lost his seat as Labour took all three seats back from the
Conservatives. Major, undeterred, still had political ambitions and
was selected as the Conservative candidate for the Labour

dominated St Pancras North constituency, where he fought in both the February and October 1974 General Elections but losing both times to Labour. Major was still determined for a career in politics and applied for selection to the safe Conservative seat of Huntingdonshire in December 1976. He won selection and started working part-time in 1978 so that he could devote more time to his constituency duties. At the May 1979 General Election, Major was returned as MP for Huntingdonshire with a large 21,563 majority. He became Secretary of the Environment Committee and also assisted with work on the Housing Act 1980, which allowed council house tenants the 'Right to Buy' their homes. In 1981, Major was appointed as a Parliamentary Private Secretary and then a junior whip in 1983. After boundary changes, Major was returned in the June 1983 General Election for the Huntingdon ward with a majority of 20,348. He was promoted to Treasury Whip in October 1984 and also in the same month he narrowly avoided the IRA's Brighton hotel bombing, having left the hotel only a few hours before the bomb went off. In September 1985 he was made Parliamentary Under-Secretary of State for the Department of Health and Social Security, before being promoted to become Minister of State in the same department in September 1986. At the June 1987 General Election Major was again returned for Huntingdon with an increased majority of 27,044 and on 13 June he was promoted by Margaret Thatcher to the Cabinet as Chief Secretary to the Treasury, gaining respect due to his ability to keep spending down. In a surprise re-shuffle on 24 July 1989, Major was appointed Foreign Secretary, succeeding Geoffrey Howe, a position he only spent three months in as he was appointed Chancellor of the Exchequer after Nigel Lawson's resignation in October 1989. Major presented only one budget (the first budget ever to be televised live) on 20 March 1990. He announced it as 'a budget for savings' and announced the Tax-Exempt Special Savings Account (TESSA) and increased taxes on alcohol, cigarettes and petrol.

In 1990, with opposition in the Conservative Party growing against Margaret Thatcher and two by-election defeats, there were doubts about a Conservative victory in an upcoming election. With a forced leadership election, Margaret Thatcher resigned as Conservative Leader and Prime Minister after the first leadership ballot and stood behind Major in the second ballot. On 27 November 1990, the second ballot was held with 187 votes being the winning target. Major fell two votes short with 185 votes of the required total, but he polled far enough ahead of both Douglas Hurd and Michael Heseltine to secure their immediate withdrawal. With no remaining challengers, Major was formally named Leader of the Conservative Party that evening and was duly appointed Prime Minister the following day. His new Cabinet was substantially different from Thatcher's and served to demonstrate that Major was looking for moderation on Europe and the desire to build a 'classless society'. One of Major's first policy decisions was to abolish the notorious Community Charge or Poll Tax and replace it with a Council Tax paid for partly by a rise in VAT. In 1992, the Conservatives were widely expected to lose the General Election to Neil Kinnock's Labour Party so Major decided to take his campaign onto the streets, famously delivering many addresses from an upturned soapbox as in his Lambeth days. This "common touch" approach stood in contrast to the Labour Party's seemingly slicker campaign and it seemed to resonate with the electorate, along with a hard-hitting negative advertising campaign focusing on the issue of Labour's approach to taxation. Major won a second period in office at the April 1992 General Election, albeit with a smaller parliamentary majority of just 21 seats (down from a majority of 102 seats at the previous election) but the Conservatives won over 14 million votes, which was the highest popular vote ever recorded. After the General Election, Major's premiership was hit with a recession, with inflation hitting 10.9% and unemployment rising to three million. With the UK's commitment to the European Exchange Rate Mechanism (ERM) constraining its ability to cut interest rates and thereby stimulate the economy, the UK was forced to withdraw from the ERM in September 1992. On 16 September 1992, a day which would come to be known as 'Black Wednesday', billions of pounds was wasted in a futile attempt to defend the value of sterling. The upheaval caused by the day's events was such that Major came close to resigning as Prime Minister. The UK was ultimately forced out of the ERM because it could not prevent the value of the pound from falling below the lower limit specified by the ERM. The disaster of Black Wednesday left the Government's economic credibility damaged and after seven months had passed it led to Major sacking Norman Lamont as Chancellor of the Exchequer and replacing him with Kenneth Clarke. At the 1993 Conservative Party Conference, Major began the "Back to Basics" campaign, which he intended to be about the economy, education and policing, but a series of sexual and financial scandals (given the catch-all term 'sleaze') hijacked the campaign and hit the Conservative party over the subsequent years. In 1994, Major's government set up the National Lottery, which up until then, all forms of gambling and lotteries in the UK had been severely restricted, however European legislation meant that lotteries from other EU countries would be able to operate in the UK. So Major's government set up a British lottery with the money being raised going to good causes within the country. On 22 June 1995, tired of the continual threats of leadership challenges, Major resigned as Leader of the Conservative Party and announced that he would contest the resulting leadership election, telling his opponents that "it is time to put up or shut up", and he continued to serve as Prime Minister whilst the leadership was vacant. John Redwood resigned as Secretary of State for Wales to stand against him, and on 14 July 1995, a vote was held, with Major winning by 218 votes to Redwood's 89, with 12 spoiled ballots and ten abstaining. This was easily enough to win and no further challenges were forthcoming. In March 1996 Major had to deal with a serious public health scare following a scientific announcement of a possible link between bovine spongiform encephalopathy (BSE, colloquially referred to as 'mad cow disease') and a form of Creutzfeldt–Jakob disease (vCJD), a serious and potentially fatal brain disease in humans. A huge cattle slaughter programme was introduced in a bid to restore faith in Britain's beef industry. In May 1996, with an EU ban in place on British beef, Major decided to withhold British cooperation on all EU-related matters until the beef situation had been resolved (the ban on British beef was not lifted until August 1999). The economy had picked up after leaving the Exchange Rate Mechanism, and, under Major, the beginning of Britain's longest period of continuous economic growth began. He also began work on engaging with the IRA to move towards a peaceful end to the conflict in Northern Ireland, his work leading the way for the Good Friday Agreement in 1998. In 1997 Major knew he would have to call a General Election by May, even though Labour were ahead in the polls and so on 17 March he announced that the election would be held on 1 May 1997. At the Election Labour under Tony Blair won by a landslide, winning 418 seats to the Conservatives 165 with the Liberal Democrats increasing their seats to 46. The Conservative Party suffered the worst electoral defeat by a ruling party since the Reform Act of 1832. Major himself was re-elected in his own constituency of Huntingdon with a reduced majority of 18,140, but the election defeat left the Conservatives without any MPs in Scotland or Wales for the first time in history. Major stood down but served as Leader of the Opposition for a further seven weeks while the leadership election to replace him was underway. His resignation as Conservative Leader formally took effect on 19 June 1997 with the election of William Hague. Major still remained active in Parliament in the following years, regularly attending and contributing in debates until he eventually stood down from the House of Commons after 22 years as an MP at the June 2001 General Election. After leaving Parliament Major actively engaged in charity work, being President of Asthma UK and a Patron of the Prostate Cancer Charity, Sightsavers UK, Mercy Ships, Support for Africa 2000 and Afghan Heroes. In the 1999 New Year Honours List, Major was made a Companion of Honour for his work on the Northern Ireland peace process, and on 23 April 2005, he was bestowed with a knighthood as a Companion of the Order of the Garter by Queen Elizabeth II.

Interesting John Major facts:

Major became the first British Prime Minister to subject himself to a leadership election while in office which he won on July 4, 1995.

Following the death of Diana, Princess of Wales in 1997, Major was appointed a special guardian to Prince William and Prince Harry with responsibility for legal and administrative matters.

Major is a long time cricket enthusiast and in 2005 he was elected to the Committee of the Marylebone Cricket Club (MCC).

Major was The youngest British Prime Minister of the 20th century At 47 he was the youngest Prime Minister since Lord Rosebery some 95 years earlier.

In 1999 he published his autobiography, covering his early life and time in office. He also wrote a book about the history of cricket in 2007 - *More Than a Game: The Story of Cricket's Early Years* and a book about Music Hall (*My Old Man: A Personal History of Music Hall*) in 2012.

In 2013 the town of Candeleda in Spain named a street (*Avenida de John Major*), after him, as he has holidayed there since 1989.

On 20 June 2008, Major was granted the Freedom of the City of Cork and he was also granted the Outstanding Contribution to Ireland award in Dublin on 4 December 2014.

Tony Blair
51st British Prime Minister

Born
6 May 1953, Edinburgh, Scotland
Period in office as Prime Minister
10 years 57 days from 2 May 1997 until 27 June 2007
Political party
Labour
Constituency Represented as MP
Sedgefield, County Durham, 1983 to 2007
Ministerial offices held as Prime Minister
First Lord of the Treasury
Minister for the Civil Service

Anthony Charles Lynton Blair (born 6 May 1953) is a British politician who served as Prime Minister from 1997 to 2007 and Leader of the Labour Party from 1994 to 2007.

Blair was born Anthony Charles Lynton Blair on May 6, 1953, in Edinburgh, Scotland, and was the second son of Leo and Hazel (née Corscadden) Blair. The Blair family moved to Adelaide, South Australia at the end of 1954 where his father lectured in law at the University of Adelaide. While in Australia Blair's sister Sarah was born. The Blair's lived in the suburb of Dulwich close to the university until the family returned to the United Kingdom in the summer of 1958. Leo, who was a successful barrister, suffered a crippling stroke in 1963 and was nursed by Hazel. His political ambitions to become a Conservative MP were dashed. Despite being born in Scotland, Blair spent the better part of his childhood in Durham, where he attended the Chorister School from 1961 to 1966. From 1966 to 1971 he attended Fettes College in Edinburgh and in 1972, at the age of nineteen, Blair enrolled for university at St John's College, Oxford, reading Jurisprudence (legal theory) for three years.

After graduating from Oxford in 1975 with a second-class Honours degree, Blair began an internship in employment law where he met fellow intern and future wife Cherie Booth, who had graduated at the top of her class from the London School of Economics. The couple married in March 1980 and went on to have four children: Euan, Nicholas, Kathryn and Leo. Blair joined the Labour Party shortly after graduating from Oxford in 1975 and to gain political experience Blair stood as the Labour candidate on 27 May 1982 in the Beaconsfield by-election. He was beaten into third place with the Conservatives winning comfortably (23,049 votes) and the Liberals finishing second (9,996 votes), Blair lost his deposit with just 3,886 votes. Despite Labour's poor showing Blair was still regarded as having fought a good campaign, and he was selected as Labour candidate for the

newly created safe seat of Sedgefield in County Durham. At the
June 1983 General Election Blair was returned as the Member of
Parliament for Sedgefield with a majority 8,281. After the election
Blair's political ascent was rapid and Labour leader Neil Kinnock
proceeded to promote Blair through the ranks. From 1984 to
1988, Blair served as the front bench spokesman on economic
and treasury affairs for the Labour Party. He also held a position
as spokesman on trade and industry in 1987. In 1988, Blair rose
to the shadow cabinet (also known as shadow front bench or
shadow ministry) in the position of Shadow Secretary of Energy
and in 1992, Blair was appointed to the position of Shadow Home
Secretary. When Neil Kinnock announced his resignation as
Labour Party leader on 13 April 1992, John Smith, previously
Shadow Chancellor, was elected as the new Labour leader but he
died suddenly on 12 May 1994 of a heart attack and Labour held
a Party leadership election on 21 July 1994. Under the 'electoral
college' system that had been introduced, which meant that the
votes of members of affiliated groups (mostly trades unions), the
members of constituency parties, and Labour MPs were all
weighted equally with 33.3% each. Blair topped all three polls
with an overall 57%, beating John Prescott (24.1%) into second
place and Margaret Beckett (18.9%) into third. In an attempt to
modernise the Labour Party, Blair announced at the end of his
speech at the 1994 Labour Party conference that he intended to
replace Clause IV (the common ownership of the means of
production and exchange) of the party's constitution with a new
statement of aims and values. At a special conference in April
1995, the clause was replaced by a statement that the party is
'democratic socialist'. Although there were signs of an economic
recovery and fall in unemployment under John Major's
Conservative government, Blair's election as leader saw a surge
in Labour support and at the 1996 Labour Party conference, Blair
famously said 'ask me my three main priorities for government
and I tell you: education, education and education'. From the
mid-nineties Labour had rebranded itself as New Labour and

published a manifesto in 1996 under the title 'New Labour, New Life for Britain'. This led into the 1997 General Election which produced the biggest Labour majority in the history of the party's existence. They won 418 seats, with a majority of 179. The main aims of the Labour manifesto including introducing a minimum wage, (the National Minimum Wage Act 1998 set a minimum of £3.60 per hour), increasing the National Health Service (NHS) spending and reducing class sizes in schools. Blair became Prime Minister with a landslide victory which ended eighteen years of Conservative Party rule and gave the Conservative's their heaviest election defeat since 1906. Blair himself was returned with a majority of 33,526 in Sedgefield. Blair's premiership started with largest majority of any party since 1935 and one of his first major initiatives was to give Gordon Brown control of the economic agenda as Chancellor of the Exchequer and grant the Bank of England independant power to determine interest rates without government consultation. Blair also replaced the then twice-weekly 15-minute sessions of Prime Minister's Question's which were held on Tuesdays and Thursdays with a single 30-minute session on Wednesdays. The government also signed the Maastricht Treaty's Social Chapter and turned its attention to brokering a peace agreement between republicans and unionists in Northern Ireland. In May 1998 Blair led a successful referendum campaign to create a new assembly for London and to establish the city's first directly elected mayor. That year Blair also helped to negotiate the Good Friday Agreement (Belfast Agreement), which was ratified overwhelmingly in both Ireland and Northern Ireland and which created an elected devolved power-sharing assembly in Northern Ireland for the first time since 1972. Blair also eliminated all but 92 of the hereditary members of the House of Lords as the prelude to more-extensive reforms of that chamber.

Blair went into the May 2001 General Election with the opposition Conservative Party, (under William Hague's leadership), deeply divided on the issue of Europe. Under the title 'Fulfilling Britain's great potential' Blair was easily re-elected in the May 2001 General Election with a 167-seat majority in the House of Commons—the largest-ever second-term majority in British electoral history. Blair's priority for the second term was to increase the pace of public sector reform, which took shape in the Prime Minister's Delivery Unit, bills on Foundation Hospitals, Academy Schools and university tuition fees along with increasing 'choice agenda'. After the 9/11 terrorist attacks in America in 2001, Blair became one of U.S. President George W. Bush's staunchest allies in the war on terror, making the case for the overthrow of Saddam Hussein and playing a key role in forming an international coalition that succeeded in driving the Taliban from power in Afghanistan. Blair and Bush tried without success to persuade other Security Council members that continued weapons inspections would not succeed in uncovering any weapons of mass destruction that were thought to be held by the Iraqi government. This led to a coalition of military forces in an attack on Iraq in March 2003, but when military inspectors failed to uncover weapons of mass destruction, the Blair government was accused of distorting ('sexing up') intelligence on which it had based its claim that Iraq was an imminent threat. At the following inquiry (Hutton Judicial Inquiry 2003) the report exonerated the government much more than had been expected by stating: 'the dossier had not been 'sexed up', but was in line with available intelligence' but that 'the wording of the dossier had been altered to present the strongest possible case for war within the bounds of available intelligence'.

Blair's Civil Partnership Act 2004 which had support from the Conservative and Liberal Democrat's, allowed legal recognition of civil partnership relationship between two people of the same sex. Blair also raised taxes to invest more money in education and healthcare and began calling attention to issues of climate change toward the end of his second term. Despite Blair's unpopular decision to go to war in Iraq, at the May 2005 General Election he led Labour into its third consecutive election victory. Although the majority fell from 167 to 66 seats, thanks to eight years of sustained economic growth, Labour had pointed to a strong economy with greater investment in public services such as education and health.

One of the most dramatic 24 hours of Blair's premiership happened on 7 July 2005, jubilation over London winning the right to host the 2012 Olympics turned to horror as the city suffered multiple suicide attacks on its transport system. Three explosions occurred on the Underground and one on a bus, killing 52 people. In a statement, Mr Blair said: "It is a very sad day for the British people but we will hold true to the British way of life". Blair suffered his first defeat as Prime Minister in the House of Commons in November 2005, when 49 Labour members of Parliament joined the opposition in voting against anti-terrorist laws that would have extended the length of time suspects could be held without charge.

In 2006, Blair under pressure from his backbenchers elected for a free vote on a UK smoking ban. As a consequence of the Health Act 2006 the smoking ban in England came into effect on 1 July 2007, which made it illegal to smoke in any pub, restaurant, nightclub, most workplaces and work vehicles anywhere in the UK.

Gradually with his popularity diminishing, Blair declared in September 2006 that he would stand down as Prime Minister within a year. On May 10, 2007—one week after Labour was defeated by the Scottish National Party in elections to the Scottish Parliament, and after suffering major defeats in English local elections, Blair formally handed over the leadership of the Labour Party to Gordon Brown at a special party conference in Manchester on 24 June 2007. Blair tendered his resignation on

27 June 2007 and Brown assumed office during the same afternoon. At the end of his last Prime Minister's questions in the House of Commons, Blair said *"Some may belittle politics but we know it is where people stand tall. And although I know it has its many harsh contentions, it is still the arena which sets the heart beating fast. It may sometimes be a place of low skulduggery but it is more often a place for more noble causes. I wish everyone, friend or foe, well and that is that, the end."*

All sides of the House gave him a rousing standing ovation.

Nonetheless, after 10 years in office as Prime Minister but still only in his early 50s, Blair was not ready to retire from the world scene. After originally indicated that he would retain his parliamentary seat, he resigned from the Commons by taking up the post of Middle East envoy for the United Nations, European Union, United States, and Russia.

In November 2007 Blair launched the Tony Blair Sports Foundation, which aimed to 'increase childhood participation in sports activities, especially in the North East of England, where a larger proportion of children are socially excluded, and to promote overall health and prevent childhood obesity'. The foundation ran for ten years training and placing 6,132 coaches with sports clubs across the north-east.

In May 2008 the Tony Blair Faith Foundation was established which is an interfaith charitable foundation. Since December 2016 the charitable work has been continued by the Tony Blair Institute for Global Change with its aim that 'by shaping the debate and offering expert advice, we aim to help political leaders build open, inclusive and prosperous societies in an increasingly interconnected world'. The idea is that 'idealism becomes the new realism', and that one of its goals is to 'counter extremism in all six leading religions: Buddhism, Christianity, Islam, Hinduism, Judaism, Buddhism and Sikhism.

Interesting Tony Blair facts:

On 16 August 2010 it was announced that Blair would give the £4.6 million advance and all royalties from his memoirs *'A Journey'* to the Royal British Legion – the charity's largest ever single donation. The book was published on 1 September 2010 and within hours of its launch had become the fastest-selling autobiography of all time

Blair didn't issue a list of Resignation Honours, making him the first Prime Minister of the modern era not to do so.

Blair made an animated cameo appearance as himself in *The Simpsons* episode, "The Regina Monologues" (2003).

Blair at 43, became the youngest person to become Prime Minister since Lord Liverpool who was Prime Minister in 1812 aged 42.

With victories in 1997, 2001, and 2005, Blair was the Labour Party's longest-serving Prime Minister and the first and only person to date to lead the party to three consecutive General Election victories.

Blair is a fan of Newcastle United football club.

While studying law at St John's College, Oxford during the early 1970s, Blair sang and played guitar in a band called the Ugly rumours.

Michael Sheen has portrayed Blair three times, in the films The Deal (2003), The Queen (2006) and The Special Relationship (2009). `

On 13 January 2009, Blair was awarded the Presidential Medal of Freedom by American President George W. Bush.

Gordon Brown
52nd British Prime Minister

Born
20 February 1951, Giffnock, Renfrewshire, Scotland
Period in office as Prime Minister
2 years 319 days from 27 June 2007 until 11 May 2010
Political party
Labour
Constituency Represented as MP
Dunfermline East 9 June 1983 – 11 April 2005 Kirkcaldy and Cowdenbeath 5 May 2005 – 30 March 2015
Ministerial offices held as Prime Minister
First Lord of the Treasury
Minister for the Civil Service

James Gordon Brown (born 20 February 1951) is a British politician who was Prime Minister and Leader of the Labour Party from 2007 to 2010. He served as Chancellor of the Exchequer from 1997 to 2007.

Brown was the son of Elizabeth Brown and John Brown, who was a Labour Party supporter and Church of Scotland minister. Born in Giffnock, Renfrewshire, Scotland, the Brown's moved to Kilkady when Gordon was three. The family of five (elder brother John and younger brother Andrew) lived in a manse (clergy house). Brown was educated first at Kirkcaldy West Primary School and then Kirkcaldy High School. At age 16 he won a scholarship to the University of Edinburgh (he was the youngest student to enter the university since World War II), where he immersed himself in student politics, eventually becoming chair of the university's Labour club. While competing in an end-of-term rugby union match, he received a kick to the head and suffered a retinal detachment leaving him blind in his left eye. Brown graduated from Edinburgh with a First-Class Honours MA degree in history and became the youngest ever Rector of Edinburgh University in 1972. *He then stayed on to obtain his PhD in history. From 1976 to 1980 Brown was employed as a lecturer in politics at Glasgow College of Technology He also worked as a tutor for the Open University.*

At the May 1979 General Election Brown stood as the Labour candidate in Edinburgh South, and although gaining 15,526 votes he lost out to the Conservative candidate Michael Ancram (17,986) to a majority of 2,460. Brown was appointed in Scottish TV as a journalist and editor in the current affairs department. (1980–83), and in 1982 he completed a doctorate in history at Edinburgh, his dissertation was titled The Labour Party and Political Change in Scotland, 1918–29.

In his second attempt to be elected to Parliament, Brown was successful as he stood in Dunfermline East as the Labour

candidate defeating the Liberals into second place with a majority
of 11,301 (18,515 votes to 7,214). In Parliament he soon became
friends with another new MP, Tony Blair, and the two of them
soon found themselves at the forefront of the campaign to
modernise Labour's political philosophy, replacing the goal of
state socialism with a more pragmatic, market-friendly
strategy. After Labour lost the June 1987 General Election (where
Brown increased his own majority to 19,589) Brown served in
Labour's shadow cabinet, first as Shadow Chief Secretary to the
Treasury (1987 to 1989) and then as Shadow Trade and Industry
Secretary. After the April 1992 General Election (in which Brown
was returned with a 17,444 majority), but was Labour's fourth
successive electoral defeat, Brown was named Shadow Chancellor
of the Exchequer by John Smith, the then Labour Party leader.
When Smith died in May 1994, Brown didn't contest the
leadership, deciding to make way for Blair in what became known
as the 'Granita pact' (Granita being a North London restaurant),
where it was rumoured that the pair forged an agreement for
Brown to not run for the Labour leadership, in exchange, Blair is
claimed to have vowed to hand over the reins of power to Brown
in his second term as Prime Minister. Brown did eventually
succeed Blair as Prime Minister, but not until mid-way through
Blair's third term in 2007.

Blair won the Labour leadership election in 1994 and after the
landslide General Election victory in May 1997, Brown took the
office of Chancellor of the Exchequer. As Chancellor he became a
formidable force, and his Spending Review in 2000 outlined a
major expansion of government spending, particularly on health
and education, tackling child poverty and getting a better deal for
pensioners. He gave the Bank of England its operational
independence, and blocked any desire to take Britain into
the euro while introducing the minimum wage. When he imposed
a windfall profits levy on the privatised utilities and later raised
national insurance contributions to bring in extra money for the

NHS, and in doing so, he showed that progressive governments were able to make tax rises that weren't unpopular. At the age of 49 Brown married Sarah Macaulay in a private ceremony at his home in North Queensferry, Fife, on 3 August 2000.

Talks of Britain adopting the Euro led to Brown bringing in the 'five economic tests' the criteria of which had to be met before entry into a monetary union was considered. After regular reviews Brown stated that the decision not to join had been right for Britain and for Europe. Brown had a strong interest in international economics, serving as the United Kingdom's governor of the International Monetary Fund and as chair of the organisation's primary decision-making committee and was instrumental in brokering a European agreement in 2005 that would double foreign aid to developing countries. At the May 2005 General Election Labour won its third consecutive election victory, although the majority fell from 167 to 66 seats, Brown was returned in the Kirkcaldy and Cowdenbeath seat with a majority of 18,216 beating the SNP into second place. After the Iraq war and a poor showing for Labour at local elections, pressure was building on Tony Blair as Prime Minister and on 7 September 2006 Blair stated that he would step down within a year. Brown subsequently pledged his support for Blair, and Blair in turn later backed Brown to succeed him as Labour Party leader and Prime Minister. Brown faced no opposition in the campaign to succeed Blair as Labour Party leader, and on June 27, 2007, three days after he officially became Labour Party leader, Brown became Prime Minister. He pledged to make reform of the National Health Service a major priority, to retain the various public-sector reforms that had been implemented by Blair, and to "wage an unremitting battle against poverty." Brown as Prime Minister was severely tested when in early October 2008, the world's financial system was on the brink of systemic collapse. Despite the announcement of a multi-million pound bail-out, major British banks were about to go bust. Wall Street suffered the worst week in its history. Stocks on the Dow lost 18% of their value in five days, London and Frankfurt were down 21% on the week. Japan's Nikkei index crashed 24%, 10 October 2008 became known as 'Black Friday'. By the end of Black Friday, John Gieve, the then deputy Governor of the Bank of England, said HBOS and RBS had 'run out of money'. After a long weekend of talks Brown's Government and the Bank of England announced a bail-out package offering £500 billion of support to banks averting a global economic meltdown. Brown later stated that if the bailout had failed he would have been forced to resign.

Brown's premiership introduced neighbourhood policing in every area, a legally-enforceable right to early cancer screening and treatment, and the world's first ever Climate Change Act, which was implemented in autumn 2008. In April 2009 British forces withdrew from the Iraq and he worked with his Irish counterpart Brian Cowen to negotiate the devolution of policing and justice powers in Northern Ireland. With Labour doing poorly in the 2008 local elections and the 2009 European elections Brown called for a General Election on 6 May 2010 (the first time the three main party leaders had taken part in a series of televised debates). A feature in the build up to the election was when Brown was caught on microphone describing a voter he had just spoken to in Rochdale as a "bigoted woman", Brown later visited the voter at her home to apologise saying he was a "penitent sinner" The election resulted in a large swing to the Conservatives and Labour lost its 70-seat majority However, none of the parties achieved the 326 seats needed for an overall majority with the Conservatives winning 306 seats (20 short of a majority), Labour 258 and the Liberals 57. This was only the second General Election since the Second World War to return a hung parliament (the first being 1974). Gordon Brown announced on the evening of Monday 10 May that he would resign as Leader of the Labour Party. Realising that a deal between the Conservatives and the Liberal Democrats was imminent, and on Tuesday 11 May Brown announced his resignation as Prime Minister, marking the end of 13 years of Labour government. Brown who had won his seat in Kirkcaldy and Cowdenbeath at the 2010 election with a majority of 23,009 (a majority that was lost to the Scottish National Party at the 2015 General Election with a 34.6% swing) stayed on in Parliament, serving as a Labour backbencher. On 1 December 2014, Brown announced that he would not be seeking re-election to parliament, and he stood down at the General Election in May 2015.

The Office of Gordon and Sarah Brown was set up in 2018 to establish their work and to facilitate their ongoing involvement in public life. This includes their charitable work which has raised over £3.5 million pounds to support good causes both locally and internationally.

Interesting Gordon Brown facts:
Brown was the first Prime Minister from a Scottish constituency since the Conservative Sir Alec Douglas-Home in 1964.

Brown was Britain's longest serving modern Chancellor of the Exchequer after being appointed in May 1997, until he took over as Prime Minister in June 2007.

Brown was the sixth post-war Prime Minister, of a total of 13, to assume the role without having won a General Election.

Brown was the youngest ever Rector of Edinburgh University in 1972.

Brown was one of only five Prime Ministers that had not attended either Oxford or Cambridge University.

Brow is the author of several books including Beyond the Crash: Overcoming the First Crisis of Globalisation, My Scotland, Our Britain and My Life, Our Times.

David Cameron
53rd British Prime Minister

Born
9 October 1966, London
Period in office as Prime Minister
6 years 64 days from 11 May 2010 until 13 July 2016
Political party
Conservative
Constituency Represented as MP
Witney 7 June 2001 to 12 September 2016
Ministerial offices held as Prime Minister
First Lord of the Treasury
Minister for the Civil Service

David William Donald Cameron (born 9 October 1966) is a British Conservative Party politician who identifies as a one-nation conservative and has been associated with both, economically liberal and socially liberal policies.

Cameron was born in Marylebone, London, and is a descendant of King William IV, being born into a family with both wealth and an aristocratic pedigree. Cameron was educated at two independent schools, Heatherdown School in Winkfield (near Ascot) and at the age of thirteen he went on to Eton College in Berkshire. Cameron passed twelve O-Levels and then three A-levels while passing the entrance exam for the University of Oxford, where he was offered an exhibition at Brasenose College in Oxford. After leaving Eton in 1984, he took a gap year before returning to Brasenose in October 1985 to take his Bachelor of Arts course in Philosophy, Politics and Economics, from which he graduated in 1988 with a first-class degree.

Between September 1988 and 1993 he joined the Conservative Party Research Department and in between in 1991, Cameron was seconded to Downing Street to work on briefing John Major for the then twice-weekly sessions of Prime Minister's Questions. In the build up to the 1992 General Election, Cameron was given the responsibility for briefing Major for his press conferences. After the success for the Conservatives in the April 1992 General Election, Cameron was rewarded with a promotion as Special Adviser to the Chancellor of the Exchequer, Norman Lamont. After Lamont was sacked at the end of May 1993 Cameron left the Treasury after being specifically recruited by Home Secretary Michael Howard, and at the beginning of September 1993, he applied to go on Conservative Central Office's list of prospective parliamentary candidates (PPCs). In July 1994, Cameron left his role as Special Adviser to work as the Director of Corporate Affairs at Carlton Communications. Carlton, which had won the ITV franchise for London weekdays in 1991, was a growing media company which also had film-distribution and video-producing arms. Having been approved for the PPCs' list, he stood as the Conservative candidate for the Stafford constituency in the 1997 General Election. Cameron lost out to Labour's David Kidney by a majority of 4,314 (24,606 vote's v 20,292). After the defeat Cameron returned to his job at Carlton but he resigned as Director of Corporate Affairs in February 2001 in order to run for Parliament for a second time. After failing to get the candidacy at Kensington and Chelsea he was selected as PPC for Witney in Oxfordshire and stood for the Conservatives at the June 2001 General Election, taking the seat with a 7,973 majority over Labour (22,153 vote's v 14,180). After entering Parliament in 2001, Mr Cameron rose rapidly through the ranks, serving first on the Home Affairs Select Committee, and which had recommended the liberalisation of drug laws. He was taken under the wing of Michael Howard, who put him in charge of policy co-ordination before promoting him to shadow education secretary. Cameron had a key role in drafting the 2005 Conservative election manifesto and also in 2005, he entered the race to succeed Mr Howard as party leader, although few initially gave him a chance. He was a distant fourth at the bookmakers behind Ken Clarke, Liam Fox and the frontrunner David Davis. It took an eye-catching conference speech, delivered without notes, in which he vowed to make people "feel good about being Conservatives again" and saying he wanted "to switch on a whole new generation" which catapulted him into the minds of the party faithful. In the first ballot of Conservative MPs on 18 October 2005, Cameron came second, with 56 votes, slightly more than expected. David Davis had fewer than predicted with 62 votes, Liam Fox came third with 42 votes, and Kenneth Clarke was eliminated with 38 votes. In the second ballot on 20 October 2005, Cameron came first with 90 votes, David Davis was second, with 57 and Liam Fox was eliminated with 51 votes. All 198 Conservative MPs voted in both ballots. The next stage of the election process was a head to head between Davis and

Cameron. The vote was open to the entire party membership.
Cameron was elected with more than twice as many votes as
Davis and more than half of all ballots issued. Cameron won
134,446 votes on a 78% turnout, to Davis's 64,398. Cameron's
election as the Leader of the Conservative Party and Leader of the
Opposition at the age of 39, was announced on 6 December
2005. He promised that the Tories, who had been out of power
for eight years, would modernise, and stop "grumbling about
today's Britain" and he would put an end to "Punch and Judy"
exchanges in the House of Commons. In July 2006 Cameron
received some mockery when he described teenaged "hoodies" as
"not a problem" in themselves, arguing they needed more
understanding, it became known as his "hug a hoodie" speech.
After almost four-and-a-half years as opposition leader, Cameron
started campaigning when Prime Minister Gordon Brown called an
election for May 2010, when the first ever televised debates
between the main party leaders in the UK was shown. Cameron
started slowly, but built up his performances and gradually
improved his ratings. At the May 2010 General Election although
voters gave the Conservatives their biggest seat gain since 1931
a hung Parliament was still returned, the first since 1974. After
days of talks between the main parties, the Tories and the Liberal
Democrats agreed to form a coalition and Cameron became the
youngest Prime Minister (43 years and 214 days) since Robert
Jenkinson in 1812 (42 years and 1 day). One of Cameron's first
moves was to appoint Nick Clegg, the leader of the Liberal
Democrats, as Deputy Prime Minister on 11 May 2010 and
between them, the Conservatives and Liberal Democrats
controlled 363 seats in the House of Commons, with a majority of
76 seats. In June 2010 Cameron described the economic
situation when he came to power as "even worse than we
thought" and warned of "difficult decisions" to be made over
spending cuts. In October his Chancellor (George Osborne)
announced a five-year austerity plan that included Britain's most
extensive spending cuts in decades, notably reductions

for policing, housing and welfare, although the National Health Service and education was "ringfenced" and protected from direct spending cuts. Cameron government's first major social innovation started to bear fruit in September 2011 with the opening of the first 24 'Free Schools' which were free to students and funded by the government, but able to operate independently of local councils. Also in 2011, Cameron had to deal with riots which erupted across the UK after the shooting by the police of Mark Duggan in Tottenham. Cameron vowed to fix a "broken society" and describes elements of it as "frankly sick". In October 2011, the retirement age was set to rise to 66 by 2020 for public-sector workers, and mandatory retirement was lifted. There was good new when unemployment in the United Kingdom began falling in the spring of 2012 and ended the year below 2.5 million, down from a peak of 2.7 million at the start of the year. In 2013, Cameron announced he would hold a referendum on membership of the European Union before the end of 2017 in order to settle the "European question" forever. Cameron introduced the *Marriage (Same Sex Couples) Act 2013*, which allows same-sex marriage in England and Wales, was passed by the UK Parliament in July 2013 and came into force on 13 March 2014. He was recognised as "ally of the year" at the PinkNews awards which were held in Westminster. At the May 2015 General Election many predictions were for a second consecutive hung parliament, but under Cameron's leadership the Conservatives won 330 seats and 36.9% of the vote share, giving them a small overall majority of 12 seats and their first outright win for 23 years. Cameron himself was returned as MP for Witney with an increased majority of 25,155. As promised in the election manifesto, Cameron set a date for a referendum on whether the UK should remain a member of the European Union, and announced that he would be campaigning for Britain to remain within a 'reformed EU'. The referendum which became known as 'Brexit' (a mix of 'British' and 'exit') was held on 23 June 2016. The result was approximately 52% in favour of leaving the

European Union and 48% against, with a turnout of 72%. Cameron addressed the country from outside 10 Downing Street on June 24, 2016 to announce his intention to resign as Prime Minister, in time for the Conservative conference in October 2016, to allow his successor time to conduct the negotiations on the British departure stating "I don't think it would be right for me to try to be the captain that steers our country to its next destination". At his final Prime Minister's Questions, his final comment was, "I was the future once" – a reference to his 2005 quip to Tony Blair, "he was the future once" and later that afternoon of 13 July 2016, Cameron submitted his resignation as Prime Minister to the Queen. He resigned his seat as MP for Witney on 12 September 2016.

Interesting David Cameron facts:

Cameron's first role after politics was as the chair of patrons at the National Citizen Service Trust, to help young people achieve their potential

Cameron was the first ever British Prime Minister to increase both their party's share of the vote and their number of seats in the House of Commons, having already served a full term as premier.

Cameron supports Aston Villa Football Club.

Cameron's released his memoir 'For the Record' on 19 September 2019. It gives an insight into his life at 10 Downing Street as well as inside explanations of the decisions taken by his government.

Cameron is married to Samantha Gwendoline Cameron (née Sheffield), the daughter of Sir Reginald Sheffield, 8th Baronet and they have had four children.
Cameron became President of Alzheimer's Research UK in January 2017.

Theresa May
54th British Prime Minister

Born
1 October 1956, London
Period in office as Prime Minister
3 years 12 days from 1 July 2016 until 24 July 2019
Political party
Conservative
Constituency Represented as MP
Maidenhead 1 May 1997 incumbent
Ministerial offices held as Prime Minister
First Lord of the Treasury
Minister for the Civil Service

Theresa Mary May, (Lady May) *née* **Brasier**, served as Britain's Prime Minister from July 2016 to July 2019, making her the first female to hold the role since Margaret Thatcher.

Theresa Mary May was born on October 1, 1956 in Eastbourne, Sussex. Her father was a vicar for the Church of England and her mother was a housewife. May grew up in Oxfordshire and initially attended Heythrop Primary School a state school, followed by St. Juliana's Convent School for Girls a Roman Catholic independent school in Begbroke. At the age of 13, she won a place at the former Holton Park Girls' Grammar School, a state school in Wheatley which became the Wheatley Park Comprehensive School. She attended the University of Oxford, studying geography at St Hugh's College, graduating in 1977 with a second class BA degree.

Between 1977 and 1983, May worked at the Bank of England, and from 1985 to 1997 at the Association for Payment Clearing Services (APACS) as a financial consultant. She served as Head of the European Affairs Unit from 1989 to 1996 and Senior Adviser on International Affairs from 1996 to 1997 in the organisation. May served as a councillor for Durnsford ward on the Borough Council of the London Borough of Merton from 1986 to 1994, where she was Chairman of Education (1988–90) and Deputy Group Leader and Housing Spokesman (1992–94). At the May 1992 General Election, May stood as the Conservative candidate at North West Durham but lost out in a safe Labour seat by a majority of 13,987. She then stood in the 1994 Barking by-election, which again was a safe Labour seat, being beaten into third place by Labour and the Liberal Democrats, receiving 1,976 votes out of 19,017 cast. Undeterred she was selected as the Conservative candidate for Maidenhead, a new seat which was created from parts of the safe seats of Windsor, Maidenhead and Wokingham. At the May 1997 General Election, May was elected as MP for Maidenhead with a majority of 11,981, beating the Liberal Democrats into second place. Upon entering Parliament May became part of William Hague's front bench opposition team, and from 1999 to 2001 she was Shadow Secretary of State for Education and Employment and later the Shadow Secretary of State for Transport, Local Government and the Regions (2001 to 2002). In 2002 May became the first woman to chair the Conservative Party, and in that capacity she strove to increase the number of female Tory MPs and to modernise the party, and in calling for change she famously said: "You know what people call us? The Nasty Party". In November 2003, after Michael Howard's election as Conservative Party and Opposition Leader, May was appointed Shadow Secretary of State for Transport and the Environment and the following year she became the Shadow Secretary of State for the Family. Following the May 2005 General Election in which she was returned with a 6,231 majority, she was made Shadow Secretary of State for Culture, Media and Sport, and in December 2005 David Cameron appointed her Shadow Leader of the House of Commons after he became Conservative leader, a position she held until 2009. In 2010 she became Parliamentary Under Secretary of State for Women and Equalities. At the May 2010 General Election she was re-elected MP for Maidenhead with an increased majority of 16,769, and on 12 May 2010, May was appointed Home Secretary and Minister for Women and Equality by Prime Minister David Cameron as part of his first Cabinet, becoming only the fourth woman to hold one of the British Great Offices of State. May became the longest-serving Home Secretary since James Chuter Ede over 60 years previously by serving until she took over as Prime Minister in 2016. As Home Secretary she pursued reform of the police, took a harder line on drug policy and introduced restrictions on immigration. After David Cameron resigned as Prime Minister in July 2016 due to the Brexit vote, May emerged along with Energy Minister Andrea Leadsom as the final candidates for the leadership which was to be voted upon by general party members by September 9. But before that process could begin in earnest, Leadsom withdrew her candidacy in response to controversy surrounding comments she had made about motherhood as a qualification for leadership (May had no children). May had won the first ballot with 165 votes against Leadsom's 66 and in the second ballot May had received 199 votes to Leadsom's 84. After Leadsom withdrew on July 13, 2016 May went through unopposed and became the new Conservative leader, and subsequently Prime Minister. Having pledged to see Brexit through to completion, her efforts ran into problems in November 2016, when the High Court ruled that she could not invoke Article 50 of the Lisbon Treaty, thus initiating negotiations on Britain's separation from the EU, without first having gained approval to do so from Parliament. Her government's appeal of that ruling was rejected by the Supreme Court in January 2017. In February a bill granting the approval was passed by the House of Commons, but, when it returned to the Commons from the House of Lords in March, it was laden with an amendment calling for a larger role for Parliament in the negotiations with the EU and with another guaranteeing EU citizens residing in the UK, could remain. May opposed the latter measure unless it was to be accompanied by a parallel guarantee for British citizens living in other EU countries. After the House of Commons rejected both of those amendments, on March 29, May formally submitted a six-page letter to European Council President Donald Tusk invoking Article 50 and opening a two-year window for negotiations between the United Kingdom and the EU over the details of separation. In the letter, May pledged to enter the discussions "constructively and respectfully, in a spirit of sincere cooperation." She hoped that a "bold and ambitious Free Trade Agreement" would result from the negotiations.

After months of rejecting calls for a parliamentary election to focus on the Brexit negotiations, in mid-April 2017, May surprised the country by calling for a snap General Election for June, saying that its results would provide stability and certainty for the United Kingdom during its crucial transition out of the EU. When the

Fixed-term Parliaments Act 2011 was introduced it brought fixed-term Parliaments to the United Kingdom, with elections scheduled every five years. This removed the power of the Prime Minister, from using the royal prerogative to dissolve Parliament before its five-year maximum length. The Act permits early dissolution only if the House of Commons votes by a supermajority of two-thirds of the entire membership of the House. A House of Commons motion to allow this was passed on 19 April, with 522 votes for and 13 against, a majority of 509 and so members of Parliament approved a snap election to be held on June 8. Parliament was dissolved on May 2 for the start of the election campaign. May's Conservatives held a slim 17-seat majority in the House of Commons but had strong showings in the opinion polls. Twice the election was interrupted (and campaigning temporarily suspended) by terrorist attacks. On May 22 an attacker detonated a bomb at a concert at the Manchester Arena, killing 22 and injuring dozens of others. Then, on June 3, only days before the election, three attackers with a vehicle mowed down pedestrians on London Bridge before moving on to Borough Market, eventually taking eight lives before being killed by police. When voters went to the polls on 8 June 2017, far from giving a clear mandate, the Conservative Party, although remaining the largest single party in the House of Commons lost its small overall majority, resulting in the formation of a minority government with a confidence-and-supply agreement with the Democratic Unionist Party (DUP) of Northern Ireland. Vowing to continue, May returned to the business of leading Britain, with the central task for her government remained formulating a cohesive approach for Brexit negotiations with the EU. In late November 2018, May was able to boast that the leaders of the EU's 27 other member countries had formally agreed to the terms of a withdrawal deal that she claimed "delivered for the British people" and set the United Kingdom "on course for a prosperous future." According to the agreement, the UK was to pay a fee to meet its long-term financial obligations to the EU. Under the plan an end would come to the freedom of movement between Britain and the EU that was central to the anti-immigration argument for Brexit. Although the UK.'s departure date from the EU was set for March 29, 2019, the agreement stipulated that Britain would continue to adhere to EU rules and regulations until at least December 2020 while the details of their long-term relationship were ironed out by the UK and the EU. This agreement had opposition from all parties in Parliament and On 12 December 2018, May faced a vote of no confidence in her leadership, she won the vote with 200 Conservative MPs voting for her, compared to 117 voting against. But following the defeat of May's Brexit deal on 15 January 2019, Jeremy Corbyn the Labour leader tabled a motion of no confidence in the Government, which was to be voted on by Parliament the following evening. The motion was defeated by 325 votes to 306, a majority of 19. Further defeats in the House on Brexit were delivered on 14 February, 12 March and 29 March 2019. This led to 70 Conservative Associations signing a petition calling for a vote of no confidence on 22 April 2019. The following month on 24 May 2019, May confirmed that she would resign as Conservative Party leader on 7 June continuing to serve as Prime Minister until she tendered her resignation to the Queen on 24 July. After leaving 10 Downing Street, May took her place on the backbenches, remaining an MP to "devote her full time" to her constituency of Maidenhead. In the 2019 General Election she was re-elected as the constituency's MP with a majority of 18,846.

Interesting Theresa May facts:

May's premiership had had 51 resignations with 33 relating to Brexit.

In September 2017, May was listed by *Forbes* as the second most powerful woman in the world, behind Germany's Angela Merkel.

Boris Johnson
55th British Prime Minister

Born
19 June 1964, New York City, New York, U.S.
Dates in office
24 July 2019
Political party
Conservative
Constituency Represented as MP
Henley-on-Thames June 2001-June 2008
Uxbridge and South Ruislip 7 May 2015 incumbent
Ministerial offices held as Prime Minister
First Lord of the Treasury
Minister for the Civil Service
Minister for the Union

Alexander Boris de Pfeffel Johnson (born 19 June 1964) is an American born British politician, author, and former journalist who has been Prime Minister of the United Kingdom and Leader of the Conservative Party since 2019. He was Foreign Secretary from 2016 to 2018 and Mayor of London from 2008 to 2016. Johnson was Member of Parliament (MP) for Henley from 2001 to 2008 and has been MP for Uxbridge and South Ruislip since 2015.

Johnson was born on 19 June 1964 in the Upper East Side of Manhattan, New York City, to his English born parents Stanley and Charlotte. In September 1964 the family moved back to Oxford, England before again moving to Washington D.C where Stanley worked with the World Bank. By this time they had two further additions to the family with Rachel being born in in 1965 and Leo born in 1967. The family again returned to England in 1969. Johnson was educated at Primrose Hill Primary school in London and the family had their fourth child when Joseph was born in late 1971. In 1977 Johnson gained a King's Scholarship to study at Eton College, the elite independent boarding school near Windsor in Berkshire where he began using his middle name of Boris. Johnson went to Oxford in 1983 having, despite his teachers' misgivings, won a scholarship to study a four-year course of the Classics, ancient literature and classical philosophy. To his later regret, he joined the Old Etonian-dominated Bullingdon Club, an exclusive drinking society notorious for acts of vandalism on host premises. In 1984, Johnson was elected secretary of the Oxford Union and in 1986, he ran successfully for president of the Oxford Union. He graduated from Oxford in 1987 with a 2:1.

In late 1987 he began work as a graduate trainee at *The Times* but when Johnson wrote an article on the archaeological discovery of King Edward II's palace for the newspaper, he invented a quote for the article which he falsely attributed to the historian Colin Lucas, his godfather. Lucas complained to the editor Charles Wilson, and Johnson was dismissed. Johnson secured employment on the leader-writing desk of *The Daily Telegraph,* the editor of which was Max Hastings who Johnson had invited to speak at the Oxford Union during his presidency. In 1989 Hastings promoted Johnson to become Brussels correspondent when he was just 25 and he continued to work in Brussels for the next five years. Johnson came back to London in 1994 and was elevated to the *Telegraph*'s assistant editor and chief political columnist (1994-1999), whilst also acquiring a column in the *Spectator*. In the May 1997 General Election Johnson stood as the Conservative candidate in Clwyd South but lost decisively to Labour by a 13,810 majority. By this time Johnson began appearing on a variety of television shows, beginning in 1998 with the BBC comedy quiz show *Have I Got News for You*. His bumbling demeanour and irreverent remarks made him an enduring favourite on British talk shows. In 1999 he was named the Spectator magazine's editor a role he continued in until 2005.

Johnson stood for Parliament in the June 2001 General Election, again as a Conservative candidate, but this time in the Henley-on-Thames constituency. He was elected to parliament by beating the Liberal Democrats into second place with an 8,458 majority. In 2004 he was appointed shadow minister for the arts. However, in November 2004, he was forced to resign over allegations of an extramarital affair, but he was reprieved in 2005 and given the position of shadow minister for education. He was returned as MP for Henley-on-Thames at the May 2005 General Election with an increased majority of 12,793. In July 2007, Johnson resigned from his position as shadow education secretary so that he would be free to stand as the Conservative candidate for Mayor of London. He was successful in beating the incumbent Ken Livingstone in May 2008 with 43.2% of the vote in the first round and 53.2% in the second round, to become only the second Mayor of London and the first London Conservative Mayor. After becoming Mayor, Johnson then announced his resignation as MP for Henley. Johnson served as London Mayor from 2008 to

2016 after being re-elected in 2012. In the May 2012 Mayoral election Johnson again defeated Ken Livingston with 44% of the vote in the first round and 51.5% in the second round. Johnson returned to Parliament in 2015, winning the west London seat of Uxbridge and South Ruislip with a majority of 10,695, in an election that saw the Conservative Party capture its first clear majority since the 1990s. Johnson continued in his role as Mayor of London until he chose not to run for re-election in 2016. He then became the leading spokesman for the "Leave" campaign in the run-up to the June 23, 2016, national referendum on whether the United Kingdom should remain a member of the European Union (becoming known as Brexit). The polls were predicting a 'Remain' win but the 'Leave' campaign won with 51.89% (17,410,742) voting for the United Kingdom to leave the EU. After the vote David Cameron announced his resignation as Prime Minister after which many observers believed that Johnson would ascend to the party leadership and the premiership. Johnson decided not to stand though, when he was deserted by his key ally and prospective campaign chairman, the Justice Secretary, Michael Gove. Gove, who had worked alongside Johnson on the "Leave" campaign, concluded that Johnson could not "provide the leadership or build the team for the task ahead" and, instead of backing Johnson's candidacy, announced his own. In July 2016 Theresa May became leader of the Conservative Party and the Prime Minister, appointing Johnson as Foreign Secretary. With the Conservatives holding a slender 17 seat majority, May called a snap General Election for June 2017 to try and "strengthen [her] hand" in the Brexit negotiations. The snap election gamble failed and resulted in the closest result between the two major parties since February 1974. Johnson retained his Uxbridge and South Ruislip with a reduced majority of 5,034 and he remained Foreign Secretary when May reshuffled her cabinet in a minority government. After a cabinet meeting in July 2018 Johnson and Brexit Secretary David Davis resigned their cabinet posts with Johnson writing *'It is more than two years since the British people voted to leave the European Union on an unambiguous and categorical promise that if they did so they would be taking back control of their democracy. They were told that they would be able to manage their own immigration policy, repatriate the sums of UK cash currently spent by the EU, and, above all, that they would be able to pass laws independently and in the interests of the people of this country....That dream is dying, suffocated by needless self-doubt'.* After resigning as Foreign Secretary, Johnson returned to the role of a backbench MP.

After failing to deliver Brexit Theresa May resigned as Prime Minister on 7 June 2019, remaining as caretaker Prime Minister until a successor was appointed. On 16 May 2019, Johnson confirmed that he would stand in the Conservative Party leadership election with initially ten candidates being whittled down to four - Johnson, Jeremy Hunt, Michael Gove and Sajid Javid. After Gove and Javid fell by the wayside in subsequent votes, Johnson and Hunt stood as the final candidates in an election in which all of the party's nearly 160,000 members were eligible to vote. On July 23 July 2019 Johnson captured some 66 percent of the vote (92,153 votes) as opposed to Hunt's 46,656 votes. On July 24 2019 Johnson officially became Prime Minister and in his victory speech, he pledged to "deliver Brexit, unite the country, and defeat (Labour leader) Jeremy Corbyn". Faced with a threat by Corbyn to hold a vote of confidence, and then confronted by a broader effort by opponents of a no-deal Brexit, to move toward legislation that would prevent that option for leaving the EU, Johnson boldly announced on August 28 that he had requested the Queen to prorogue Parliament. On 11 September, three Scottish judges ruled the prorogation of the UK Parliament to be unlawful. Johnson's main commitment was still to take the UK out of the EU by 31 October 2019 – saying he would rather 'die in a ditch than ask for a Brexit extension'. However, Johnson lost his first six votes in Parliament and a bill to block a no-deal exit passed the Commons on 4 September

2019, causing Johnson to propose a General Election on 15 October. His motion was unsuccessful as it failed to command the support of two-thirds of the House. Johnson was able to find common ground with the EU on a renegotiated agreement that greatly resembled May's proposal but replaced the backstop with a plan to keep Northern Ireland aligned with the EU for at least four years from the end of the transition period. On October 22 the House of Commons approved Johnson's revised plan in principle but then quickly hindered his effort to push the agreement through to formal Parliamentary acceptance before the October 31 deadline. Johnson was therefore compelled to ask the EU for an extension of the deadline, which was granted for January 31, 2020. With no-deal Brexit off the table, an early election was scheduled for December 12 2019. The Conservative General Election victory proved to be more decisive than anyone had expected. In winning 365 seats (43,6% of the votes), the party increased its presence in the House of Commons to an 80 seat majority recording its most commanding win in a parliamentary election since 1987. Johnson himself was returned as MP for Uxbridge and South Ruislip with an increased majority of 7,210. The COVID-19 pandemic emerged as a serious crisis within the first few months of Johnson's second term, and on 20 March 2020, Johnson with regret, requested the closure of pubs, restaurants, gyms, entertainment venues, museums and galleries, saying "We're taking away the ancient, inalienable right of free-born people of the United Kingdom to go to the pub". On 23 March, this was strengthened into a "stay at home" order throughout the UK, except for a few limited purposes, backed up by new legal powers for a period of up to 2 years. The UK was amongst the last major European states to progressively encourage social distancing, close schools, ban public events and order a lockdown.

On 27 March, it was announced that Johnson had tested positive for COVID-19 and on 5 April, with his symptoms persisting, he was admitted to St Thomas' Hospital in London for tests. The next day, his condition having worsened, he was moved to the hospital's intensive care unit and Dominic Raab was appointed to deputise for him. The Prime Minister was seriously unwell, his breathing had deteriorated and he spent three days in intensive care. Johnson left intensive care on 9 April, and left hospital three days later stating that the NHS had saved his life "no question". In October 2020 with Covid 19 cases rising Johnson declared another lockdown on Thursday 5 November until Wednesday 2 December.

At the point of finishing this book Johnson was heading into 2021 with two major issues to deal with: the Covid 19 infections and Brexit...

Interesting Boris Johnson facts:

In 2016 Johnson renounced his American citizenship.

In 1987 Johnson married Allegra Mostyn-Owen. The marriage lasted less than a year. It was dissolved in 1993. He married the barrister Marina Wheeler later the same year. They have two sons—Theodore Apollo (born 1999) and Milo Arthur (born 1995)—and two daughters—Lara Lettice (born 1993) and Cassia Peaches (born 1997). After Johnson and Wheeler split he became engaged to Carrie Symonds in late 2019. Their first son was born on 29 April 2020. He was born at University College Hospital in London. His name is Wilfred Lawrie Nicholas Johnson.

BoJo is a name for Johnson which often used by the press.

Johnson has written numerous books including *The Churchill Factor: How One Man Made History* detailing the life of the former Prime Minister Winston Churchill.

Johnson was portrayed by Stuart McQuarrie in the 2005 television film *A Very Social Secretary*.